CONTESTED WORDS

Contested Words

Legal Restrictions on Freedom of Speech in Liberal Democracies

IAN CRAM
University of Leeds, UK

ASHGATE

Published by
Ashgate Publishing Limited
Gower House
Croft Road
Aldershot
Hampshire GU11 3HR
England

Ashgate Publishing Company
Suite 420
101 Cherry Street
Burlington, VT 05401-4405
USA

Ashgate website: http://www.ashgate.com

British Library Cataloguing in Publication Data
Cram, Ian
Contested words : legal restrictions on freedom of speech in liberal democracies. - (Applied legal philosophy)
1. Freedom of expression 2. Constitutional law - Philosophy
I. Title
342'.0853

Library of Congress Control Number: 2006921288

ISBN 0 7546 2365 3

Printed and bound in Great Britain by MPG Books Ltd, Bodmin, Cornwall.

Contents

Preface

The origins of this book stem in a significant way from a module *Free Speech, Constitutions and the Law* that is offered to students studying the LLM in International and European Human Rights at the School of Law, Leeds University. On this module, students are encouraged to immerse themselves in the distinctive constitutional cultures of the United States, Canada and Australia, as well as the supra-national norms that characterize the European Convention on Human Rights. Over the several years that I have taught this module, I have been encouraged by students' interest in the legal regulation of freedom of expression in other liberal democracies and their clear desire to understand the wider political and historical contexts which inform the various regulatory stances of these jurisdictions. In writing this book, I intended to concretize some of my own thoughts about the difficult and controversial line-drawing exercises that fall to courts and legislatures in liberal democracies in free speech disputes. One of my hopes is that the following pages will stoke further the many lively and thoughtful conversations that the module has generated in class.

The book draws on and develops some work published previously either in journal articles or at conferences. Colleagues at the Human Rights Research Unit here at Leeds have also been kind enough to contribute their thoughts to a paper that straddled materials to be found in the first two chapters of this monograph and was delivered at a seminar hosted by the Unit. Professor Colin Munro generously agreed to read an earlier draft version of the chapter on hateful expression and provided some valuable feedback. Professor Tom Campbell, the Applied Legal Philosophy Series Editor at Ashgate read through the manuscript and offered helpful suggestions which are gratefully acknowledged. At Ashgate, a debt of gratitude is also owed to Jacqui Cornish, the Senior Desk Editor who efficiently saw this book through to completion. I would like in addition to thank Jane Read who was meticulous in her proof-reading of the manuscript and spotted errors that I had overlooked.

My final thanks go to my wife Aurora, son Seumas and daughter Fiona. Without them, this book might have been finished earlier. At the same time, without them, this book might never have been written at all.

Ilkley Moor, April 2006

Series Editor's Preface

The objective of the Applied Legal Philosophy series is to publish work which adopts a theoretical approach to the study of particular areas or aspects of law or deals with general theories of law in a way which focuses on issues of practical moral and political concern in specific legal contexts.

In recent years there has been an encouraging tendency for legal philosophers to utilize detailed knowledge of the substance and practicalities of law and a noteworthy development in the theoretical sophistication of much legal research. The series seeks to encourage these trends and to make available studies in law which are both genuinely philosophical in approach and at the same time based on appropriate legal knowledge and directed towards issues in the criticism and reform of actual laws and legal systems.

The series will include studies of all the main areas of law, presented in a manner which relates to the concerns of specialist legal academics and practitioners. Each book makes an original contribution to an area of legal study while being comprehensible to those engaged in a wide variety of disciplines. Their legal content is principally Anglo-American, but a wide-ranging comparative approach is encouraged and authors are drawn from a variety of jurisdictions.

Tom D. Campbell
Series Editor
Centre for Applied Philosophy and Public Ethics
Charles Sturt University, Canberra

Chapter 1

Current Controversies in Freedom of Expression

Introduction

Under what circumstances, if any, is the state entitled to curb the speech of racists? Should Holocaust denial be made a specific offence or does this invade too far upon cherished notions of liberty of expression? Ought the claims of the producers and consumers of virtual child pornography that they are protected by freedom of expression to be accepted? What about other forms of sexually explicit expression? Are bans on tobacco advertising ever justified? What limits, if any, is the state entitled to place on the election expenditure of relatively wealthy parties or their donors? Should the state do more to facilitate the expression of economically weak groups in order to enrich debate on matters of politics and social affairs? This book is intended as a contribution to some current debates on freedom of expression. It seeks to explore from a comparative constitutional law perspective attempts at line-drawing in modern liberal democracies in these difficult areas. Importantly, the discussion attempts to situate its analysis within a broader context that acknowledges the role played by underlying traditions and currents in political philosophy that frame the treatment of speech problems in constitutional courts. This work hopes to throw light on the fundamental values that inform the interpretation of open-ended constitutional declarations of freedom of expression. Do courts in liberal democracies conceive of expression guarantees as primarily concerned with maintaining the conditions of informed popular sovereignty, as means of promoting democratic accountability over public office holders or, alternatively, are they linked more closely to the idea of individual autonomy, as a necessary mechanism for enabling the intellectual and emotional growth of persons? If the former, how far is the state entitled to go in creating the circumstances for enhanced public discourse and at what cost to individual liberty? Where an emphasis on public discourse is evident, does this mean that state regulation of non-political expression is considered to be relatively unproblematic, with the result that legislative/executive abridgements of commercial expression or sexually explicit expression raise few constitutional issues? Conversely, if we see speech/expression guarantees as more intimately linked to individual autonomy, does this mean that the state is not justified in redressing obvious inequalities in private power that become reflected in distorted or dominant patterns of discourse?

Constitutional protection for freedom of expression is usually accompanied by statements of other fundamental rights and freedoms. I have in mind here those constitutional provisions that proclaim a commitment to equality, dignity and diversity. What relationship, if any, do these guarantees have to freedom of expression? As we will see in Chapter 5, which deals with the regulation of hateful expression, a number of jurisdictions accept that freedom of expression is mediated by countervailing constitutional principles such as equality and dignity. The commitment to equality may, however, simply be cast in negative terms as a formal requirement obliging the state to remain neutral between conflicting viewpoints. That is, the state may not assist the dissemination of opinion with which it is in agreement. More radically, equality can be read in a different way to authorize state intervention between unequal speakers, either to silence some of the expression of the powerful or to enhance the speech of marginalized individuals/groups.

The Crisis of Liberal Democracy, Virtuous Citizenry and Freedom of Expression

According to classical liberal theory, to function effectively, liberal democracies required merely that the appropriate institutional mechanisms were in place (such as bicameral legislatures; checks and balances) and that constitutional doctrines were respected and enforced (separation of powers; the rule of law). Liberal democracies, so the argument went, did not need an especially virtuous citizenry to function effectively. Individuals could in fact pursue their private self-interests without threatening the well-being of the liberal state.[1]

A reassessment of this position has occurred, however, within liberal thinking. The pursuit of private well-being is no longer seen to be sufficient and the notion of the individual as a bearer of rights without any reciprocal obligations to society has come under attack. Some have argued that, without the development of certain forms of virtuous conduct, the ability of liberal society to operate successfully will diminish. The example is given of the environment where it is said that the state cannot protect the environment 'if citizens are unwilling to reduce, reuse and recycle in their consumer choices …'.[2] In the sphere of electing governments, voter apathy already threatens to undermine the democratic legitimacy of political institutions. In Britain, for example, there has been a steady decline in the numbers of persons voting in general elections. Statistics from the House of Commons Parliamentary Research Services indicates that in 1992 77.7 per cent of those eligible voted. This dropped at the following election in 1997 to 71.4 per cent before crashing in

1 Kant, for example, subscribed to the view that the right institutional mechanisms could overcome the private conduct of a 'race of devils', *Perpetual Peace – First Supplement* (1903, Allen & Unwin, London). See further *The Federalist* Papers Nos. 10–51, where the clash of private interests was also thought beneficial in general terms: J Madison, A Hamilton and J Jay, *The Federalist Papers* (1987, Penguin Books, London).

2 W Kymlicka, *Contemporary Political Philosophy – An Introduction* (2nd edn, 2002 OUP, Oxford) 285. Other examples include the fields of personal health and personal finances where unchecked irresponsible attitudes, if widespread, may outstrip the ability of the state to provide remedial help.

June 2001 to 59.4 per cent.[3] In the 2005 general election, this figure rose slightly to 61.3 per cent – a fact attributable in part to the introduction of postal voting, although this produced concerns about fraud and the role of local political parties in distributing ballot papers.[4] Falling levels of voting are not confined to the UK. Across the Atlantic, US Presidential elections in the 1950s and late 1960s regularly boasted a turnout figure of between 59 and 61 per cent. In the 1970s and up to the mid-1980s this dropped to around 55 per cent. In the 1996 and 2000 contests, the figures fell to 49 per cent and 51.1 per cent respectively.[5] Federal elections in Canada in 2000 saw the lowest ever figure of just 61 per cent of eligible voters casting a ballot, prompting a research paper from the Centre for Research and Information on Canada entitled *Voter Participation in Canada – Is Canadian Democracy in Crisis?*[6] The paper concluded that young Canadians were far less likely to vote than were their parents and grandparents when they were young. Disengagement from or non-engagement with electoral politics is worrying for a number of reasons. Apart from undermining the legitimacy of legislative rule-making, it may be indicative of wider alienation from the community and a retreat into the private spheres of family, career and other personal projects. Moreover, where interest in political matters is shared by relatively few persons, this may induce a belief on the part of those in authority that abuses of power are less likely to attract significant public censure.

Theorists such as Shklar, Galston and Kymlicka have begun to consider the sorts of virtues which liberal society requires of its citizens or, at least, a significant proportion of those citizens and how, once identified, these may be encouraged. In the context of this book's concern with freedom of expression, the work of William Galston is worthy of closer study.[7] His account of liberal virtues identifies among the political virtues needed of citizens in representative democracies the capacity to discern the talent and character of candidates vying for public office and the ability to evaluate the performance of those who have attained office. Galston additionally refers to the virtue of being willing to engage in open public discourse which involves listening and understanding others as well as seeking to persuade others to our point of view. Stephen Macedo, for his part, has stressed the importance of 'public reasonableness' in liberal constitutionalism. Alongside toleration, law-bound liberty and a rights-oriented conception of justice, liberal institutions

> … provide the settings for ongoing efforts to formalize, clarify, contest, justify, refine, and extend liberal principles … In a liberal regime, criticism of the government is accepted

---

3 *British Electoral Facts 1832–1999* Parliamentary Research Services, House of Commons.

4 See further The Electoral Commission, *Securing the Vote* (2005) available electronically at http://www.electoralcommission.org.uk/files/dms/Securingthevote_17643-12944__E__N__S__W__.pdf.

5 There was a rise in 2004 however to 60 per cent.

6 (2001, Centre for Research and Information on Canada, Ottawa).

7 *Liberal Purposes* (1991, CUP, Cambridge), especially Ch. 10.

> and even encouraged, and liberal citizens expect to be answered with reasons rather than mere force or silence.[8]

This more active, 'talk-centric' version of liberal democracy with its authority-questioning citizen represents a shift away from 'vote-centric' approaches to democracy in which citizens were conceived of as passive and uncritical and whose fixed preferences were translated into support for political parties via the electoral system.[9] In 1995 Jon Elster was able to write that 'the idea of deliberative democracy, or decision-making by discussion among free and equal citizens, is having a revival', a trend he attributed to the work of Jurgen Habermas.[10] Consequently, political scientists have been much occupied with designing mechanisms and procedures to facilitate deliberative decision-making.[11] The benefits which are said to accrue from deliberation-enhancing devices include better decision-making (since more persons with informed insights would be able to influence outcomes) and greater societal cohesiveness (fewer persons would feel excluded from the process; also the fact of participation itself might connect citizens to others and encourage empathy with others' concerns). The most optimistic accounts hold out the hope of greater consensus across key issues confronting the polity. Whether this is a realistic aspiration or not,[12] most can agree that, if properly inclusive, deliberative procedures may result in greater legitimacy for resultant policy choices. Unsurprisingly, these various advantages have united a diverse set of theorists, including liberals, communitarians and feminists, in advocating enhanced structures of deliberative decision-making.

At this juncture, however, proponents of deliberative democracy must respond to two distinct sorts of questions. The first concerns the question of how to ensure that there are enough individuals who are informed, critical of authority in a non-dogmatic way and committed to mutual understanding through a process of public deliberation. A second issue relates to the precise form and size of structures and mechanisms needed to facilitate more deliberative decision-making.[13] Here, from the perspective of constitutional law, the stance of the courts towards legislative

---

8 *Liberal Virtues* (1990, Clarendon Press, Oxford) 40–41.

9 The terms 'vote-centric' and 'talk-centric' are to be found in Kymlicka *supra.* It has been suggested by one US academic that modern democracies may be compared to a public lavatorial exercise in which a bursting electorate manage every few years to relieve themselves in private at the ballot box before continuing thereafter with their private lives: B Barber, *Strong Democracy: Participatory Politics for a New Age* (1984, University of California Press, Berkeley) 188.

10 J Elster 'Introduction' in J Elster (ed.) *Deliberative Democracy* (1998, CUP, Cambridge) at 1.

11 See, for example, J Dryzek, *Deliberative Democracy and Beyond: Liberals, Critics and Contestations* (2000, OUP, Oxford).

12 For a much more sceptical analysis of the potential of deliberative structures, see J Johnson, 'Arguing for Deliberation' in J Elster (ed.) *Deliberative Democracy* (1998, CUP, Cambridge) Ch. 7.

13 See J Elster, 'Deliberation and Constitution-making' in J Elster (ed.) *Deliberative Democracy* (1998, CUP, Cambridge) at 107–109.

regulation of expressive activity will be important. An argument that will be made in this book is that the courts do have *some* role to play in safeguarding the conditions in which democratic deliberation among citizens can flourish.

Liberals, Communitarians and Deliberative Democracy

Although united by the commitment to more deliberative decision-making processes, liberals, communitarians and others differ on the crucial question of how this is to be achieved. These differences reflect profound disagreements in political philosophy about the appropriate role of the state and its relationship with the individual. The task of engendering a virtuous citizenry poses particular difficulties for liberal thinkers. The liberal way of life supposedly frees its citizens from centrally directed notions of worthwhile or wasteful life choices. Individuals need to be left free to make their own lifestyle choices and thus cannot be forced to become active participants in debates about politics. The political life is not to be privileged above other forms of life as especially fulfilling. So the crucial question for liberal theorists becomes one of how liberal society might inculcate the sorts of virtues needed for the long-term success of representative democracies without resort to coercion. Some scholars within this tradition have looked to civil society, the market, schools, private associations and religious organizations as pre-existing *loci* of civic virtue and sought to strengthen them. Each of these, however, reveals limitations which hinder its respective effectiveness as 'seedbeds of virtue'. Take, for instance, the claim that the virtues of personal responsibility and mutual obligation (which are required of citizens in democratic society) are engendered in religious organizations. Notwithstanding this fact, churches also teach deference to authority, meaning that the civility which is learnt springs too often from hierarchical relations. Religious organizations also teach intolerance of other faiths and lifestyles when they clash with prescribed beliefs. At bottom, it may simply be expecting too much of a church whose purpose is to attend to the spiritual needs of its members to train persons for citizenship in a deliberative democracy.

Perhaps more fundamentally than the 'how to inculcate virtue' question, liberals have to provide an answer to the question of why citizens would choose in a non-coerced manner to act virtuously (including participating in decision-making and accountability structures) when withdrawing from the public sphere and behaving in a disrespectful, discriminatory or even threatening manner might bring them more of what they need to pursue their conception of the good life. The answer is a shared commitment to the principles of justice at the heart of which is a belief in the equal worth of individuals.

Communitarian accounts of civic virtue and how this may be engendered differ radically from the foregoing. In a communitarian society, the state is not neutral between conceptions of the good life, but seeks to promote a substantive version of the 'common good' and actively strives to create the public and private virtues needed for society to attain that end.[14] Liberal ideas of personal autonomy, underpinned by notions of individual rights, are rejected as missing the collective dimension of existence and fostering instead alienated and atomized hedonism. Conversely, communitarians perceive individuals as having social characters grounded in the communities in which they live.[15] The good of the individual is not conceivable unless understood within some broader view of the good of the community. This 'embeddedness' of persons stands in sharp contrast to the liberal view of individuals as free to step back from social roles and relationships and to question whether these are worth pursuing. One variant of communitarian thinking to have gained recent prominence – particularly in US academic circles – is civic republicanism. Broadly speaking, in its modern guise,[16] civic republicanism is committed to the concept of an inclusive community of political equals who search through open deliberation and dialogue for a reasoned understanding of the common good. Civic republicanism rejects what it labels the 'pluralist' view of politics whereby legislation, rather than being the product of enlightened and undistorted discourse between equals, merely reflects the balance of pre-existing individual preferences and interests. One of civic republicanism's leading proponents, Cass Sunstein, set out the four organizing principles of civic republicanism: deliberation in politics; equality of political actors; universalism and citizenship.[17] Deliberation in politics can only occur where citizens show 'civic virtue'; that is, where (without necessarily abandoning private interests) citizens bring critical scrutiny to bear on these and seek outcomes which will serve the whole community, rather than elements of it.[18] Thus stated, civic virtue serves primarily an instrumental interest – that of promoting deliberation, rather than being concerned to improve individual character. The principle of deliberation also requires as pre-conditions certain constitutional guarantees such as freedom of expression on

---

14 On communitarian thinking in general, see M Sandel, *Liberalism and the Limits of* Justice (1982, CUP Cambridge); C Taylor, *Philosophy and the Human Sciences: Philosophical Papers, Vol ii* (1985, CUP, Cambridge); M Walzer, *Spheres of Justice: A Defence of Pluralism and Equality* (1983, Blackwell, Oxford).

15 A McIntyre, *After Virtue: A Study in Moral Theory* (1981, Duckworth, London).

16 For an Aristotelian account of civic republicanism, see A Oldfield, *Citizenship and Community: Civic Republicanism and the Modern World* (1990, Routledge, London). For a view that civic republicanism ideas derive from a world differing vastly from our own, see T Sandalow, 'A Skeptical Look at Contemporary Republicanism' (1989) 41 *Fl L Rev* 523.

17 'Beyond the Republican Tradition' (1988) 97 *Yale L J* 1539.

18 Some advocates of deliberative structures emphasize that the views and positions that participants bring to public deliberation must be 'reasonable'. Amy Guttman for example has stated that advocacy of 'the routine murder of innocents, arbitrary arrests, systematic deception…' falls outside of the bounds of what counts as reasonable, disqualifying the speaker from contributing: see 'The Challenge of Multiculturalism in Political Ethics' (1993) 22 *Philosophy and Public Affairs* 171. On the idea that a commitment to deliberative democracy entails certain *substantive* principles as well as laying down the *processes* for making political decisions, see A Guttman and D Thompson , 'Deliberative Democracy Beyond Process' in J S Fishkin and P Laslett (eds) *Debating Deliberative Democracy* (2003, Blackwell, Oxford).

matters of politics and public affairs, as well as the right to vote. Sunstein's second principle – political equality of participants – is adduced to eliminate sharp disparities in the influence that different actors would otherwise have in deliberative structures. All individuals and groups are required to have access to the political process, although economic equality is not however a pre-condition of political equality. At the same time, Sunstein is not hostile to the redistribution of existing wealth and entitlements, when necessary, to reduce the political influence of the powerful and afford a voice to weaker members of the community. Thus, in a section dealing with the financing of electoral campaigns, he argues that a 'principal threat' to a well-functioning system of free expression lies in government inaction which permits disparities in private wealth to have an extensive influence in the political process.[19] Civic republicanism is committed to promoting deliberation among a multitude of voices.[20] Whilst many would endorse in principle the idea of some equalization of the ability to be heard (especially at election time), in practice it raises a number of difficult questions about state aid for political parties and expenditure ceilings for electoral campaigning. A closer look at some legislative schemes to limit the distorting impact of private wealth upon election campaigns (and the constitutional disputes they have spawned) occurs in Chapter 4 of this book.

The third principle of Sunstein's civic republicanism is universalism, understood as

> … a belief in the possibility of mediating different approaches to politics, or different conceptions of the public good, through discussion and dialogue. The process of mediation is designed to produce substantively correct outcomes, understood as such through the ultimate criterion of agreement among political equals. It is because of the belief in universalism that republican approaches posit the existence of a common good, to be found at the conclusion of a well-functioning deliberative process.[21]

In other words, ethical relativism and scepticism are rejected.

The fourth principle is citizenship, which is manifested in guaranteed rights of participation. These are necessary for citizen control over the conduct of elected representatives' behaviour so that there is a limit on the risks of factionalism and self-interested representation. Participation is also valuable for Sunstein because it offers the chance to exercise and inculcate certain characteristics such as empathy, virtue and feelings of community. It follows that the exclusion of certain sections of society (such as prisoners) from the franchise may in fact hinder re-integration into society and affect levels of re-offending. A commitment to this notion of 'citizenship' may demand close judicial scrutiny over legislative restrictions on the right to vote. This matter is considered further in Chapter 3.

Although keen to stress the compatibility of civic republicanism with elements of liberal thinking, Sunstein's claims provoked considerable criticism from among liberal scholars. A major controversy which has arisen centres upon his belief in

---

19 *Ibid.*, at 1577.

20 *Ibid.*, at 1571.

21 *Ibid.*, at 1554.

an objectively derivable common good/civic virtue attainable through deliberation among political equals. Unlike more conservative, communitarian-determinative theories which equate the common good with the community's own perception of the common good and would therefore permit regulation of individual liberty that commanded popular support,[22] Sunstein's 'common good' permits only those restrictions that can point to objective justification as moral truths.[23] Instead, without fully articulating the theoretical basis of his 'common good', he points to the values inherent in broadcast regulation (such as the fairness doctrine to guarantee access to a wide range of viewpoints),[24] environmental measures and anti-discrimination law as attesting to the republican belief in universalism.[25] Critics have seized on this external standard aspect of Sunstein's model as fundamentally at odds with the premise of self-determination.[26] The criticism is as follows: either civic virtue is an objective value or it is not. If it is, the community of equals could save itself much time and effort by allowing an enlightened and benign dictator to reveal the conclusion of political debate in advance. If it is not, civic virtue is capable of being given whatever meaning the citizens wish to give it and the deliberative process becomes crucial once more. This criticism misses the point that Sunstein is concerned primarily to rule out certain conclusions, not produce unanimity on all questions for all time. A community of political equals made up of different ethic groups and sexual orientations could not, acting in a manner consistent with the equal worth and dignity of all individuals, uphold access to public goods such as housing or transport on a racial- or gender-discriminatory basis.

---

22 The communitarian-determinative model thereby allows societal self-determination, see M Redish and G Lippman, 'Freedom of Expression and the Civic Republican Revival in Constitutional Theory – The Ominous Implications' (1991) 79 *Cal L Rev* 267, 290–95. see also M Sandel, 'Morality and the Liberal Ideal' (1984) 190 *New Republic* 15. As Greenawalt notes, conservative communitarianism is to be found when judges decline to interfere with rules laid down by legislatures on the twin bases that the values of the local/national community are best reflected by legislatures and ought to be preserved. See K Greenawalt, *Fighting Words; Individuals, Communities and Liberties of Speech* (1995, Princeton University Press, Princeton NJ) 133.

23 For an example from a fellow civic republican that popular consent alone cannot be the basis of limitations on individual liberty, see Frank Michelman's attack on the Supreme Court's decision in *Bowers* v *Hardwick* 478 US 186 (1986) upholding the law of Georgia which criminalized consensual homosexual activity in the privacy of the home: 'Law's Republic' (1988) 97 *Yale LJ* 1493.

24 Republicanism is hostile to the exclusive use of the market to regulate media access.

25 (1988) 97 *Yale LJ* 1539, 1555. He is careful to note that not all political disputes are resolvable in this way. Sometimes compromises will be necessary. In other instances, such as religious issues, different conceptions of the good life should not be mediated through politics. Some commentators point to the fact that most republican theorists are positioned on the political left to suggest that left-of-centre values would be prominent in any statement of the common good. See further S Gey, 'The Unfortunate Revival of Civic Republicanism' (1993) 141 *U Pa L Rev* 801, 865.

26 S Gey, *ibid*., at 809–10.

The various and contrasting implications of liberal, communitarian and civic republican thinking for freedom of expression run through the remaining chapters of this book. A political culture that is communitarian will perhaps find it easy to impose restraints upon expression where these are considered by the majority to cause offence. In the case of civic republicanism, the possibility appears to exist of viewpoint bans imposed not because a majority in the polity dislikes/disagrees with the expression in question but because the expression advocates objectively 'bad' answers to societal problems. Also the prioritization of political discourse in civic republican thinking has ramifications for the degree of protection conferred on other speech forms such as commercial expression. For liberals, viewpoint discrimination is objectionable because it limits the autonomy of individual speakers and listeners alike to decide for themselves what they wish to communicate/hear. As will be seen in Chapter 5, which deals with the problems posed by hateful expressive forms, if the state is permitted on the basis of content/viewpoint to decide which communicative acts may be heard, the risk arises that certain disfavoured topics/positions could be excised from public discourse altogether. The tensions between the competing claims of individuals and community are a recurrent theme in this book.

Chapter 2

Rights-based Judicial Review, Constitutional Cultures and Expressive Freedom

Introduction

> Complaints are everywhere heard from our most considerate and virtuous citizens … that our governments are too unstable, that the public good is disregarded in the conflicts of rival parties, and that measures are too often decided, not according to the rules of justice and the rights of the minor party but by the superior force of an interested and overbearing majority.[1]

To some, it might seem paradoxical to place responsibility upon the judicial sphere (an undemocratic, unrepresentative institution) for maintaining the conditions of deliberative democracy and individual liberty in preference to trusting the elected representatives of the people and, more generally, political processes. Thus, in a recently published monograph on the British constitution, Adam Tomkins claims that, despite its monarchical outward form, the constitution is in fact deeply influenced by republican values. It is just that the dominant mode of constitutional scholarship has tended to neglect the role and value of political forms of accountability, emphasizing instead (and wrongly) legal forms of control.[2] In *Our Republican Constitution* he sets out to demonstrate the current vitality of republican ideals and advocates a series of reforms to prerogative powers, open government, party discipline and the Crown to bring about a more genuinely republican style constitution.[3] A major target of Tomkins's polemic is something that he labels 'legal constitutionalism'. Among its other tenets, a key aspect of legal constitutionalism for Tomkins is the notion that 'the law should control government through the enforcement of specific rules and general principles of legality (such as human rights)'.[4] Apart from restating well-worn criticisms of unelected, unrepresentative judges and the limitations of the

1 J Madison, Paper 10, in J Madison, A Hamilton and J Jay, *The Federalist Papers* (1987, Penguin, Harmondsworth).

2 *Our Republican Constitution* (2005, Hart Publishing, Oxford).

3 Some of these – such as the abandonment of the party whipping system – belong to the realms of utopian thinking and as such are of scant practical value.

4 *Ibid.*, at 11.

courtroom as a forum for making legal policy, he asserts that the record of the judges in human rights cases shows that

> … legal constitutionalism promises more than it is able to deliver; that in practice it is able neither to secure liberty nor act as an effective check on the government of the day.[5]

Citizens, we are informed, enjoy no greater liberty now than they did prior to the 1998 *Human Rights Act*. In the course of this chapter, we will return to see whether this analysis of outcomes of inhuman rights cases is credible. For the time being, it can be remarked that Tomkins's commitment to a truly deliberative and open democracy is something which many public law scholars aspire to. The suggestion that constitutional courts have little or no role to play in attaining this state of affairs is, however, highly debatable. It is the contention of this chapter, in contrast to Tomkins, that rights-based judicial review can play some part – albeit within the limitations imposed by judicial structures – in promoting the conditions for vigorous democratic debate among a community of political equals.

In unravelling the apparent paradox between open, deliberative government and judicially determined rights, it is worth recalling the potential for majoritarian political processes to act in ways that are destructive of these ends. Certainly, Madison seems to have been aware of the problem. Further back in history, as John Laws recounted in an article published in *Public Law*, the loss of 25 Athenian ships at the battle of Arginusae led to a trial of eight Athenian generals before an Assembly of the People.[6] The strength of public feeling against the generals was such that, instead of being given separate trials as they were legally entitled to, the generals were tried together. When a challenge was brought to the procedure, the presiding committee yielded to public anger and proceeded by way of a single trial. The generals were subsequently sentenced to death. In order that certain basic rights deemed characteristic in a democracy (such as the right to a fair trial and freedom of expression) might prevail, the lesson of the Arginusae generals is, it seems, that we should be prepared to countenance limits upon majoritarian processes.

A commitment to a truly deliberative democracy among political equals may also require that action be taken to enable to some extent at least those with less communicative power to have their voices heard on matters relating to public affairs. On this account, any evaluation of the outcome of judicial review ought to take account of the extent to which judicial intervention promotes or hinders democratic deliberation among citizens as political equals, a feature of judicial review not generally acknowledged by the critics of legal constitutionalism. This matter is looked at more closely in Chapter 4 in the context of constitutional challenges to election campaign finance laws and Chapter 5 in relation to hate speech controls.

In attempting to make some general points about the impact of judicial review across a number of liberal democratic states, the chapter also addresses issues concerning the distinctiveness of national constitutional practice and culture. There

5 *Ibid*., at 31.

6 'Law and Democracy' (1995) *PL* 72.

is a view in comparative constitutional scholarship that national legal cultures are sufficiently distinct to prevent much meaningful insight being gained from the norms and values of specific cultures. The predominantly sceptical note sounded in a collection of essays by distinguished scholars on the prospects for importing aspects of First Amendment jurisprudence into English/European Convention freedom of expression law bears recent testimony to the academic respectability of this stance.[7] Concerns about the inappropriateness of (mainly US) legal transplantation have similarly been voiced by Canadian and Australian commentators.[8] Apart from textual/structural differences in constitutional documents and respective common law traditions, these sceptics point, with some justification, to divergences in underlying political values. What is seen as the rampant individualism of the US is contrasted with more obviously collective values encountered elsewhere. Under these circumstances, it is considered inappropriate to seek to apply the rights-based model of judicial review developed in the US outside that jurisdiction. Thus, in a chapter entitled 'The Use and Abuse of American Constitutional Theory in *Charter* Analysis', the Canadian academic Patrick Monahan expressed the view that American writing on judicial review did not and could not provide

> ... adequate answers to the difficult interpretative questions which arise under the Charter. The Charter is a uniquely Canadian document. The key to unlocking its secrets does not lie in an alien culture but in the Canadian political culture.[9]

Whilst it is entirely right to highlight and respect the significance of nations' distinctive cultural, political and institutional facets, this approach runs the danger of over-hasty dismissal of insights in constitutional adjudication offered by other jurisdictions.[10] In the context of freedom of expression, for example, the stress on cultural distinctness can mean that the rich and principled discussion of the underlying purposes of expressive freedom that is to be found in foreign legal writing is all too easily discarded. Public lawyers in England and Wales will need no reminding of the period pre-dating the obligation under s.2 of the *Human Rights Act* 1998 on the courts to 'take account' of European Court of Human Rights (ECHR) jurisprudence when English judges routinely asserted that the common law had nothing of value to learn from European judges on questions relating to

---

7 I Loveland (ed.) *Importing the First Amendment* (1998, Hart Publishing, Oxford).

8 See thus D Rolph, 'The Message, Not the Medium: Defamation, Publication and the Internet in *Dow Jones & Co* v *Gutnick*' (2002) 24 *Sydney Law Review* 262, defending the Australian High Court's refusal to allow First Amendment norms to prevail over the state of Victoria's defamation law.

9 *Politics and the Constitution – The Charter, Federalism and the Supreme Court of Canada* (1987, Carswell, Toronto) at 74. See also his remark that 'General Motors may be able to ignore the Canadian–American border but Ronald Dworkin cannot', at 95.

10 For the view that the benefits of judicial review are contingent on features and circumstances specific to each particular country, see W Sadurski, 'Judicial Review and Protection of Constitutional Rights' (2002) 22 *OJLS* 275.

freedom of speech or other liberties. Somewhat condescendingly, senior judges declared that the European Convention on Human Rights amounted to nothing more than 'the articulation of values already recognised at common law.'[11] Thus in *Derbyshire County Council* v *Times Newspapers*,[12] Lord Keith of Kinkel declared that, at common law, a local authority was not entitled to sue for libel. He stated that he had reached this conclusion 'upon the common law of England, without finding any need to rely upon the European Convention'.[13] Three years later, in *John* v *MGN Ltd*, the then Master of the Rolls Sir Thomas Bingham likewise considered the relevance of Convention jurisprudence to be at best confirmatory. There, he referred to the idea that ECHR case law might 'buttress' the soundness of conclusions already arrived at via the wisdom of English common law.[14] For Murray Hunt, these statements raised the troubling prospect that international human rights norms and the jurisprudence accompanying them would be marginalized in domestic proceedings. He argued conversely that those norms should be accorded a central role in the development of English common law.[15] As it turned out, alongside s.2 of the *Human Rights Act* 1998 the strong interpretative obligation laid down by s.3(1) of the same Act sounded the death knell for this somewhat complacent approach.

The basis from which this chapter proceeds is the very modest one that proper respect for cultural and historical differences need not lead always to the wholesale rejection of other jurisdictions' insights into constitutional conflicts. The manner in which foreign courts have conceptualized and analysed conflicts in public law can, as Feldman has argued, suggest approaches without necessarily dictating an outcome.[16] This claim would appear to be especially relevant in the context of political expression. After all, the institutions of representative government in liberal democracies by definition draw their authority from the consent of the people. This would seem to require a sufficient number of critically engaged citizens enjoying access to a range of information and opinions about public affairs. It also demands that no arbitrary and permanent barriers be erected to limit political discussion and that citizens be free to participate effectively in the political process, regardless of race, ethnicity, gender or wealth. Significantly in this regard, Hare has identified a set of normative propositions to emerge from courts in Australia, Canada, the UK, the US and the European Court of Human Rights in Strasbourg, any of which

---

11 M Hunt, *Using Human Rights Law in English Courts* (1998, Hart Publishing, Oxford) at 303.

12 [1993] AC 534.

13 *Ibid.*, at 551.

14 [1996] 2 All ER 35, 58.

15 See thus J Laws, 'Is the High Court the Guardian of Fundamental Constitutional Rights?' (1993) *PL* 59.

16 'The Internationalization of Public Law and its Impact on the United Kingdom' in J Jowell and D Oliver (eds), *The Changing Constitution* (5th edn, 2004, OUP, Oxford).

could, without too much difficulty, be taken to represent legal doctrine in each of the others.[17] These include the following:

> Freedom of communication on matters of government and politics is an indispensable incident of that system of representative government which the Constitution creates;[18] … It is difficult to imagine a guaranteed right more important to democratic society than freedom of expression … The vital importance of the concept cannot be over-emphasised;[19] … [F]reedom to disseminate and receive information on political matters is essential to the proper functioning of the system of parliamentary democracy cherished in this country;[20] … [D]ebate on public issues should be uninhibited, robust, and wide open, and that may well include vehement, caustic and sometimes unpleasantly sharp attacks on government and public officials;[21] … [F]reedom of political debate is at the very core of the concept of a democratic society which runs through the Convention.[22]

These statements appear to make it plain that political expression across the common law world is entitled to a high level of constitutional/legal protection, more so by implication than other forms of expression such as commercial speech or sexually explicit speech. [23] Certainly, it is difficult to find equivalent foundational claims being made on behalf of product advertisements or the publishers of *Playboy* magazine. A powerful reason why this must be so lies in the concept of a modern, deliberative democracy. As the US First Amendment scholar Cass Sunstein has observed, the people's representatives do not mechanically convert constituents' preferences into legal form.[24] Instead, they come together with other representatives and are exposed to additional information, others' experiences and perspectives. It is in this context that law-making occurs. An earlier exposition of this position is to be found in Edmund Burke's 'Address to the Electors of Bristol' in which he famously attacked the idea of Parliament as a gathering of mandated agents with different and hostile interests which each agent was duty-bound to maintain in the face of opposition from others. For Burke,

> [P]arliament is a deliberative assembly of one nation, with one interest, that of the whole; where not local purposes, not local prejudices, ought to guide, but the general good, resulting from the general reason of the whole. You choose a member indeed;

17 I Hare, 'Is the Privileged Position of Political Expression Justified?' in J Beatson and Y Cripps (eds), *Freedom of Expression and Freedom of Information – Essays in Honour of Sir David Williams* (2002, OUP, Oxford).

18 *Lange* v *Australian Broadcasting Company* (1997) 189 CLR 520, 599, *per* Brennan CJ.

19 *Edmonton Journal* v *Alberta AG* (1989) 64 DLR (4th) 577, 607, *per* Cory J.

20 *Reynolds* v *Times Newspapers* [1999] 3 WLR 1010, 1022, *per* Lord Nicholls.

21 *New York Times* v *Sullivan* 376 US 254 (1964) at 270, *per* Brennan J.

22 *Lingens* v *Austria* (1986) 8 EHRR 407, at para 42.

23 I Hare, 'Is the Privileged Position of Political Expression Justified?' in J Beatson and Y Cripps (eds), *Freedom of Expression and Freedom of Information – Essays in Honour of Sir David Williams* (2002, OUP, Oxford) at 108.

24 *The Partial Constitution* (1993, Harvard University Press, Harvard MA) 22–3.

> but when you have chosen him, he is not member of Bristol, but he is a member of parliament … .[25]

The freedom to exchange ideas and reasons in the public sphere cannot not be limited to elected representatives however. The justifications offered for rule-making in democracies have to be intelligible to all citizens. As was noted in Chapter 1, William Galston's account of the political virtues needed of citizens to sustain liberal democracy stressed the importance of citizens' capacities to discern the talent and character of candidates seeking public office and to evaluate the performance of those already in power.[26] Likewise rejecting the idea that decision-making ought simply to reflect the outcome of clashes between pre-existing, private interests, Stephen Macedo has maintained that citizens in a liberal regime expect to be able to criticize government and to be provided with reasoned explanations for government conduct rather than being met with force or silence.[27] The central importance of maintaining the conditions for an effective deliberative democracy may from time to time call for constraints to be placed on ruling majorities when they are tempted to silence the expressive activities of others. Unorthodox political expression is especially prone to interference. This criterion calls for stringent scrutiny of censoring measures enacted by temporary political majorities since it is quite clear that a model of judicial review that sought to reflect community values only might well fail to protect unorthodox political expression to the detriment of wider debate.

The existence of a clear cross-jurisdictional consensus on the freedom of speech implications of representative democracy should not obscure the fact that difficult questions of definition will from time to time arise as to the ambit of 'political expression', although most of these would appear to be resolved by reading the term broadly to include matters of public concern more generally.[28] More importantly perhaps, the non-absolute nature of freedom of expression must be confronted within each jurisdiction. No one seriously argues for an unlimited freedom to reveal damaging military information or expression which renders impossible the administration of justice. Few either would be prepared to tolerate speech that caused imminent and widespread social disorder. Outside these fairly unproblematic areas, modern democracies face common and difficult problems in relation to the regulation of hate speech, the buying of political influence, expression that is critical of political leaders and commercial advertising on behalf of demonstrably harmful

---

25 Speech of 3 November 1774 republished in *The Works of the Right Honourable Edmund Burke* (1854–56, Henry G Bohn, London).

26 *Liberal Purposes* (1991, CUP, Cambridge), especially Ch. 10. See also S Macedo, *Liberal Virtues* (1990, Clarendon Press, Oxford).

27 *Ibid.*

28 The House of Lords in *Reynolds* rejected the idea of a generic privilege for 'political information' in defamation law partly on account of the fact that the category would not be extensive enough to cater for all matters of serious public concern. Hare himself raises some of the definitional difficulties at 108–12, *ibid.* See also C Munro, 'The Value of Commercial Speech' (2003) 62 *CLJ* 134.

products. It is also to be expected that the construction of boundaries on these and other questions will reflect specific, national political cultures, as well as procedural and substantive legal doctrines. The precise context in which the contested expression occurs will also be highly significant. Speech that touches on the subject matter of immigration, for example, might at the outset be deemed worthy of considerable protection from external interference but where the speaker intends or is aware that his/her words may inflame others to act in a way which puts others in fear of their physical safety and the speech occurs against a general backdrop of attacks on racial/ethnic minorities, the claim to high-level protection is much less compelling.

Judicial Review and Constitutionalism

> A bill of rights is what the people are entitled to against every government on earth.
>
> (Thomas Jefferson, 1787)[29]

Where once politicians, judges and academics alike contested at length the wisdom of entrusting to unelected judges the power to gainsay the policy choices of elected legislatures, the debate has, with some notable exceptions, moved on. Of course, for some jurisdictions (including Canada and South Africa), the express vesting of judicial review over primary legislation in a constitutional document has provided some degree of closure on the issue.[30] When 'the people' have spoken and made a solemn undertaking as in the adoption of new a constitution with a clear separation of powers, the government or the legislature may not simply act in disregard of the courts' custodial function in preserving the decisions of 'the people'. On this view,

---

29 PL Ford (ed.), *Writings of Thomas Jefferson* (1892, GP Putnam's Sons, New York) 4, 477.

30 In the case of Canada, see s.24(1) of the *Canadian Charter of Rights and Freedoms* and s.52(1) of the *Constitution Act* 1982. Christopher Manfredi – a Canadian critic of judicial supremacism – has commented that 'it is too late in Canadian constitutional development to question whether the Charter should have been entrenched. Indeed, it is precisely because that question was resolved in favour of the Charter that attention must be paid to the manner in which the judges interpret and apply this document of open-ended rights …': *Judicial Review and the Charter – Canada and the Paradox of Liberal Constitutionalism* (2nd edn, 2000, OUP, Toronto) at 22. See also B McLachlin, 'Courts, Legislatures and Executives in the Post-Charter Era' (1999) *Policy Options* 42. For notable dissents on this point, see both M Mandel, *The Charter of Rights and the Legalization of Politics in Canada* (1989, Wall & Thompson, Toronto) and A Hutchinson, 'Supreme Court Inc. – The Business of Democracy and Rights' in G W Anderson (ed.) *Rights and Democracy – Essays in UK–Canadian Constitutionalism* (1999, Blackstone Press Ltd, London). Mandel criticizes the Canadian Charter for undermining representative democratic institutions and failing to constrain private power. Hutchinson similarly slams 'rights-talk' as a diversion and encourages instead greater attention to 'championing a style of and substance of politics that takes seriously the virtues of democratic dialogue over the vices of rights-talk', at 44.

the government acting alone or in concert with the legislature are no longer 'the people' and lack the power to disturb the constitutional settlement.[31]

Of course, the absence of such express authority in other constitutions has not prevented the judiciary arrogating to itself the power of review. Ever since the ruling of Chief Justice Marshall in *Marbury* v *Madison*[32] the US Congress and subsequently the state legislatures have enacted laws in the knowledge that their provisions were susceptible to constitutional challenge. Whilst much debate has centred upon the question of how the power to review has been exercised by nine Supreme Court justices, few today question the fact of review.[33]

Even supposedly unentrenched (and therefore majoritarian-friendly) bills of rights such as those encountered in the UK and New Zealand have within a relatively short space of time acquired characteristics that have begun to worry the defenders of legislative supremacy. Take New Zealand for example. The *New Zealand Bill of Rights Act* 1990 (hereafter *NZBORA*) does not confer on the New Zealand courts a power to strike down an Act of the New Zealand Parliament. Instead, it merely requires under s.6 that legislation be interpreted consistently with the *NZBORA*'s terms. Thus, where a statutory provision can be interpreted in more than one way, the courts will prefer the interpretation that is 'most in harmony' with *NZBORA*.[34] It should be noted that, unlike the position under s.3(1) of the *Human Rights Act* 1998 in the UK, s.6 does not permit a strained interpretation of legislation to ensure conformity with *NZBORA*.[35] Where an *NZBORA*-compliant reading of an Act cannot be given, *NZBORA* explicitly rules out the prospect that the Act could be invalidated, impliedly repealed or disapplied. Section 4 states:

> No court shall, in relation to any enactment (whether passed or made before or after the commencement of this Bill of Rights):

---

31 D Davis, M Chaskalason and J De Waal, 'Democracy and Constitutionalism: The Role of Constitutional Interpretation' in D van Wyk, J Dugard, B de Villiers and D Davis, *Rights and Constitutionalism – The New South African Order* (1995, Clarendon Press, Oxford).

32 (1803) 5 US (1 Cranch) 137.

33 Eugene Rostow commented that judicial review 'has been exercised by the Court from the beginning … And it stands now, whatever the Founding Fathers may in fact have meant, as an integral feature of the living constitution' in 'The Supreme Court and the People's Will' (1958) 33 *Notre Dame Law Review* 573, 576. See further E Rostow, 'The Democratic Character of Judicial Review' (1952) 66 *Harv L Rev* 193.

34 *GA Moonen* v *Film and Literature Board of Review* [2000] 2 NZLR 9 at para.16 *per* Tipping J and see for comment I Cram, 'Film Licensing in New Zealand and the Limits of Constitutional Protection for Artistic Expression' (2004) 15 *Ent L Rev* 243.

35 A Butler (2000) *EHRLR* 249. Section 3 (1) states: 'So far as it is possible to do so, primary legislation and subordinate legislation must be read and given effect in a way which is compatible with the Convention rights.' See further Lord Lester, 'The Art of the Possible – Interpreting Statutes under the Human Rights Act 1998' (1998) *EHRLR* 665.

(a) Hold any provision of the enactment to be impliedly repealed or revoked, or to be in any way invalid or ineffective; or
(b) Decline to apply any provision of this enactment by reason only that the provision is inconsistent with any provision of this Bill of Rights.[36]

Remarkably, however, in 2001 three (out of seven) Court of Appeal judges held in *R* v *Pora* that, in cases raising issues within the ambit of the *Bill of Rights Act* 1990, the doctrine of implied repeal no longer applied.[37] This led one critic to splutter, somewhat incredulously, 'To an extent unimagined before the Bill of Rights Act's passage, New Zealand now has the regular exercise of political value judgments by unelected judges'.[38] This response to *Pora* reminds us (if reminding was needed) that judicial determination of human rights in democracies is problematic on account of its blatant counter-majoritarianism. In reply, defenders of judicial review challenge the notion that majoritarianism alone captures the meaning of democracy. Instead, a broader vision of democracy than that offered by majoritarianism is posited in which the powers of transient political majorities can be constrained by appeals to constitutionalism and rights. Essentially, constitutionalism makes the normative claim that certain values/principles are so fundamental to the democratic process that they should be beyond the power of passing political majorities to alter. Bruce Ackerman, for one, has pointed to the importance of safeguarding the participation of all citizens in the political process, regardless of talent, ability or economic resources.[39] Limits on majoritarian policy-making can also be agreed to in advance by the members of a society in recognition of medium and long-term needs for effective political debate.[40] Obvious limits in this sense include the rights to freedom of expression, association and assembly. In these areas, there is a strong case for active judicial

36 For background see PA Joseph, *Constitutional and Administrative Law in New Zealand* (1993, Law Book Company, Sydney), Ch. 26; and A Butler, 'Interface between the Human Rights Act 1998 and other Enactments: Pointers from New Zealand' (2000) *EHRLR* 249.

37 [2001] NZLR 37, and see J Evans, 'Questioning the Dogmas of Realism' (2001) *NZULR* 145. Others have even looked on with alarm at the refashioning of the common law to reflect the Bill of Rights in cases such as *Lange* v *Atkinson* [1998] 3 NZLR 424; [2000] 3 NZLR 385; see for example J Allan, 'The Author Doth Protest Too Much' (2003) 20 *NZULR* 519, 525.

38 J Allan, *ibid.*, at 525. See also Andrew Butler who faulted the approach of the three judges as failing to understand the limits on statutory construction placed by *NZBORA* to preserve a particular vision of parliamentary sovereignty, 'Implied Repeal, Parliamentary Sovereignty and Human Rights in New Zealand' (2001) *PL* 586.

39 B Ackerman, *We the People* (1991, Harvard University Press, Harvard MA). See, in a Canadian context, Justice (now CJ) B McLachlin, 'The Canadian Charter and the Democratic Process' in C Gearty and A Tomkins (eds), *Understanding Human Rights* (1996, Mansell Publishing Ltd, London) at 26–30.

40 S Holmes, *Passions and Constraints: On the Theory of Liberal Democracy* (1995, University of Chicago Press, Chicago IL).

policing of legislative/executive infringements.[41] Most closely associated with John Hart Ely's *Democracy and Distrust*, this defence of judicial oversight emphasizes the democracy-reinforcing potential of judicial review in modern representative democracies.[42] Other constraints suggested by the idea of constitutionalism include those on the scope of authority (as for example contained in federal constitutions allocating legislative, executive and judicial functions between central and regional authorities) and procedural requirements for exercising power.[43] In most democracies where elected representatives' constituencies include a diverse set of electors in terms of religion, ethnicity, race, sexual orientation and other characteristics, one of the advantages held out by constitutionalism is the prospect of judicial safeguarding of the rights of minority groups and their members from prejudiced incursion by the majority.

The Joe McCarthy Problem and Other Institutional Capability Issues

Those who would prefer the task of determining constitutional rights questions be left to the elected representatives of the people (hereafter 'majoritarians') have sooner or later to confront what some US commentators have referred to as the 'Joe McCarthy problem', namely how can those who are concerned to uphold constitutional principles be content to vest ultimate authority in those with little or no interest in constitutional values or, much worse, those who hold certain core precepts in contempt.[44] One response to this is simply to point, as Mark Tushnet has, to the more notorious occupants of the highest judicial offices,[45] as well as to some fairly spectacular failures to defend constitutional values (ironically in the case of the US during the McCarthy era when a supine Supreme Court upheld convictions under federal laws prohibiting the advocacy of revolution).[46] Most would agree with Tushnet that both legislatures and judges can make mistakes. The real issue, he argues, is 'whether in general legislatures or courts make more, and more important constitutional mistakes.' Related to this results-based evaluation – although worthy of consideration in its own right – is the issue of the institutional features of

41 C Sunstein, *The Partial Constitution* (1993, Harvard University Press, Harvard MA) 142.

42 (1980, Harvard University Press, Harvard MA).

43 In a non-federal context, an argument for 'auto-limitation' of government power was made by Patrick McAuslan and John McEldowney in 'Legitimacy and the Constitution: The Dissonance between Theory and Practice' in P McAuslan and J McEldowney (eds), *Law, Legitimacy and the Constitution* (1985, Sweet & Maxwell, London).

44 See thus M Tushnet, *Taking the Constitution Away from the Courts* (1997, Princeton University Press, Princeton NJ) at 55–57.

45 According to Tushnet the US Supreme Court list would include the anti-Semite James McReynolds who broke with the Court custom of shaking the hands of fellow justices because he could not bear to shake hands with Justice Brandeis (*ibid.*).

46 *Dennis* v *United States* 341 US 494 (1951).

rights regulation. Are courts – because they are courts – simply better placed than legislatures to settle constitutional arguments?

To begin with, I want to explore some criticisms of judicial review offered by majoritarians favouring legislative resolution of constitutional questions. I will start by outlining the views of the legal philosopher Jeremy Waldron before turning to consider an argument against judicial supremacy first made in the nineteenth century. Underlying these various majoritarian arguments is a commonly held and optimistic account of the potential of the political sphere and democratic politics to provide a forum for an informed and public discussion of key rights issues.[47] It is not clear, however, that the empirical evidence supports this presumption as strongly as majoritarians would have us believe.

In *Law and Disagreement* Waldron sets out to restore the reputation of legislatures and ordinary legislation as the best way of resolving disputes about rights. Waldron's central argument is that it is impossible to obtain agreement among all individuals on what counts as just or morally correct. Atheists, to take one example, refuse to accept that religious persons have a superior conception of justice. The disagreement persists because the premises underpinning a claim to have a right answer are always going to be disputed. The intractable nature of moral disagreement erects a barrier that no master theory can overcome. Instead of seeking in vain for such a theory, effort ought to be directed towards the development of procedures which, whilst not settling questions of right and wrong, will nonetheless resolve disputes in a way that is respectful of the contending factions' positions. It is Waldron's position that these procedures are to be found in legislatures where it is not required that 'anyone's sincerely held view be played down or hushed up because of the fancied importance of consensus'.[48]

Waldron's objection to judicial review is that, ultimately, it is tied to an unconvincing account of human capacities. It sets the judges up as sufficiently superior in thinking to the rest of the population on rights questions when this cannot ever be satisfactorily be shown to the disagreeing parties or the wider community. For Waldron, this means that judicial review amounts to nothing more than the imposition of judges' personal opinions. At the same time, judicial review manages to evince considerable disrespect to individual rights-bearers. His argument here is that it is incongruent on the one hand to confer rights on individuals and treat each person as worthy of holding rights whilst, on the other, transferring (under judicial review)

47 See thus Waldron who asserts of both England and the US that there are 'robust and established traditions of political liberty (which have flourished in the often despite the best efforts of the judiciary); and in both countries there are vigorous debates about political structures that seem able to proceed without threatening minority freedoms': *Law and Disagreement* (1999, OUP, New York) at 290.

48 See also on this point K Ewing in 'Human Rights, Social Democracy and Constitutional Reform' in C Gearty and A Tomkins (eds), *Understanding Human Rights* (1996, Mansell Publishing Ltd, London). Ewing refers to the 'right of equality in decision-making' as the basic principle of social democratic constitutionalism which favours allowing Parliaments and not courts the final say on rights matters, at 42–4.

decision-making power away from the popularly elected assemblies. The latter denial of participation in political decision-making points up a distrust of citizens and their reasoning that cannot easily be reconciled with the notion of individual rights. It follows that there is an undeniable 'democratic' cost when judges decide matters, even if the decision that is made bolsters or contributes to the maintenance of that democracy.

Aside from Waldron's criticisms of judicial review, other assaults on the validity of judicial intervention from an institutional perspective have been clustered around the idea of the problematic consequences of 'judicial overhang' on legislatures and wider public debate. On this view, judicial review is said to impact negatively on the treatment of constitutional issues in legislatures by inducing variously a lack of legislative responsibility, distorted law-making and distorted legislative discussion. Elected representatives' lack of ultimate authority to say what the constitution means may, in the final analysis, deaden wider, public discussion of rights-related issues since the views of expert judges on the meaning of the Constitution is all that matters. This line of criticism is most closely associated with the nineteenth-century US legal scholar James Bradley Thayer.[49] Legislatures ought to take constitutional questions seriously but, in practice, Thayer claimed they paid little attention to such matters, knowing that the courts would correct any misconceptions. This disinclination to take constitutional questions seriously could be traced directly to judicial supremacy.[50] Where, alternatively, legislatures have tried to address the constitutional implications of their rule-making, a later generation of constitutional scholars have contended that judicial review works to distort both the ultimate form that legislation assumes as well as influencing the nature of deliberative discussion. The skewing effect on legislative form springs from the desire to offer the judges minimal grounds for taking constitutional offence. Elected assemblies will shy away from enacting what may be considered to be best policy, adopting instead the least risk-laden alternative. Accordingly, the deliberation which precedes the enactment of any particular policy will frequently be occupied by the issue of constitutional compatibility. Expert lawyers may be called before the legislature to predict whether a measure is 'narrowly tailored' or 'proportionate' within the meaning most recently

49 'The Origin and Scope of the American Doctrine of Constitutional Law' in *Legal Essays* (1908, The Boston Book Co., Boston). Thayer supported an extremely limited form of judicial review in those instances where the legislature had made a very clear mistake, one which was not open to rational question. See subsequently in the same vein Leonard Levy who considered that judicial resolution of such issues lulled the people 'into apathy on matters that are fundamentally their concern': *Original Intent and the Framers' Constitution* (1988, Macmillan, New York) at 362–3. See further, in a Canadian context, A Hutchinson, 'Supreme Court Inc. – The Business of Democracy and Rights' in G W Anderson (ed.), *Rights and Democracy – Essays in UK–Canadian Constitutionalism* (1999, Blackstone Press Ltd, London).

50 This failure has been characterized by Tushnet as 'democratic debilitation'. See his 'Policy Distortion and Democratic Debilitation: Comparative Illumination of the Counter-Majoritarian Difficulty' (1995) 94 *Mich L Rev* 245.

afforded to those terms by the courts. The crucial feature of this deliberative phase is the fact that it occurs within judge-made confines.

Apart from these negative features of judicial overhang, supporters of majoritarianism also point more positively to the advantages of unencumbered legislative policy-making. These usually include a lengthy pre-legislative period of gestation in which affected persons and groups will be afforded opportunities to make representations on the content of proposed rules to government and opposition members of the legislature. Empirical evidence may also be gathered by participants in the debate to bolster arguments. The diversity of groups and individuals who come forward will normally ensure that a range of viewpoints is heard. Finally, by the time the government has brought specific reforms forward for enactment into law, an informed discussion occurs in the legislature which is characterized by a careful weighing of arguments and supporting evidence. Waldron, for example, has claimed that the legislative phase reveals a respectful set of procedures characterized by

> … [o]pinionated disagreement – a noisy scenario in which men and women of high spirit argue about what rights we have, what justice requires, and what the common good amounts to, motivated in their disagreement not by what's in it for them but by a desire to get it right.[51]

This is contrasted against judicial determination of the constitutionality of legislative policy where the adversarial structure of legal procedures and judges' limited capacities to analyse and foresee the full ramifications of their rulings makes the courts much less competent to forge new rules.

In the following sections I look at institutional and results-based defences of judicial review – a typology that may suggest a clearer distinction than exists in practice between the two defences. After all, the attractiveness of the institutional argument for judicial review would surely diminish if, notwithstanding a constitutional settlement that laid down a clear separation of powers and gave guarantees of an independent judiciary, in reality the judges adopted a consistently pro-executive approach to state versus individual liberty disputes. This may indicate that the predominant justification is the results-based one or merely that the judiciary has the potential to act as a check on executive/legislative action. With this caveat in mind, we can look to these two main defences.

Institutional Defences of Judicial Review

The leading institutional defence of judicial review remains the account of Alexander Bickel.[52] He argued that the US legislature and the executive were called upon to articulate and defend enduring constitutional values but had too

51 *Law and Disagreement* (1999, OUP, New York) 305.

52 AM Bickel, *The Least Dangerous Branch – The Supreme Court at the Bar of Politics* (1962, Bobbs-Merrill Co., Indianapolis IN).

often in the past acted out of expediency, rather than principle.[53] They had been purposely designed to respond to the clash of interests that occurs in democratic politics. This fact inclined legislatures and executives to act with a short-term perspective. The courts, on the other hand, enjoyed certain advantages in dealing with matters of principle, including their insulation from daily political affairs and their training to give expression to enduring values in actual disputes to come before them.[54] Insulation is valuable because it helps resist popular pressure. Individual liberty is at risk when elected politicians come under intense pressure to 'respond' to the disquiet of vocal and powerful interests by enacting appeasing measures that curtail freedoms of unpopular minorities in ways that are considered to assist retention of political power.[55] In the UK, examples from both main parties' tenure of office are not difficult to find. The Conservative Party's determination when in office to appear 'tough' on criminals was such that it led to a series of legal challenges in the field of prison administration.[56] In the case of Labour, the tightening of asylum rules in response to media-led claims of large-scale migration from Eastern Europe and elsewhere offers a more recent example of 'responsive' policy-making. With an embarrassing frequency, it has fallen to the courts, within the confines of the doctrine of parliamentary sovereignty and, more recently, the *Human Rights Act* 1998, to strike down a number of executive policies and decisions that disfavoured the interests of prisoners[57] and asylum seekers.[58] The ruling by the House of Lords in *A* v *Secretary of State for the Home*

53 For criticism of this view as historically shaky, see J Hart Ely, *Democracy and Distrust – A Theory of Judicial Review* (1980, Harvard University Press, Harvard MA).

54 For much the same argument, see R Dworkin, *A Matter of Principle* (1996, Clarendon Press, Oxford) Ch. 2.

55 J Choper, *Judicial Review and the National Political Process* (1980, University of Chicago Press, Chicago IL) at 67–70.

56 S Livingstone, T Owen and A McDonald, *Prison Law* (3rd edn, 2003, OUP, Oxford) Ch. 16. And note Livingstone's comment elsewhere that 'Politicians find votes in being "tough" on prisoners even if they never visit a prison: displaying more progressive views on prisons is rarely a vote-winner.' 'Prisoners' Rights' in D Harris and S Joseph, *The International Covenant on Civil and Political Rights and United Kingdom Law* (1995, Clarendon Press, Oxford) at 295.

57 See infamously, *R* v *Secretary of State for the Home Department ex parte Venables* [1997] 3 All ER 97, where the Home Secretary's willingness to take account of a petition organized by the tabloid press urging him to impose a higher sentence than those imposed by either the trial judge or the Lord Chief Justice in the case of the murderers of James Bulger meant that the Minister's decision was struck down as unfair. See also *Pierson* v *Secretary of State for the Home Department* [1997] 3 All ER 577, where the Home Secretary's attempt to increase a life sentence prisoner's tariff was retrospectively ruled unlawful once the Minister had conceded that an aggravating feature of the offence was not present.

58 For instance, *Regina (Salih)* v *Secretary of State for the Home Department* (2003) as reported in *The Times* of 13 October – Minister's policy of not informing failed asylum seekers of the availability of discretionary statutory support for accommodation was held to be unlawful); *Regina (Q) and others* v *Secretary of State for the Home Department* [2004]

Department that the indefinite detention provisions of the Labour Government's anti-terrorism laws were discriminatory and contrary to the ECHR is but the latest in a line of high-profile judicial defences of individual liberty.[59] Once more, in the face of a dominant executive authority using its parliamentary position to force through controversial and corrosive legislation in an era of heightened public anxiety, it has fallen to the judicial sphere, not the political sphere, to act as the bulwark of individual liberty. Against this background, it is hard to share the faith of Tomkins and an earlier generation of scholars such as John Griffith in the political processes. Time and again these processes have failed vulnerable persons. From the perspective of an immigrant, asylum seeker or detainee under terrorism laws, to claim that rights-based litigation has achieved little of note is frankly wide of the mark.

In addition to its checking function, Bickel further maintained that the Supreme Court performed a valuable legitimating role when it confirmed legislative action as within the scope of Congress's powers. This function would be meaningless if the court had no power to strike down *ultra vires* measures.

Supporters of judicial review also challenge the descriptions of legislative bodies' conduct invoked by their adversaries. They deny, for example, that law-making by popularly elected assemblies always reflects the ideal of a careful and informed weighing of policy alternatives in which affected parties have had ample and equal opportunity to make representations to the government and elected representatives. It is well established that differences in resources, expertise and insider contacts among pressure groups (for example) will impact to create unequal access to the policy-making process. As Michael Rush has commented in the case of the UK,

> Inevitably, advantages will accrue to the organizations which have regular or frequent contact with Parliament, because they are likely to be familiar with the system and have established contacts upon whose services they can call.[60]

QB 36 – refusal of support for asylum-seekers under the *Nationality, Immigration and Asylum Act* 2002 held to be unlawful where it had been assumed that the failure to claim asylum at the port of entry would justify in itself the refusal of support; *R (on the application of Adam)* v *Secretary of State For Home Department* [2004] EWCA Civ 540; (2004) *The Times* 26 May – Home Secretary's policy under 2002 Act of not providing support to destitute asylum seekers who had not sought asylum as soon as was reasonably practicable amounted to inhuman or degrading treatment under Article 3 of ECHR where it was clear that no charitable assistance was on hand and the applicant would experience imminent and severe suffering. See further M Symes and P Jorro, *Asylum Law and Practice* (2003, Butterworths, London) Ch. 10.

59 [2005] HRLR 1. Indeed it may be argued that it was the forceful rejection in *A* of the indefinite detention measure that prompted a principled discussion in both Houses of Parliament about the deprivation of liberty at times of public emergency.

60 M Rush (ed.), *Parliament and Pressure Politics* (1990, Clarendon Press, Oxford) at 263.

Equally at odds with reality is Jeremy Waldron's rose-tinted view of 'respectful' legislative debate set out in *Law and Disagreement*, noted earlier. Few observers of contemporary political debate in the UK and beyond would recognize this description of their respective legislative assemblies where the reality of heavy legislative programmes and active 'whipping' ensure that individual conscience plays a minimal part in either members' contributions to legislative discussion or voting patterns. That the 'democratic' cost of majority curtailment of others' freedoms and rights – when 'the people' act in a way that damages the interests of democracy – happens to be downplayed by Waldron is hardly surprising. Instances of 'rights-holders' behaving disrespectfully towards other 'rights-holders' through their elected representatives can be found in many jurisdictions. This, however, is to move away from a purely institutional account of judicial review. The actual record of judges and legislatures is considered in greater detail below.

Earlier, we noted Thayer's objection to judicial review that it bred an irresponsible or disinterested attitude towards constitutional questions. Were this to prove empirically true, we should expect modern civic republicans to have serious objections to judicial review on account of its ability to undermine structures of popular discussion and deliberation. Others conversely have argued judicial review enhances the participatory nature of politics by permitting popular discussion of the topic decided before the court to commence from the court's principled analysis of the competing rights and interests raised by the litigation. This allows for a much higher quality of national debate in the media and elsewhere in the aftermath of the ruling than would have occurred if the matter had been resolved exclusively by the legislature. An advocate of judicial review in these terms – Ronald Dworkin – cites the example of *Roe* v *Wade* to claim that, as a result of the constitutional litigation, American citizens understand better the distinction between questions regarding the issue of the morality of abortion and other questions concerning the government's ability to prohibit it.[61]

Unsurprisingly, this counter-claim is resisted by majoritarians. Jeremy Waldron, for example, disputes entirely the empirical basis for Dworkin's position. In his view, national debates about abortion in the UK and New Zealand are just as robust and informed as they are in the US, perhaps more so because they are not so constrained by efforts to construct principles from the 'scraps of some sacred text in an exercise of tendentious exercise of constitutional calligraphy'.[62] He rejects the idea that the public requires a moral debate to focus at the outset on the meaning to be ascribed to constitutional principles before it can be conducted in an enlightened manner. Another majoritarian, Hutchinson, refers more broadly to the 'attenuated discourse of rights-talk' before the courts and urges people to aspire instead to a 'truly democratic polity that will enable them to become full citizens in an expansive civic dialogue

61 410 US 113 (1973). In the same vein, see also B McLachlin, 'Courts, Legislatures and Executives in the Post-Charter Era' (1999) *Policy Options* 42.

62 *Law and Disagreement* (1999, OUP, New York) at 290.

over the terms and conditions of social living'.[63] The empirical truth on these matters is difficult to discern. It is probably fair to say that the institutional arguments are inconclusive. In any event – and this seems to be significant from a civic republican perspective – even if it is granted that the exercise of a power by a few black-robed judges may be guaranteed to engage an articulate population in principled discussion, it does not alter the fact that the debate which does ensue among that section of the population is largely impotent.[64] Ineffectual participation in public discourse among the highly educated is not what civic republican society claims to offer to its citizens. At the same time, upbeat, majoritarian accounts of legislative procedures remain, at best, naive. Moreover, in the absence of reform, it is difficult to see how current unequal patterns of access to law-making in legislatures can usher in Hutchinson's wished-for era of 'expansive civic dialogue'.

Results-based Arguments For and Against Judicial Review

Is the UK worse off for not having established (outside of EU law) judicial review of primary legislation, or are the records of those countries where such review is possible noticeably superior to our own?[65] A survey of the field of academic commentators produces some unlikely bedfellows. Taking first the critics of judicial review, those on the political left point with alarm to the use of litigation by corporations and economically powerful individuals to protect their putative constitutional rights.[66] The UK critics among them look backwards with considerable disdain to decisions of the Privy Council when it acted as a constitutional court for countries within the Commonwealth, accusing it of 'veering between indefensible interference with democratic decisions … and indefensible abstention in the face of illiberal and oppressive conduct by Commonwealth regimes'.[67] Those hostile to judicial review from the political right cite with equal concern the tendency to confer protection

63 'Supreme Court Inc. – The Business of Democracy and Rights' in GW Anderson (ed.), *Rights and Democracy – Essays in UK–Canadian Constitutionalism* (1999, Blackstone Press Ltd, London) at 44.

64 *Law and Disagreement* (1999, OUP, New York) at 291.

65 One survey which concluded that no such rights-gains were evident in jurisdictions where judicial review of primary legislation occurred is that of the 1986 Reith lecturer Lord McCluskey in *Law, Justice and Democracy* (1987, Sweet & Maxwell, BBC Books, London).

66 See thus Sir S Sedley, 'Human Rights: a 21st Century Agenda' in R Blackburn and J Busuttil (eds), *Human Rights for the 21st Century* (1997, Pinter, London); K Ewing 'Human Rights, Social Democracy and Constitutional Reform' in C Gearty and A Tomkins (eds), *Understanding Human Rights* (1996, Mansell Publishing Ltd, London) at 44–5; A Hutchinson, 'Supreme Court Inc. – The Business of Democracy and Rights' in GW Anderson (ed.), *Rights and Democracy – Essays in UK–Canadian Constitutionalism* (1999, Blackstone Press Ltd, London); and A Hutchinson and A Petter, 'Private Rights/Public Wrongs: The Liberal Lie of the Charter' (1988) 38 *Uni Toronto Law Journal* 278.

67 Sir S Sedley, 'Human Rights: a 21st Century Agenda', *ibid.*, at 4.

on homosexuals, convicted prisoners and trades unions as eroding the capacity of representative assemblies to reflect community standards.[68]

A test of these critics' principled opposition to judicial review of rights questions would occur however if, over time and across a number of issues, having seen their favoured policy outcomes rejected by the peoples' representatives in favour of antithetical alternatives, those alternatives were then regularly struck down by the courts with clear hints to adopt the critics' preferred policies. If opposition to judicial review was maintained in such circumstances, it would clearly be of a sort closer in nature to Waldron's institutional argument against judicial review. The suspicion must be, though, that much opposition to judicial review is results-based.[69] It is possible then to concur with Tushnet's observation of the tendency among a significant tranche of constitutional theorists to urge minimal judicial review and vigorous democratic dialogue on those issues where it is believed that the latter are likely to yield a favoured substantive policy outcome.[70] The argument that will be made in this book is that a more principled approach to the fact and intensity of judicial scrutiny in freedom of expression cases may be possible, which is in keeping with the primacy of democratic deliberation across representative democracies but which, at the same time, is respectful of distinct traditions and particular cultures.

How to Review? A Best-fit Approach to Judicial Oversight

To its supporters, judicial review is legitimate because it forces governments and/or legislatures to adhere to the rule of law in the sense that wherever there is a failure to act according to law, the courts uphold the constitution by granting an effective remedy to the party whose rights were violated. Thus where the government improperly obliges a tobacco company to carry health warnings, the courts can strike down this obligation on the ground that it violates the tobacco company's freedom of expression. And yet the language of constitutional guarantees is rarely so precise as to point unequivocally to one solution in such cases.

In those liberal democracies where the courts are given powers to adjudicate in constitutional disputes involving relatively open-ended provisions ('Everyone has the right to freedom of expression', 'Congress shall make no law abridging the freedom of speech or of the press'), questions inevitably arise about the values (implicit or explicit) which inform the resolution of the dispute in hand. In a number of liberal democracies outside the UK, the debate has ceased to be about whether judicial review over primary legislation can be justified but rather is focused on

68 C Manfredi, *Judicial Power and the Charter – Canada and the Paradox of Liberal Constitutionalism* (2nd edn, 2001, OUP, Toronto).

69 A point made elsewhere by Justice L'Heureux-Dubé, 'Judicial Independence and Judicial Activism' in F L Morton (ed.), *Law, Politics and the Judicial Process in Canada* (3rd edn, 2002, University of Calgary Press, Calgary) at 614.

70 'Policy Distortion and Democratic Debilitation: Comparative Illumination of the Counter-Majoritarian Difficulty' (1995) 94 *Mich L Rev* 245.

the kind of judicial review that should occur. Even in the UK where the courts lack the power to invalidate primary legislation, much academic and judicial ink has been spilt on the issue of the appropriate intensity of court controls over executive discretion where fundamental human rights are engaged.

A common theme in the work of judges and free speech scholars from diverse theoretical perspectives is that the abstract or open-textured nature of certain constitutional guarantees obliges each generation of judges to look beyond the terms of the written Constitution to acquire an understanding of the central themes or settled values which underpin the corpus of earlier jurisprudence and then to apply that understanding to the individual cases that come before them.[71] This 'non-interpretivist' approach is to be contrasted with an 'interpretivist' view in which, to be legitimate, judicial interpretation must be based upon the actual language and original meaning of the framers.[72] The latter position endorses a minimal form of review. Judicial striking down of the acts of the legislature is only ever legitimate when the constitutional impropriety of the legislature's proposed law can clearly be shown to derive from the original words of the framers or their implicit and uncontested intentions.[73] Today, interpretivism is not considered to provide a workable theory of judicial review of primary law. Alongside difficulties in establishing the precise intention of the framers in the absence of full historical records, it is immediately apparent that, even if these gaps were to be remedied and a clear understanding of the framers' (presumably unanimous) intentions were to be arrived at, they would have a negligible dispositive impact on claims arising out of contemporary societal conditions. How does an interpretivist reading of the Fourteenth Amendment of the US Constitution (Equal Protection Clause) help to resolve a dispute when that Amendment is invoked by a Hispanic or Jewish US citizen? The historical record indicates a desire to confer protection on black slaves only.

At the opposite end of the spectrum to interpretivism, strong support for the non-interpretivist approach to constitutional adjudication is to be found in the work of Robert Dworkin and Michael Perry. Each has, in his own distinct way, talked up non-interpretivist contributions of the judicial sphere to human rights law. Perry, for example, has claimed that the 'status of constitutional human rights is almost wholly a function, not of constitutional interpretation but constitutional policymaking by the

71 Sometimes referred to as the 'non-interpretivist' approach to constitutional adjudication. For justification see, for example, W Brennan, 'The Constitution of the United States: Contemporary Ratification' (1986) *S Texas L Rev* 433; AM Bickel, *The Least Dangerous Branch – The Supreme Court at the Bar of Politics* (1962, Bobbs-Merrill, Indianapolis IN); R Dworkin, *Freedom's Law – The Moral Reading of the American Constitution* (1996, OUP, Oxford) especially the Introduction; J Hart Ely, *Democracy and Distrust – A Theory of Judicial Review* (1980, Harvard University Press, Harvard MA) Ch. 2.

72 See thus E Meese, (1986) *Pub Admin* L R 701; R. Bork, *The Tempting of America: The Political Seduction of America* (1990); and for an overview D Barnum, *The Supreme Court and American Democracy* (1993, St Martin's Press, New York) Ch. 14.

73 For Bork, the publicly understood meaning of the constitutional text at the time it was written is the crucial meaning.

Supreme Court'.[74] Dworkin, for his part, conceives of judicial review as holding out the promise that the most fundamental conflicts between individual and society can be resolved by judges acting out of a principled concern for justice. More broadly, writers from a variety of points on the political spectrum appear to support the idea that, in order to be legitimate, rights-based judicial review has to meet a test of 'fit', by which is meant that judicial interpretation has to accord with the jurisdiction's traditions and practices (as elaborated in part by previous constitutional decisions) and that judges are not free to give rein to their personal values by placing a meaning on a section of the constitution that departs from a hitherto clearly established view of the provision.

Whilst the best 'fit' may be a matter of dispute (reasonable people will disagree with particular outcomes), there is excluded a range of outcomes that accord little or not at all with past practice. For Dworkin, the task of the judges in constitutional litigation is likened to the task of writing the next chapter in a chain novel. The judge must make a contribution that makes sense in view of the overall story thus far and advances the narrative in a plausible way. The requirement of constitutional integrity, however, prevents judges from simply giving effect to their own values when construing the Constitution. If this is accepted, it follows that each jurisdiction will have its own distinct narrative that is unlikely to fit exactly with the narratives of other states. What is interesting to discover is the extent to which, if at all, judges charged with reading and applying the constitution do manage to provide 'best fit' solutions to the disputes before them. In the next section, having sought to justify my selection of Canadian Supreme Court jurisprudence, I identify core elements of Canadian political culture before going on to explore some leading constitutional litigation under the *Canadian Charter of Rights and Freedoms* with a view to ascertaining whether that culture is reflected in Supreme Court's adjudications. The extent to which it corresponds to a civic republican model of judicial review is also considered. I then conclude by looking at the more limited form of UK judicial review to have emerged under the *Human Rights Act* 1998.

Canada and the 'Dialogue' between the Supreme Court and the Peoples' Representatives

For more than 20 years, Charter-based judicial review litigation has yielded valuable insights into judicial line-drawing in rights disputes. Academic discussion of the Canadian Supreme Court's record is to be found in a number of monographs originating both within and beyond the jurisdiction, including the UK.[75] Canada's

---

74 *The Constitution, the Courts and Human Rights: An Inquiry into the Legitimacy of Constitutional Policymaking by the Judiciary* (1982, Yale University Press, New Haven CT).

75 These include GW Anderson (ed.), *Rights and Democracy – Essays in UK-Canadian Constitutionalism* (1999, Blackstone Press Ltd, London), and individual chapters in other edited collections such as J Fudge, 'The Canadian Charter of Rights: Recognition, Redistribution and the Imperialism of the Courts' in T Campbell, KD Ewing and A Tomkins (eds), *Sceptical*

heritage as a former dominion territory, modelled in part on Westminster notions of responsible parliamentary government, and the absence of a comprehensive written statement of individual rights and freedoms offer an obvious set of background reasons to explain UK interest. Particular attention to Canadian constitutional design can be traced more specifically to 1994 with the Labour Party's preference (while in opposition) for a partially entrenched Canadian-style Charter of Rights with its balance of judicial determinations of rights questions on the one hand and retention of a legislative veto in the form of a 'notwithstanding' clause on the other.[76] Despite Labour's belated realization on attaining office in 1997 that judicial review of primary legislation was in fact out of keeping with the UK's constitutional tradition and the consequent accommodation of rights within the principle of parliamentary sovereignty, interest in Canadian judges' rights discourse remains. The fact that, unlike their Canadian equivalents, the UK courts are explicitly barred from disapplying provisions of domestic statute law found to be Convention-non-compliant has not discouraged careful judicial inspection of Canadian rights jurisprudence to ascertain how balances between individual freedom and countervailing societal interests can be struck.

Canadian Political Culture

Patrick Monahan's evaluation of Canadian Supreme Court jurisprudence has sought to discover the extent to which it is informed by the values and norms that he argues belong to Canadian political culture. One central element Monahan identified is a commitment to representative democracy. This led him to contend that judicial review could legitimately be used to protect existing opportunities for democratic debate and, further, open up new avenues of public discourse. Stringent scrutiny needed to be exercised over government policies that impeded participation in the political process or over policies where full participation was not present. By the same reasoning, it followed that any form of judicial review that invited judges to test legality of political outcomes by reference to normative standards not inherent in wider political culture would improperly limit popular participation and control of the constitution.

Beyond this commitment to representative democracy, Monahan argued that the political culture of Canada out of which the Charter emerged was much less individualistic than that found in the US. Like their UK counterparts, Canadian citizens, we are told, do not in general subscribe to the view that a strong state is necessarily inimical to personal liberty. Individuals plainly possess rights but these

Essays on Human Rights (2001, OUP, Oxford). See also B McLachlin, 'The Canadian Charter and the Democratic Process' in C Gearty and A Tomkins (eds), *Understanding Human Rights* (1996, Mansell Publishing Ltd, London).

76 T Blair, *The Guardian* (1994) 16 July.

may be limited for the sake of the greater public good.[77] To return to the labels of political philosophy referred to in Chapter 1, it may be said that Canada is closer than the US to a communitarian model of society in which the individuals are more 'embedded' within their communities and where citizens are seen not merely as the holders of rights and entitlements but also the carriers of obligations for the benefit of others. Monahan maintained that Canadian politics has always placed a particular emphasis on the value of community, one aspect of which is the more active role assumed by the state in promoting freedom. The emergence of socialist parties at provincial and federal levels was also claimed to be further evidence of the prevalence of collective values. Monahan's account contested the view of some on the left that the 1982 Charter represented a complete break with the collectivist tradition and ushered in an era of individual rights. He characterized this reading of the Charter as 'vastly oversimplified' and an 'error of the highest proportions'.[78] Whilst indeed containing guarantees of individual rights understood in the classic liberal sense of a freedom from state interference, the Charter also endorsed the idea of state regulation and intervention to secure substantial community goals. It further conferred constitutional protection on the collective rights of particular communities such as the equal status of French and English as official languages in Canada in ss.16–23 of the Charter, the rights of aboriginal peoples in s.25 and the rights of denominational, separate and dissentient schools in s.29.[79] The Charter was also to be interpreted in a manner 'consistent with the preservation and enhancement of the multicultural heritage of Canadians.'[80] Looking more closely at the Charter's language guarantees for instance, Monahan argued that, although these rights are couched in individualistic terms (for example, s.19(2) 'Either English or French may be used by any person in, or in any pleading in or process issuing from, any court of New Brunswick'), the freedom only makes sense if situated in its social setting with others who hear us and speak to us in turn.[81] As Dickson CJ noted in *La Société des Acadiens du Nouveau Brunswick Inc* v *Association of Parents for Fairness in Education*:

> What good is the right to use one's language if those to whom one speaks cannot understand … We speak and write to communicate to others. In the courtroom, we speak to communicate to the judge or judges. It is fundamental, therefore, to any effective and coherent guarantee of language rights in the courtroom that the judge or judges understand,

77 See for example B. McLachlin, 'The Canadian Charter and the Democratic Process' in C Gearty and A Tomkins (eds), *Understanding Human Rights* (1996, Mansell Publishing Ltd, London).

78 *Politics and the Constitution, The Charter, Federalism and the Supreme Court of Canada* (1987, Carswell, Toronto) 13.

79 On the meaning of collective rights, see M Freeman, 'Are there Collective Human Rights?' in D Beetham (ed.), *Politics and Human Rights* (1995, Blackwell, Oxford).

80 S.27.

81 *Politics and the Constitution, The Charter, Federalism and the Supreme Court of Canada* (1987, Carswell, Toronto) 112–13.

either directly or through other means, the language chosen by the individual coming before the courts.[82]

Aside from substantive and interpretative provisions which bolstered community values, the Charter could also be said to provide two main mechanisms by which individual rights might be subordinated to wider community interests. The first is provided by the override or 'notwithstanding' clause in s.33 of the Charter which allows determined legislators to press ahead with policies interfering with freedom of expression and 'legal rights' recognized in ss.7–15 of the Charter in the face of an adverse judicial ruling. The second is the catch-all s.1 'reasonable limits' clause of the Charter which permits legislative restriction of any Charter right where 'demonstrably justified in a democratic society'. Both will now be considered.

Constitutional Protection for Community Interests

Section 33 of the Canadian Charter of Rights and Freedoms This states:

> (1) (1) Parliament or the legislature of a province may expressly declare in an Act of Parliament or of the legislature … that the Act or a provision thereof shall operate notwithstanding a provision included in section 2 or sections 7–15 of this Charter.

This override applies to fundamental rights (including expression) and legal rights (against unreasonable search, seizure, arbitrary arrest or imprisonment, and so on) and endures for five years,[83] although it may be renewed.[84] It cannot be used to nullify constitutional protection for the democratic rights (such as those to vote for and stand in elections), mobility rights (of Canadian citizens to enter, remain in and leave Canada), language rights and the right to sex equality. Supporters of the override claim that it forms an integral part of a balanced set of constitutional mechanisms so that, in those occasional situations where the judiciary 'goes awry', the legislature can have the final say. The clause was added at a late stage of the Charter's drafting in response to fears voiced by political leaders in the provinces that judicial review would impede their legislative programmes. As one leading defender of the override put it,

> Most often we will accept the decisions of the courts on these [Charter] rights issues. But occasionally situations will arise in which the citizenry through a responsible and accountable process conclude that a judicial resolution of a rights issue is seriously flawed and seek to reverse it .[85]

---

82 [1986] 1 SCR 549, 566, cited by Monahan, *ibid.*

83 S.33(3).

84 S.33(4).

85 P Russell, 'Standing up for Notwithstanding' (1991) 29 *Alberta L Rev* 293, reprinted in FL Morton, *Law, Politics and the Judicial Process in Canada* (3rd edn, 2002, University of Calgary Press, Calgary) at 588. See also L Weinrib, 'The Supreme Court of Canada in the Age of Rights: Constitutional Democracy, the Rule of Law and Fundamental Rights

The override clause is said by some to promote debate and public participation among a politically active citizenry by forcing legislatures to consider how to respond to judicial reverse on constitutional matters. After all, judicial striking down of a law on Charter grounds leaves a legislature with several choices – to reverse the ruling in question, to modify the ruling or to avoid it altogether. This 'dialogue' theory of Canadian judicial review may be traced to an influential article written by Hogg and Bushell in 1997 which looked at the empirical impact of Supreme Court rulings on legislatures. They concluded that the effect of the Charter

> ... is rarely to block a legislative objective, but rather to influence the design of implementing legislation. Charter cases cause a public debate in which Charter-protected rights have a more prominent role than they would have if there had been no judicial decision. The process is best regarded as a 'dialogue' between courts and legislatures.[86]

The 'dialogue' theory has been seized upon by members of the Supreme Court as a means of playing down the significance of judicial intervention in legislative policy-making.[87] Supporters of dialogue theory cite *Ford* v *Quebec* as an example of the robust re-assertion of majoritarian or collective interests where the Supreme Court had invalidated a law which prohibited the display of commercial signs in English on the ground that it interfered disproportionately with the s.2(b) Charter rights of English-speakers.[88] The response of the Quebec National Assembly was to enact a new law that prohibited the use of English on all outdoor signs (a measure hardly less invasive of s.2(b) rights) but which was effectively rendered immune from Charter challenge by the insertion of a s.33 notwithstanding clause. Thus, it is argued that, after a period of further reflection prompted by the Canadian Supreme Court, the National Assembly was able to promote the French language in accordance with

---

under Canada's Constitution' (2001) 80 *Can Bar Rev* 699, where the override is contrasted favourably to the lack of an equivalent mechanism in the US Constitution. Weinrib argues that this clause 'designates legislatures as constitutional actors but only, as is appropriate, to the extent of their time-limited electoral mandate' at 728.

86 P Hogg and A Bushell, 'The *Charter* Dialogue between Courts and Legislatures' (1997) 35 *Osgoode Hall Law Journal* 75. For a critical response see C Manfredi and J Kelly, 'Six Degrees of Dialogue: A response to Hogg and Bushell' (1999) 37 *Osgoode Hall Law Journal* 513. Hogg and Bushell's response in turn may be read at 'Reply to Six Degrees of Dialogue' (1999) 37 *Osgoode Hall Law Journal* 529.

87 See thus the remarks of McLachlin and Iacobucci JJ in *R* v *Mills* [1999] 3 SCR 668 at para. 57. For a view that the empirical focus of Hogg and Bushell on legislative responses to constitutional adjudication is too narrow, see J Fudge, 'The Canadian Charter of Rights: Recognition, Redistribution and the Imperialism of the Courts' in T Campbell, KD Ewing and A Tomkins (eds), *Sceptical Essays on Human Rights* (2001, OUP, Oxford). Fudge argues that such data may still fail to capture another dimension of the Charter, namely its impact of the Charter on the political discourse and practices of the very social movements (including the litigation strategies of women's and gay and lesbian groups) which invoke the Charter.

88 [1988] 2 SCR 712 and see L Weinrib, 'Learning to Live with the Override' (1990) 35 *McGill L J* 541.

majoritarian preferences.[89] Even where a legislature ultimately opts not to employ a s.33 override in the face of an adverse judicial ruling, the fact that the choice to do so exists in itself can promote a wide political debate about the wisdom of overturning the decision. Such claims were made in the aftermath of the Albertan legislature's decision not to reverse the Supreme Court's decision in *Vriend* v *Alberta*. The Court had held that Alberta's human rights legislation infringed the Charter guarantee of equality by omitting to outlaw discrimination based on sexual orientation.[90] Although the override was not ultimately invoked, the fact that it was available for use was nonetheless said to have prompted a valuable public debate about the issue of discrimination on sexual orientation grounds.

For majoritarian critics of the Charter, s.33 has in practice fallen far short of the goal of promoting a partnership between the courts and legislatures in which each reviews and reacts to the other's vision of the Constitution. Despite a series of controversial decisions from the Supreme Court, s.33 has fallen into virtual desuetude. Research carried out for the non-partisan Institute for Research on Public Policy by Leeson concluded that s.33 is a 'paper tiger'.[91] Writing in 2000, he noted that only the Quebec legislature has shown any willingness to make use of s.33.[92] By 2004, even Quebec, with its particular history of struggle for autonomy from federal control, had not resorted to s.33 for 16 years. Leeson advances three possible explanations for the reluctance to use s.33. First, as recommendations on how to respond to adverse court decisions come to ministers of justice from government lawyers who, in addition to being traditionally deferential in their dealings with courts, may see their future careers as lying in the judicial sphere, the advice that is tendered may be cautious in nature. Second, as polls consistently indicate that Canadians hold judges in higher regard than politicians, the latter may be unwilling to risk conflict with Supreme Court judges for fear of falling even lower in public esteem. Related to this, Leeson advances a third explanation, namely the potential for adverse political reaction in the media and popular opinion if apparently independent judicial decisions are tampered with by partisan politicians. In truth, however, the reasons why, in any particular instance, s.33 is not resorted to may be quite case-specific, drawing on some, all or possibly none of these explanations.

Section 1 and the concept of reasonable limits By virtue of s.1 of the Charter, the rights guaranteed by the Constitution are subject to 'such reasonable limits prescribed by law as can be demonstrably justified in a free and democratic society'. In *R* v *Oakes* the Supreme Court interpreted s.1 as requiring a two-stage

89 Defenders of current judicial review arrangements in Canada make much of the potential for s.33 override as offering a real majoritarian check on an over-mighty judiciary. For a recent offering see K Roach, *The Supreme Court On Trial: Judicial Activism or Democratic Dialogue* (2001, Irwin Law, Toronto). For a critical review of Roach, see J Allan, 'The Author Doth Protest Too Much' (2003) 20 *NZULR* 519.

90 [1998] 1 SCR 548.

91 'Section 33, the Notwithstanding Clause: A Paper Tiger?' (2000) 6 *Choices* 17.

92 Saskatchewan did use s.33 once in 1986 to force striking workers back to work.

test for limitations on Charter rights to satisfy.[93] At the first stage, the objective behind a restriction must be shown to be of sufficient importance; that is, to constitute a pressing and substantial concern in a democratic society. Then, at stage 2, a three-limbed test of proportionality is applied. A limitation (i) must be rationally connected to its objective; (ii) should impair the right as little as is necessary to meet the objective; and, finally, (iii) the effect of the measures must not be out of all proportion to that which is gained by securing the government objective.

In practice, the extent to which s.1 secures the triumph of legislative infringements of individual rights has come to hinge upon the intensity of judicial scrutiny applied by the Court, particularly at the stage 2 proportionality analysis. Here once again, majoritarian critics have found fault with what is perceived to be excessive judicial intervention in legislative policy-making. Others maintain conversely that the Court has generally been aware of the need to leave scope for a more narrowly tailored legislative response.[94] Manfredi, an opponent of judicial supremacy, does however make the telling point in relation to s.1 that whenever a legislative response is attempted, this in turn must also be judged according to the judicial sphere's view of what constitutes a proportionate interference with Charter rights. Ultimate authority having been conferred on the judiciary to determine the meaning of the Constitution, the considered judgments of democratically elected representatives in legislatures across the breadth of Canada thus remain vulnerable to the views of nine unrepresentative figures sitting in a courtroom in Ottawa.

Evaluation of the 'fit' between political culture and the Supreme Court's freedom of expression jurisprudence Detailed consideration of the specific impact of Charter jurisprudence on aspects of freedom of expression in Canada occurs in several places throughout other chapters in this monograph. In this section, in anticipation of the fuller discussion which appears elsewhere in this book, a brief and general overview of the Court's record in s.2(b) Charter disputes will be set out. The purpose of this section of materials is to assess to what extent, in discharging its adjudicative duties under the Charter, the Court has managed to uphold the value of representative democracy and balance in an appropriately Canadian way, competing claims of individual rights and community interests. After an initial burst of activity in the 1980s, it is commonly accepted that the Court became more deferential to

93 [1986] 1 SCR 103.

94 P Monahan, 'The Supreme Court of Canada in the 21st Century' (2001) 80 *Can Bar Rev* 374, 394. For the view that the Court has sometimes been too deferential to the legislature and has allowed traditional ideas of consensus and community to 'overwhelm' the notion of judicially protected rights, see L Weinrib, 'The Supreme Court of Canada in the Age of Rights: Constitutional Democracy, the Rule of Law and Fundamental Rights under Canada's Constitution' (2001) 80 *Can Bar Rev* 699.

legislative policy-making and the exercise of executive discretion.[95] For his part, Patrick Monahan believes the Court to have assumed its Charter mandate

> … in a serious but measured manner, attempting to balance the need to protect rights vigorously with a recognition that legislative bodies must continue to govern in the public interest. The continuing broad support for the Court and for the Charter amongst Canadians is an indication that the balance has been very close to the mark.[96]

Evidence of the Court's commitment to a participative representative democracy is apparent in the strict scrutiny applied by a majority of the Court in a number of political expression cases. This is exemplified *inter alia* by *Osborne* v *Canada* in which restrictions on partisan political activity by civil servants were deemed to have been drafted too broadly.[97] Voting regulations which disenfranchised whole categories of prisoners were similarly faulted on proportionality grounds in the 2002 case of *Sauvé* v *AG of Canada (No. 2)*.[98] This ruling followed the Court's earlier affirmation of lower court decisions in *Sauvé* v *AG for Canada* and *Belczowski* v *Canada* in which a blanket ban on voting by inmates in penal institutions was struck down.[99] Likewise, the majority's finding in *Thomson Newspapers Co.* v *Canada* that a federal ban on the broadcasting, publication or dissemination of opinion survey results during the final three days of an election campaign constituted an unwarranted infringement of s.2(b) was explicitly founded on the high constitutional importance of political speech in a democracy and the formidable obstacles faced by legislatures wishing to curtail such expression.[100] The Court's decision in *Libman* v *Quebec* to quash the third party expenditure limit of $600 in referenda as a disproportionate means of achieving the legislature's legitimate goal of safeguarding the fairness of referenda campaigns might also be characterized as a strong defence of political speech (or, more accurately, the autonomy of speakers with the financial means to engage in effective speech).[101] For some, however, Libman represents an unwelcome judicial foray into the detail of legislative policy-making in defence of private capital and in disregard of the skewing effect that imbalances in funding have on the voters'

---

95 D Beatty, 'The Canadian Charter of Rights: Lessons and Laments' in GW Anderson (ed.), *Rights and Democracy – Essays in UK–Canadian Constitutionalism* (1999, Blackstone Press Ltd, London), 21–3; P Monahan, 'The Charter Then and Now' in P Bryden, S Davis and J Russell (eds), *Protecting Rights and Freedoms* (1994, University of Toronto Press, Toronto); L Weinrib, 'The Supreme Court of Canada in the Age of Rights: Constitutional Democracy, the Rule of Law and Fundamental Rights under Canada's Constitution' (2001) 80 *Can Bar Rev* 699.

96 P Monahan, 'The Supreme Court of Canada in the 21st Century' (2001) 80 *Can Bar Rev* 374, 397–8.

97 [1991] 2 SCR 69.

98 [2002] 3 SCR 519. Also joined to the action was *McCorrister and others* v *AG for Canada and others*.

99 [1993] 2 SCR 438.

100 [1998] 1 SCR 877.

101 [1997] 3 SCR 569.

access to campaign groups' messages. The Quebec legislature's assessment of harms caused by non-affiliated persons' expenditure to the democratic process at referendum time was successfully impugned in a curiously pedantic judgment which accepted at the same time that the imposition of an alternative ceiling set at a limit just $400 higher would have passed judicial scrutiny. Subsequently, in *AG* v *Harper* the Court has seen fit to accept legislative judgments about the measures needed to promote electoral fairness in the context of federal elections. There the federal Parliament's limits of $3000 and $150,000 on third party election advertising at electoral district and national levels respectively were held to constitute a permissible limitation on freedom of expression.[102] An accompanying ban on third party advertising on polling day was also upheld for similar reasons. The Court's clear support for the federal limits chosen to minimize the distortion in communicative impacts caused by differentially funded third party expenditure is plainly welcome. *Harper* may come to be seen as a welcome nod in the direction of the civic republicanism principle of political equality, part of which requires that the voices of economically weaker individuals/groups are not drowned out in political debate.

If the Court's record in respect of expression closely connected to the practice of representative democracy is generally thought to be respectable, it is doubtful whether the same could consistently be said in relation to individual right/community interest balances struck in recent years in cases involving hate speech, commercial and sexually explicit expression.[103] Thus, the Court has been criticized for the ready extension of s.2(b) protection to corporate expression, sexually explicit imagery, in the face of legislative restrictions designed to advance public interests in raising health awareness and protecting vulnerable children from sexual exploitation and abuse. Indeed, in *RJR McDonald Inc.* v *Canada*, the invalidation of statutory provisions that required cigarette manufacturers to insert unattributed health warnings and a list of toxic ingredients on cigarette packets was said by one critic to show greater concern for corporate speech than the need to protect people's health from threats posed by addictive products.[104] It was 'an insult' to the notion that the Charter enhanced ordinary Canadians' rights and liberties. In the case of advertising directed at children, the Court has taken a more deferential stance towards legislative encroachments upon commercial expression. In *Irwin Toy Ltd* v *AG of Quebec*, a provincial law prohibiting commercial advertising aimed at persons under 13 years of age was narrowly upheld.[105] The majority stopped short of demanding unambiguous empirical evidence of a link between advertising and purchasing patterns of children's toys. Neither did they ask the state to show that

102 [2004] 1 SCR 827.

103 An interesting account of the ambivalent stances of the Court in the commercial speech cases is to be found in GW Anderson, 'Understanding Constitutional Speech: Two Theories of Expression' in GW Anderson (ed.), *Rights and Democracy: Essays in UK–Canadian Constitutionalism* (1999, Blackstone Press Ltd, London) at 50–73.

104 [1995] 3 SCR 199. A Hutchinson, 'Supreme Court Inc. – The Business of Democracy and Rights' in GW Anderson (ed.), *Rights and Democracy: Essays in UK–Canadian Constitutionalism* (1999, Blackstone Press Ltd, London) at 42.

105 [1989] 1 SCR 927.

a ban was the least intrusive means of securing Quebec's objective. Instead, to pass constitutional muster, it was required to be shown that the prohibition was a reasonable choice among other policy options.[106] The latitude shown to the Quebec legislature may to a considerable extent be accounted for by the fact that children were deemed to fall within a group that is particularly vulnerable to manipulation through advertisements.

Elsewhere, the claims to dignity and equal worth of other groups – members of ethnic and racial minorities – has also prompted a more relaxed form of judicial scrutiny in challenges to restraints on the wilful promotion of hatred against an identifiable group laid down in the *Criminal Code*.[107] In *Keegstra*, an anti-Semitic Alberta school-teacher who taught his students that the Jews were money-loving, treacherous and had invented the Holocaust to gain sympathy was convicted under the Code. His claim that the conviction violated his constitutional entitlement to freedom of expression was rejected by four votes to three in the Supreme Court.[108] Aside from furthering dignity and equality claims, the offence of wilful hatred signalled the state's constitutional commitment to multiculturalism in s.27 of the Charter. Shortly after *Keegstra*, however, a more broadly drawn provision of the Code which criminalized the wilful spreading of false news 'likely to cause injury or mischief to a public interest'[109] was narrowly struck down in *Zundel*.[110] The majority's reasoning focused on, among other matters, the question of proportionality and in particular upon the chill on protected expression caused by the uncertain reach of the prohibition.

UK Constitutional Culture

The wider constitutional culture within which rights adjudication is situated in the UK bears similarities to pre-Charter Canada (minus the federal aspects). Thus, the overarching themes of the constitution were and still are encapsulated in the doctrines of parliamentary sovereignty, the rule of law and the separation of powers. The legitimacy of the sovereign Parliament is crucially underpinned by a representative democracy in which all electors participate as political equals to select members of the legislature who, in turn, are required to submit themselves for re-election at regular intervals. Ministerial responsibility serves to call the executive in Parliament to account for its actions.

As with Canadian political culture, attachment to a representative democracy is accompanied by a more positive conception of the role of the state in pursuing

---

106 See in comparison the dissent of McIntyre and Beetz JJ who seemed to place commercial speech on an equal footing with political expression and allow for its suppression only in the most urgent and compelling cases and then only to the extent necessary for others' protection. *Ibid*., at 1009.

107 S.319(2).

108 *R* v *Keegstra* [1990] 3 SCR 697.

109 S.181.

110 [1992] 2 SCR 731.

community goals (as for example in promoting racial tolerance). In this conception, citizens are the bearers not only of rights over others but of duties towards other citizens. The creation of the welfare state after the Second World War can be seen as a prime example of this commitment to the general good. The enduring appeal of collective values is also apparent in the electoral successes of the Labour Party, certainly in the 1960s and 1970s. Today, however, many would question the Labour Party's commitment to be the champion of collective values as, increasingly, market-based solutions to economic and social policy questions are adopted.[111]

Protecting Rights UK Style

Earlier in this chapter, it was noted that the role of the judges under the *Human Rights Act* 1998 is more limited than that enjoyed by their Canadian or US counterparts. The Government's explicit commitment to retain the fundamental constitutional principle of parliamentary sovereignty made during debates in both Houses of Parliament[112] was given statutory expression in ss.3(2)(b) and (c) (interpretative clause), 4(2) (declaration of incompatibility) and s.6(2) (public authorities' duties to act compatibly with Convention rights) of the 1998 Act. In sum, where the only possible interpretation of domestic statutory law results in an applicant's Convention rights being breached, the courts are powerless to do anything other than apply domestic law. However, at the same time as reaffirming the predominance of the will of transient political majorities as expressed in legislation, the 1998 Act clearly envisaged some increase in the power of the courts.[113] Two interrelated features of the Act point to such an increase. First, there is the obligation on the courts in s.3, 'so far as it is possible to do so', to read and give effect to primary and secondary legislation (both past and future) in a European Convention-compliant way.[114] The wording of this obligation is significant. As Lord Lester has remarked, it demands a Convention-compliant reading in 'so far as it is possible to do so', not in 'so far as it is reasonably possible to do so'.[115] The second feature of the 1998 Act which suggests an increase in the role of the judges is the power of the higher courts under s.4(2) to grant a 'declaration

111 S Ludlam and MJ Smith (eds), *Governing as New Labour – Policy and Politics under Blair* (2003, Palgrave Macmillan, Basingstoke).

112 See the Lord Chancellor, HL Debs (1997–98) Vol. 582, col. 1229, and the Home Secretary, HC Debs (1997–98) Vol. 307 cc. 771–2.

113 C Gearty, 'Reconciling Parliamentary Democracy and Human Rights' (2002) 118 *LQR* 248.

114 S.3(1), (2)(a) HRA 1998.

115 'The Art of the Possible: Interpreting Statutes under the *Human Rights Act* 1998' (1998) *EHRLR* 665.

of incompatibility'.[116] Somewhat disparagingly referred to as a 'booby prize',[117] a declaration is available when a provision of primary or subordinate legislation cannot be given a Convention-compliant reading.[118] Although the declaration cannot prevent the application of the Convention-infringing provision(s) of domestic law to the dispute,[119] it was purposely inserted into the Act in order to prompt a dialogue between the courts and the legislature on the matter of rights and countervailing interests.[120] Indeed, the White Paper which preceded the Act (*Rights Brought Home: The Human Rights Bill*) observed that a declaration 'will almost certainly prompt the Government and Parliament to change the law'.[121] Post-October 2000, legal commentators have looked to discover trends in the granting/refusal to grant s.4(2) declarations in order to ascertain whether the Act heralds a significant new epoch in relations between the judicial and legislative branches of the constitution in which, by the very act of issuing a declaration, the courts might be understood to all intents and purposes to be requiring Parliament to change the law.[122]

The interpretative obligation laid down in s.3 of the Act goes beyond the previous approach to statutory interpretation with its presumption that Parliament did not intend to enact legislation at odds with obligations in international law. This presumption, it will be recalled, was deployed to resolve ambiguities in domestic law and was rebutted only where the legislature had used clear words.[123] The White Paper made it clear that no ambiguity was needed before a court was required to provide a Convention-compliant interpretation of domestic law, a position confirmed in subsequent case law.[124] Only in those cases where the legislation was 'clearly incompatible' with the Convention would a compliant interpretation be impossible.[125] The subsequent use to which s.3 has been put has however sparked a fundamental debate among judges and academic commentators about the nature and limits of the courts' interpretative function in a modern democracy. Two schools of thought

---

116 In England, Wales and Northern Ireland, the House of Lords, Court of Appeal and High Court: in Scotland, the Court of Session and the High Court of Justiciary sitting otherwise than as a trial court, s.4(5).

117 G Marshall, 'Two Kinds of Incompatibility; More about s.3 of the HRA 1998' (1999) *PL* 377, 382.

118 In the case of subordinate legislation, a declaration of incompatibility follows only when the primary legislation prevents removal of the incompatibility, s.4(4)(b).

119 Moreover, a declaration does not bind the parties to the proceedings in which it was made, s.4(6)(b).

120 See the remarks of the Home Secretary at HC Debs. (1997–98) Vol. 314, c. 1141.

121 (1997) Cm 3782, para. 2.10.

122 F Klug, 'Judicial Deference under the Human Rights Act 1998' (2003) *EHRLR* 125.

123 For a view that the s.3 still requires the presence of ambiguity, see G Marshall, (1999) *PL* 377 and 'The Lynchpin of Parliamentary Intention: Lost, Stolen or Strained' (2003) *PL* 236.

124 *In re S; In re W* [2002] 2 WLR 720, 731 *per* Lord Nicholls of Birkenhead.

125 *Rights Brought Home: The Human Rights Bill* (1997) Cm 3782, para. 2.7.

have emerged in judicial circles. The first is associated with Lord Steyn in *R* v *A* (*Complainant's Sexual History*)[126] and envisages an expansive role for the judges in not only reading down express language in a statute but also implying provisions into the same in order to achieve a Convention-compliant interpretation of the Act.[127] This may entail adopting a linguistically strained interpretation of legislation. On this view, a declaration of incompatibility would then be avoided unless it was plainly impossible to give a provision a Convention-compliant reading.[128]

Against this view, Lord Hope of Craighead has sought to advance a more constrained version of the judges' interpretative role, notably in *R* v *A* and *R* v *Lambert*. In the latter, he spoke of the need to construe statutes impacting on protected human rights in a way that respected the will of the legislature 'so far as this remains appropriate and to preserve the integrity of statutes so far as is possible'.[129] Resort to the s.3(1) obligation would not be possible if the legislation contained words or phrases which expressly or impliedly contradict the meaning which the court would have give the provision in order to render it compatible. Lord Hope's position is said to invoke the plain intention of Parliament as a brake on s.3 interpretative duty.[130] Section 3(1) does not allow judges 'to overrule decisions which the language of the statute shows to have been taken on the very point at issue by the legislator'.[131]

The qualitative differences between Lords Steyn and Hope on s.3 are neatly encapsulated by their contrasting analyses in *R* v *A* which concerned the proper interpretation of the so-called 'rape shield' laid down in s.41 of the *Youth Justice and Criminal Evidence Act* 1999. The provision restricts the ability of defendants charged with sexual offences to cross-examine a complainant and lead evidence relating to the complainant's past sexual conduct. The restriction operates by way of narrowing the discretionary powers of trial judges. For Lord Steyn, as s.41 currently stood it had an excessive reach, one which infringed defendants' Article 6 fair trial rights. In order to render s.41 *Human Rights Act*-compatible, a provision would have to be implied into the 1999 Act (via s.3, *Human Rights Act*) which allowed trial judges an additional discretionary power to admit evidence or questioning that was required to secure a fair trial. In contrast, Lord Hope started from the proposition that Parliament's intention in enacting s.41 was to lean towards the complainant when striking a balance between the probative value of evidence of past sexual conduct and its potential for prejudice. The legislature's intention was to address the previous law's tendency to divert juries' attention away from the central issues in the trial by allowing a focus on the complainant's sexual history. The insertion of additional

126 [2001] 2 WLR 1546.

127 On reading down – the technique by which an Act is made to conform with the Convention by the adoption of a narrow or modified interpretation – see R Edwards, 'Reading Down Legislation under the Human Rights Act' (2000) 20 *LS* 353.

128 [2001] 2 WLR 1546, 1563.

129 [2001] 3 WLR 206, 233.

130 K Starmer, 'Two Years of the Human Rights Act' (2003) *EHRLR* 14.

131 *R* v *Lambert* [2001] 3 WLR 206, 234.

discretionary grounds to admit such material by way of Lord Steyn's implication flew in the face of the clearly demonstrated will of Parliament.

Since *R* v *A* and *R* v *Lambert*, Lord Hope's 'deference to the will of Parliament' approach has enjoyed greater favour than Lord Steyn's more activist alternative. Thus in *Re S*; *Re W* the House of Lords was critical of the Court of Appeal's innovatory supervisory scheme for looking after children who are the subject of care orders under the *Children Act* 1989.[132] The creation of the scheme would have conferred on the courts a supervisory role which was not authorized by the 1989 Act. This approach had been justified by the Court of Appeal as a legitimate exercise of its interpretative powers under s.3 of the *Human Rights Act* to imply into the 1989 Act saving, Convention-compliant procedures. On appeal to the House of Lords, the introduction of the new scheme was held to be beyond the interpretative duties of the Court of Appeal. Lord Nicholls reminded the lower court of the outer limits of the s.3(1) duty. He pointed out that s.3(2) presupposed that not all legislation would be rendered Convention-complaint. Under the scheme of the *Human Rights Act*, the amendment of statutes remained a task for Parliament. Interpretation of statutes was the task of the courts. As to identifying the moment when judicial construction of a statute crossed over the boundary from interpretation to amendment, Lord Nicholls suggested that this occurred when a meaning was given which 'depart(ed) substantially from a fundamental feature of an Act …'[133] and would be especially apparent when the departure had important practical repercussions which the courts were not equipped to assess. On the facts in *Re S* this boundary had been crossed when the Court of Appeal created its new scheme, the ramifications of which were impossible to assess. By way of comment, it may be noted that neither camp directly canvasses the possibility that the subject matter of the statute under construction might influence the permissible bounds of judicial creativity. Statutes touching on fundamental Convention rights are not to be approached any differently than those regulating more peripheral entitlements.

Logically, the approach of Lords Hope and Nicholls would appear to make s.4(2) declarations of incompatibility from the higher courts more likely than under Lord Steyn's more robust alternative. The legislature ought to find itself being invited more regularly to consider the introduction of amending legislation as a uniquely UK-style 'dialogue' is opened up between the courts and Parliament. One leading commentator has gone so far as to suggest that the Act empowers the courts

> … to deliver a wound to Parliament's handiwork that will often prove mortal, even though life support for the legislation must be switched off by the government or Parliament, not the courts.[134]

---

132 [2002] 2 WLR 720.

133 *Ibid.* at 731. See also his remarks in *Ghaidan* v *Godin-Mendoza* [2004] UKHL 30 at para. 33 where he spoke of permitted modifications as ones which could be characterized as going with 'the grain of the legislation'.

134 A Bradley, 'The Sovereignty of Parliament – Form or Substance?' in J Jowell and D Oliver (eds), *The Changing Constitution* (5th edn, 2004, OUP, Oxford) at 58.

In practice, whilst a number of s.4(2) declarations have been made, a significant percentage of these have been overturned on appeal.[135] In respect of the small clutch of declarations whose legality has not been challenged (or, if so, have survived appeal) the Parliamentary/executive reaction has tended to be constructive. For example, in *R* v *Mental Health Review Tribunal (North and East London)* the reverse onus of proof in mental health review tribunal procedure requiring detained persons to show why continued detention is not justified was deemed by the Court of Appeal to violate Article 5(1) and (4) of the Convention.[136] In response to the s.4(2) declaration, not only was a Remedial Order brought into force putting the onus of proof on the state,[137] but the Secretary of State set up an *ex gratia* compensation scheme for those who had been adversely affected under the previous rule. Likewise, the automatic penalty scheme created under the *Immigration and Asylum Act* 1999 and imposed on persons transporting clandestine entrants to the UK was found in *International Transport Roth GmbH* v *Secretary of State for the Home Department* to be incompatible with Article 6(2) of the Convention.[138] Parliament's response to the incompatibility is to be found in the *Nationality, Immigration and Asylum Act* 2002.[139] The respective declarations of incompatability in *Bellinger* v *Bellinger* (voiding of male-to-female transsexual's marriage to her husband under the *Matrimonial Causes Act* 1973 held to be incompatible with Articles 8 and 12 of the Convention[140] and *R (on the application of Anderson)* v *Secretary of State for Home Department* (Home Secretary's powers to control the release of mandatory life prisoners under section 29 of the *Crime Sentences Act* 1997 held to be in breach of the need for an independent and impartial tribunal under Article 6) have since prompted legislative reform. As a result of *Bellinger*, the *Gender Recognition Act* 2004 was passed to allow transsexual females to marry their male partners whilst the *Criminal Justice Act* 2003 has removed the Home Secretary's power to control the release of mandatory life prisoners.[141]

---

135 See thus *R (on the application of Uttley)* v *Secretary of State for Home Department* [2004] 1 WLR 2278; *Wilson* v *First County Trust Ltd* [2004] 1 AC 816; *A* v *Secretary of State for Home Department* [2004] QB 335; *Mathews* v *Ministry of Defence* [2003] 1 AC 1163; *R* v *Secretary of State for the Environment, Transport and the Regions ex parte Holding and Barnes plc* [2001] 2 WLR 1389.

136 *R (H)* v *London North and East Mental Health Review Tribunal* [2002] QB 1. The infringing provisions were ss.72–3, *Mental Health Act* 1983.

137 *Mental Health Act* 1983 Remedial Order 2001/3712, Art.3.

138 [2003] QB 728.

139 Schedule 8.

140 [2003] 2 AC 467 and see D Nicol, 'Gender Reassignment and the Transformation of the Human Rights Act' (2004) 120 *LQR* 194.

141 *Criminal Justice Act* 2003, ss.303(b), 332 and Schedule 37(8) para 1. See further A Kavanagh, 'Statutory Interpretation and Human Rights after Anderson: A More Contextual Approach' (2004) *PL* 537, and 'The elusive divide between interpretation and legislation under the Human Rights Act 1998' (2004) *OJLS* 259.

Conclusion

Within the context of core human rights such as freedom of expression, it is apparent that the 1998 Act has provided fresh impetus for members of the judiciary wishing to subject executive discretion to heightened levels of judicial scrutiny. This is most obviously true in developments in the doctrine of proportionality that have allowed judges to go beyond the limited notion of 'Wednesbury unreasonableness' to consider the balance struck by the executive between individual rights and collective interests, the weight accorded to particular factors.[142] Even Lord Hope accepted in *R* v *Director of Public Prosecutions, ex parte Kebilene and Others* that the degree of deference due on democratic grounds to elected or administrative bodies was subject-matter-dependant and would be reduced where the action/decision complained of engaged 'rights of high constitutional importance'.[143] The extent to which judicial reasoning under the 1998 Act has made good the promise of heightened scrutiny will be considered in the remaining chapters of this book.

Beyond this, attention will be focused on comparative freedom of expression jurisprudence more generally to ascertain how the notion of a representative democracy serves as a basis for ascribing weight to, and differentiating between, claims to expressive freedom.[144] How far have the courts in Western liberal democracies gone to defend forms of political expression? What level of scrutiny has been applied to restrictions on the smaller parties' political broadcasts and the political activities of civil servants? Have corporate claims to freedom of expression received greater protection than the advance of fairness in electoral campaigns/public health awareness programmes? How have the claims of ethnic (and other) minority members to dignity, equality and individual respect fared in the face of insulting and abusive speech? The theme of this book is that, contrary to the position of Tomkins and others, judicial intervention can and does secure real advances that promote a more genuinely participative democracy. That it does not always achieve this end, or that it may only move in incremental steps in highly fact-specific litigation towards this goal is not disputed. What is contested is the assertion that rights-based judicial intervention and the achievements of legal constitutionalism are in the final analysis insignificant.

---

142 [2001] 2 AC 532, 547 *per* Lord Steyn.

143 [2002] 2 AC 326.

144 For an opposing view that rejects the need to develop a theory of judicial deference in respect of rights adjudication, see F Klug, 'Judicial Deference under the Human Rights Act 1998' (2003) *EHRLR* 125.

Chapter 3

Political Expression: Political Parties, Voters and Candidates

Introduction

Laws which regulate the expression of political opinion at election time strike at what is perhaps the most fundamental set of expression interests in modern democracies – the right of speakers on the one hand to set before the electorate their political programmes or other opinion/information, and the undoubted interest of the electorate in receiving the widest possible range of views and information when deciding how (if at all) to cast their vote. Any provision which appears to limit the flow of such core political expression threatens the notion of informed political choice. In this and the following chapter, I consider a variety of controversial legislative restrictions on political expression in a number of western liberal democracies and look in detail at the basis of constitutional challenges to their validity/enforcement. The restrictions discussed in this chapter include outright bans on political parties, taste and decency controls on party election broadcasts, issue advocacy restraints and limits on the right to vote and stand for election. In Chapter 4, some constitutional issues surrounding the imposition of donation and expenditure controls on political expression are examined.

Political Parties in Democratic States

Political parties fulfil several functions in a modern democratic state. One crucial function is to provide a mechanism for the participation of ordinary individuals in the political life of their community and nation.[1] As the German Constitutional Court has noted, parties constitute the 'political units of action which a democracy needs in order to unite electors into groups capable of political action …'.[2] They participate

1 Of course, this is not to say that parties function perfectly in this regard. Moreover, other forums which channel citizens' political activity exist, including national and local pressure groups, neighbourhood associations, etc. These too have expressive interests that may be threatened by incumbent political forces.

2 8 *BVerfGE* 51 (1958). Article 2 of the Law on Political Parties defines political parties as 'organisations of citizens who, permanently or for protracted periods seek to exert influence on the political opinion-forming process … and to participate in the representation of the people …' The constitutional basis for this law is provided by Article 21 of the Basic Law.

in the forming of the political will of the electorate by generating competing sets of policies which are then offered to voters at elections. The significance of political parties in ensuring pluralism and thereby safeguarding the proper functioning of democracy has also been noted by the European Court of Human Rights.[3] Ewing has likened political parties to a 'transmission belt' for policy development and its carriage into legislation.[4] Parties that attain an overall majority in the legislature provide a link between the government and the governed. MPs on the government side provide a channel through which the party in power may retain a sense of, and respond to voter opinion. Minority parties form the opposition and perform the valuable functions of calling the government to explain its policies and actions and presenting an alternative vision of how the nation's affairs might conceivably be managed.

It follows that the range of restrictions on parties' freedom of expression considered in this chapter can be extremely damaging to democratic self-governance. These might impede the opportunities for developing individuals' capacities for constructive participation in community and national affairs. Restraints might also curtail the formation and development of alternative policies, thereby restricting the flow of information and ideas to the electorate and reducing the options on offer to voters. Incumbent parties could be tempted to lessen the opportunities that their rivals have to expound their alternative vision in an effort to hold onto office.[5] Nonetheless, it should be acknowledged that the state may have entirely legitimate reasons for wanting to regulate the expressive activities of political parties, extending in the most serious cases to dissolution. Such an extreme stance might be warranted where a party's aims or the activities of its supporters seriously threaten the existence of the state or core, democratic values. After all, unlike other organizations which enter the political arena, political parties alone have the capacity to transform the essential character of society upon coming to power.[6] As students of European history are all too aware, totalitarian movements organized as political parties have prospered under democratic conditions only to do away with fundamental democratic values and freedoms upon coming to power. This potential for subversion of democratic values may justify the outlawing of extremist parties. Thus, the Article 21(2) of the Basic Law of the German Constitution makes provision for the banning of political parties which,

---

3 *United Communist Party* v *Turkey* (1998) 26 EHRR 121.

4 KD Ewing, 'Transparency, Accountability and Equality – The Political Parties, Elections and Referendums Act 2000' (2001) *PL* 542, 544.

5 See in this regard the original provisions of s.93 of the *Representation of the People Act* 1983 which allowed an incumbent MP who took part in a programme about an election in his/her constituency to have an effective veto over the broadcast of the programme. For an unsuccessful attempt to achieve this, see *Marshall* v *BBC* [1979] 3 All ER 80. The amended version of s.93 now gives the broadcasters a freer hand (in consultation with the Electoral Commission) to adopt a code of practice to regulate this matter.

6 Recognized by the European Court of Human Rights in *Refah Partisi (The Welfare Party)* v *Turkey* (2003) 37 EHRR 1, paras 87, 99.

> … by reason of their aims or the conduct of their adherents, seek to impair or do away with the free democratic basic order or threaten the existence of the Federal Republic of Germany shall be unconstitutional. The Federal Constitutional court shall rule on the question of unconstitutionality.[7]

Three parties have been banned under this provision: the neo-Nazi *Sozialistiche Reichspartei* in 1951;[8] the Communist Party (KPD) after much delay in 1956,[9] and the Nationalist Front in 1992.[10] Claims that the far right National Democratic Party (NPD) was implicated in a spate of physical attacks on disabled persons and immigrants prompted Chancellor Schroeder's Social Democratic Government in December 2000 to apply to the federal Constitutional Court to have the NPD banned.[11] Although the ban had been agreed by the Bundestag, proceedings in the Constitutional Court were postponed in 2003 when doubts emerged about the reliability of the evidence supplied by a leading witness.[12]

The disbanding of political parties has also come under scrutiny at supra-national level by the European Court of Human Rights in Article 11 freedom of association proceedings. In a 1998 case *United Communist Party* v *Turkey*, the Court, whilst reminding national authorities of the essential role played by political parties in promoting dialogue and public debate in a democracy, nonetheless accepted the possibility that states might exceptionally impose a ban where it was convincingly established that a party posed a 'real threat' to democratic society or the state.[13] A real threat was subsequently found to exist in *Refah Partisi (The Welfare Party)* v *Turkey* when the Court upheld the Turkish Constitutional Court's dissolution of the applicant party.[14] The leaders of Refah Partisi had done little to

---

7 Article 43 of the Law on the Federal Constitutional Court. For background, see N Foster, *German Law and Legal System* (1993, Blackstone Press Limited, London) at Ch. 6.

8 2 *BVerfGE* 1 (1952).

9 5 *BVerfGE* 85 (1956).

10 See further Y Meny and A Knapp, *Government and Politics in Western Europe* (3rd edn, 1998, OUP, Oxford) 91–2. For discussion of the first two bans, see D Currie, *The Constitution of the Federal German Republic* (1994, University of Chicago Press, Chicago IL) at 215–21.

11 F Hanschmann, 'Federal Constitutional Court to Review NPD Party Ban Motion' (2001) 2 *German Law Journal* 17.

12 W Buttner, (2003) 'German Helsinki Committee for Human Rights, Security and Cooperation in Europe', available electronically at www.ihf-hr.org/viewbinary/viewdocument.php?doc_id=5519.

13 *United Communist Party* v *Turkey* (1998) 26 EHRR 121. On the facts of this case, the requisite degree of evidence did not reach this standard and the ban on the United Communist Party was held to be in breach of Article 11. See further J G Merrills and AH Robertson, who argue that a ban would be justified where a party 'advocates violence or rejects democratic principles in some other way': *Human Rights In Europe – A Study of the European Convention on Human Rights* (2001, Manchester University Press, Manchester) at 185 and K Sawyer 'Rejection of Weimarian Politics or Betrayal of Democracy?' (2003) 52 *Am Uni Law Rev* 1531.

14 (2003) 37 EHRR 1. Refah's party leaders were banned from holding similar office in any other party for five years.

dispel the ambiguity in other party members' published remarks about the use of violence to seize power and set up a legal regime based on shariah for the Muslim community alongside the existing secular legal system. Shariah, the Court found, was fundamentally incompatible with Convention values, particularly in respect to criminal law and procedure, its treatment of women and its application of religious principles to all aspects of public and private life. It followed that a political party that advocated the introduction of shariah could not be regarded as complying with the democratic ideal underpinning the Convention. In view of the fact that Refah's popular support levels indicated that it had a 'real' prospect of coming to power on its own without the need to compromise its policies in an alliance with another party,[15] the danger to democracy was all the more tangible and immediate.[16]

In other sets of cases, a political group may fall short of threatening the very existence of the state but nonetheless find itself subject to restrictions on account of a close connection between particular expressive activity and immediately ensuing public disorder or threats to the rights and freedoms of others. In the UK, incitement to racial hatred laws in particular, and public order legislation more generally, would seem to provide a set of constraints on extremist political expression.[17] In this context it is also relevant to note that, short of dissolution, national authorities may take measures to restrict on contents grounds the expressive activities of political parties without infringing the Convention rights of speakers. Thus, it is clearly established that the right to claim Article 10 protection in respect of forms of racist expression is subject to the overriding provisions of Article 17 of the Convention which affords the Court a basis for declaring as manifestly ill-founded Convention claims which are 'aimed at the destruction of any of the rights or freedoms set forth herein'.[18] Article 17 is considered in further detail in Chapter 5 of this book.

Restrictions on Political Broadcasting and Advocacy Advertising

Party Political Speech

In the UK at present, political parties enjoy free access to a number of party political and party election broadcasts (PPBs/PEBs). In the period before and

---

15 At the time it was dissolved, the party had secured 35 per cent of the votes in local elections, whilst an opinion poll carried out two months later put its support at 38 per cent. (2003) 37 EHRR 1 at para 107.

16 *Ibid.*, at para. 132.

17 For more detail on UK law in this area see Chapter 5.

18 Article 17 states 'Nothing in this Convention may be interpreted as implying for any state, group or person any right to engage in any activity aimed at the destruction of the rights and freedoms set forth herein or at their limitation to a greater extent than is provided for in the Convention.' See further *Glimmerveen & Hagenbeek v Netherlands*, Application Nos. 8348/78 and 8406/78, 18 DR 187. On the meaning of Article 17 more generally see *Lawless v Ireland* (1979–80) 1 EHRR 1.

during the 2001 general election campaign, licence holders regulated by the Independent Television Commission (ITC) were obliged to carry party political/election broadcasts as part of their programme output, observing 'such rules as the (ITC) may determine'.[19] In drawing up its rules, the ITC was to have regard under the *Political Parties, Elections and Referendums Act* 2000 to the views of the Electoral Commission.[20] For its part, the BBC was not under any formal obligation to offer PPBs/PEBs[21] although in practice, it carried the same number of PEBs/PPBs, the total having been agreed in advance by all broadcasters. In the 2001 general election, the major parties were given in each of the home nations five PEBs each.[22] The smaller parties were entitled to a PEB in each of the nations of the UK if they were fielding candidates in at least one-sixth of the seats in that nation.[23]

In *R* v *BBC ex parte ProLife Alliance* the House of Lords reversed a decision of the Court of Appeal and upheld by a majority of four to one the BBC's ban on the transmission of a party election broadcast deemed 'offensive' within the meaning of paragraph 5.1(d) of the Licence and Agreement.[24] The clash between the Court of Appeal and House of Lords has rightly prompted fresh examination of the case for maintaining restrictions on political expression in general (including what has been termed advocacy advertising) and the means, if any, by which these should be policed.[25] The matter did come under review during the parliamentary passage of the *Communications Act* 2003 in relation to consideration of the functions of OFCOM – the successor to the Independent Television Commission. Tessa Jowell, the Secretary of State for Culture, Media and Sport, was however unable to confirm

19 *Broadcasting Act* 1990, s.36.

20 *PPER* 2000, s.11.

21 The annual allocation of PPBs tends to reflect key moments in the political calendar such as the Budget, Queen's Speech, etc.

22 ITC (now OFCOM) Programme Code s.4.1 (iii) does not specify how many broadcasts the major parties will be offered, referring merely to 'a series of broadcasts before each election'. See also *Communications Act* 2000, s.333.

23 *Ibid.* The regional formula avoided the problem of subjecting all UK electors to the PEBs of regional parties when the majority of those electors would not be able to vote for those parties. This of course takes a narrow view of the purpose of PEBs, namely to inform the *electoral* choice of voters. Narrowly conceived as such, the rules may nonetheless hinder informed voting. Thus, a voter in England may be denied access to certain broadcast views about the government's relations and dealings with nationalist parties in Scotland and Wales. Yet this material might be considered by an elector in an English constituency to be relevant to his/her voting intentions.

24 [2003] 2 WLR 1403 (HL); [2002] 3 WLR 1080 (CA).

25 On the issue of 'good taste', the equivalent restriction for broadcasters licensed formerly by the Independent Television Commission was laid down in the *Broadcasting Act* 1990, s.6(1)(a) which imposed a 'best endeavours' obligation on the ITC to secure that 'nothing is included in … (licensees) programmes which offends against good taste or is likely to encourage or incite to crime or to lead to disorder or to be offensive to public feeling'.

that the 2003 Act was compatible with Convention rights on account of a provision retaining the ban on political advertising.[26]

The gulf between the Court of Appeal (which had unanimously struck down the ban as unjustified censorship of political expression) and the House of Lords points up a prior and more profound debate about the courts' role as constitutional guardians of free political debate in the *Human Rights Act* era which was examined in Chapter 2. Two of the leading judicial protagonists in this debate – Lord Justice Laws (an enthusiastic advocate of judicial guardianship of fundamental rights) and Lord Hoffman (an altogether more sceptical onlooker) – continued in *ProLife Alliance* to set out their respective lines of activism/restraint in ways that will be examined shortly. In the meantime and by way of setting the context for this disagreement, it can be noted that the retention of restrictions on 'political advertising' sits uneasily with the importance which is now commonly attached to the freedom of political expression, particularly given recent pronouncements from the European Court of Human Rights.[27] In *Verein gegen Tierfabriken* v *Switzerland*,[28] for example, a unanimous Court found that the national authority's ban on the applicant animal welfare association's television commercial intended for national television (which showed pigs in small pens and likened conditions to those found in concentration camps) to have violated the applicant's Article 10 rights. The advertisement had urged viewers to 'eat less meat, for the sake of your health, the animals and the environment'. The Court considered this to constitute a form of 'political expression' in respect of which the Swiss authorities enjoyed a relatively narrow margin of appreciation when assessing whether there was a 'pressing social need' to regulate. The need for close scrutiny was reinforced by the fact that the ban prevented the applicant using the one medium that allowed for communication with the whole of the Swiss population. Whilst recognizing the importance of preventing powerful financial groups securing commercial advantages through advertising and any resultant economic pressures on broadcasters' freedom of expression, it had not been shown that the applicant association was so financially powerful that it posed a danger to the independence of the broadcaster.[29] In consequence, the restriction had not been shown to be 'necessary in a democratic society'.

Against this European backdrop of increased scrutiny of restrictions on political advocacy, the House of Lords was called upon in *R* v *BBC ex parte ProLife Alliance* to consider the legality of the BBC's refusal to show in Wales images from a party

26 *Communications Act* 2003, ss.319(2)(g), 321 (2).

27 A Scott, '"A Monstrous and Unjustifiable Infringement"? Political Expression and the Broadcasting Ban on Advocacy Advertising' (2003) 66 *MLR* 224. One pre-HRA era ruling that ought to be reconsidered is *R* v *Radio Authority ex parte Bull and another* [1998] QB 294. This is discussed below. It may be worth noting that Amnesty did pursue their complaint to Strasbourg but settled when the government indicated its willingness to re-consider the ban on political advertising. See *Press Release* 8 December (1999) cited in Scott, *ibid*., at fn 68.

28 (2002) 34 EHRR 159.

29 It was not suggested by the Swiss authorities that the content of the commercial was in any way disturbing.

election broadcast by the ProLife Alliance.[30] The images in question were undeniably disturbing, consisting of the mangled and mutilated bodies of aborted foetuses. An accompanying soundtrack explained the processes involved. This soundtrack was not objected to and was broadcast alongside a blank screen bearing the word 'censored' five days before the 2001 General Election.[31] In subsequent proceedings, a unanimous Court of Appeal granted a declaration that the refusal to transmit the original broadcast was unlawful.[32] In a strongly worded judgment, Laws LJ declared that this was a case about the constitutional justification for the BBC's 'act of censorship'. The BBC had failed to give proper weight to the applicant's strong common law entitlement to engage in political speech at election time. Citing Lord Steyn's remarks in *R* v *Home Secretary ex parte Simms* that freedom of speech is the 'lifeblood of democracy', Laws LJ noted the special responsibility of the courts to act as the constitutional guardian of political debate, a duty which became particularly acute at the time of a general election.[33] Graphic and disturbing images could not by themselves form the basis of the censorship that was imposed in this case.[34] After all, the original PEB merely showed what happened in an abortion. It did not misrepresent what occurred. Considerations of taste and decency could triumph over free speech at election time in the most exceptional circumstances only. The BBC had failed to show that such exceptional circumstances were present.

On appeal to the House of Lords, the BBC was found not to have acted unlawfully. Its application of the taste and decency obligations to the proposed broadcast did not reveal grounds for judicial intervention such as arbitrariness, discrimination or unreasonableness. In Lord Hoffman's eyes, whilst 'untutored opinion could differ' on the application of taste and decency standards, 'broadcasters were particularly experienced in making such decisions'.[35] The Court of Appeal was faulted for having asked itself the wrong question. The BBC was not required to carry out a full proportionality examination in which the benefits of allowing the party to transmit a political message in the speaker's chosen form was to be weighed against the likely shock and disgust of the viewing public (or sections of it). Instead, and proceeding from the premise that Parliament was entitled to impose

---

30 The ProLife Alliance was entitled to a PEB broadcast in Wales, having fielded six candidates there.

31 The ProLife Alliance prepared two revised versions of the PEB containing progressively more blurred images. Neither was considered acceptable.

32 Overturning the refusal of Scott Baker J in the High Court.

33 [2002] 3 WLR 1080, 1096–7. For Laws LJ's earlier stated views on the courts' role in protecting fundamental rights, see 'Is The High Court the Guardian of Fundamental Rights?' (1993) *PL* 59.

34 In his concurrence at 1103, Simon Brown LJ observed that the Broadcasting Standards Commission had earlier approved an ITV programme which showed harrowing scenes of bodily mutilation in the aftermath of a bomb blast in Nairobi. The use of powerful scenes was held to have 'represented the true horror of terrorism' and thus 'served an important public interest and educative function'.

35 [2003] 2 WLR 1403, 1415.

standards of taste and decency on all broadcasts (including PEBs), the majority of their Lordships could find nothing to fault in the broadcaster's conclusion that the Alliance's images would have been offensive 'to a very large number of viewers'.[36] In an academic commentary subsequently cited with approval by Lord Hoffman in the House of Lords, Andrew Geddis argued that the Court of Appeal had fallen into error when it conflated the broadcaster's duty as a rule-applier to check that the proposed broadcast met taste and decency conditions with the role played by Parliament and the Secretary of State for National Heritage in setting standards or rule-making.[37]

The House of Lords' focus upon the reasonableness of the broadcasters' assessment of the taste and decency issues raised by the PEB had the effect that, despite the undoubted interference with an exercise of party political expression at election time, a comparatively relaxed standard of judicial scrutiny was applied to the BBC's decision-making processes. In terms of the general argument advanced in this book in favour of contextualized review, this approach to BBC regulation looks to have paid lip service only to the overarching importance of political speech in a democracy. It is worth probing the reasons offered/implicit in the majority's relaxed scrutiny stance to see whether this charge is unfounded.

At the outset it should be noted that the applicant did not seek to persuade the Court that the taste and decency rules were incompatible *per se* with Article 10. It is difficult to argue, then, that the Alliance wished to challenge at the level of rule-making as Geddis suggests. Rather, objection was taken with the application of the taste and decency standard in the context of a PEB. Even if a challenge had been taken to the legality of the rule itself, the most that could have resulted from the application would have been a declaration of incompatibility under s.4 of the *Human Rights Act* with the legal status of the rules left unaffected. This may account for why the argument was not made, although it is perhaps better explained on the ground that the 'rights of others' exception in Article 10(2) has been given a broad interpretation by the Strasbourg Court in the past. In *Otto Preminger Institut* v *Austria*, for example, the majority of the Court upheld the seizure and forfeiture of a film which it deemed was 'gratuitously offensive' to the religious feelings of others (including Roman Catholics) as a lawful restraint on the applicant film institute even though it was only shown to a paying audience with an interest in this type of film who had, in any event, been given prior warning of the nature of the film.[38] The Alliance broadcast, by contrast, would have been transmitted directly into viewers' homes, raising the

36 The phrase is Lord Hoffman's at [2003] 2 WLR 1403, 1423: he lent especial credence to the fact that the principal figures involved in the decision-making processes at the BBC were both women who were better placed than 'elderly male judges' to decide whether the images would be considered offensive to other women.

37 A Geddis, 'What Future for Political Advertising on the United Kingdom's Television Screens?' (2002) *PL* 615. For Geddis's response to the House of Lords' ruling see 'If Thy Right Eye Offend Thee, Pluck it Out': *R* v *BBC ex parte ProLife Alliance* (2003) 66 *MLR* 885.

38 (1995) 19 EHRR 34.

real possibility of confronting its audience with graphic imagery.[39] Any warning delivered in advance of the programme would plainly not protect those viewers who switched on after its announcement. Nonetheless, in liberal democratic states committed to pluralism, considerations of taste and decency constitute a problematic starting point for the imposition of conditions on political parties' electoral broadcasts. Election time in a democracy ought to constitute the moment when the electorate are exposed to the fullest range of opinions and ideas. Certainly it is true that parties campaigning on platforms that challenge aspects of a consensus among the main parties (particularly on moral issues) are clearly going to run greater risks in offending voters' sensibilities, especially with a pervasive and powerful medium like television.[40] Yet perhaps at election time, more so than at other times, there exist compelling reasons to be more than usually tolerant of 'offensive' expression.[41] For a court to approach a broadcaster's application of taste and decency standards at election time with something short of a rigorous scrutiny standard makes the flow of information (in this case factually accurate information) and ideas contingent on listeners' and viewers' sensibilities or, more precisely, the broadcaster's assessment of the same. In this sense, majority attitudes can acquire a censoring capacity, preventing the electorate as a whole obtaining access to information that may prove relevant to their electoral choice. The potential for stultification of informed debate looms large. Finally, proper respect for the means and tone chosen by the parties to convey their manifesto commitments also points to the need for a close judicial look at a regulator's restrictions. It is important to recall in this regard the oft-stated observation of the European Court of Human Rights that speakers are to be left to decide for themselves how to present ideas/information and that this is to be understood as extending to a degree of provocation or exaggeration.[42]

Viewed against such considerations, the case for declining to interfere with the broadcaster's judgment rests upon either a contentious judicial assessment of the democratic interest advanced by the prohibited material (Lord Hoffmann)[43] or a

---

39 Even Lord Scott of Foscote, the dissenting judge in the House of Lords, recognized that the 'rights of others' was 'well capable of extending to a recognition of the sense of outrage that might be felt by ordinary members of the public who in the privacy of their own homes had switched on the television set and been confronted by gratuitously offensive material': [2003] 2 WLR 1403, 1425. On the facts of the present case, however, the unsensational, factually accurate nature of the proposed broadcast led his Lordship to hold the BBC's fear of viewer offence to be unfounded.

40 The ability of television to make the viewer feel a participant in the events it depicts is commonly thought to justify subjecting the medium to tougher contents controls than other media. See Lord Hoffmann in *ProLife Alliance* and, earlier in a different context, Stevens J in *FCC v Pacifica* 438 US 726, 748 (1978).

41 I do not suggest, however, that this tolerance ought to stretch to the advocacy of values in direct opposition to democratic values.

42 *Bergens Tidende* v *Norway* (2001) 31 EHRR 16; *Thoma* v *Luxembourg* (2003) 36 EHRR 21.

43 See also Lord Walker of Gestingthorpe.

disregard for the importance in democratic life of protecting political expression at election time (Lords Nicholls and Millet). Thus, in the case of Lord Hoffmann, an implicit theme running through his speech is that the Alliance is not a serious political party and seeks somewhat manipulatively to field candidates in parliamentary elections in order to gain free publicity for its views.[44]

Of crucial importance to the majority's reasoning is the premise that the Alliance had no right under Article 10 to broadcast on television. There is, to use the phrase of Lord Hoffmann, 'no human right to use a television channel'. The Alliance enjoyed the same freedom of expression as every other citizen. By virtue of its registration as a political party and numbers of candidate deposits lodged in Wales, the party was already afforded more access to the electorate through a PEB than other citizens and single-issue groups.

The fact that the Alliance had no right to a broadcast did not mean, however, that Article 10 ceased to be relevant to the regulation of PEBs altogether. Citing the European Commission decisions in *Haider* v *Austria*[45] and *Huggett* v *United Kingdom*,[46] the majority found that the applicant was nonetheless entitled not to be denied access to broadcast media on discriminatory, arbitrary or unreasonable grounds. Lord Hoffman did accept that, whilst neutral in the sense of being applicable to all PEBs, taste and decency rules impacted unevenly against a party 'which feels the need to breach the standards in order to get its message across'. In such cases, the question was whether the condition imposed on taste and decency grounds was 'objectively justified'.[47] This required an assessment of the impact of the condition upon the democratic interest which lies behind PEBs, namely encouraging an informed choice at the ballot box. It is here that the analysis offered by Lord Hoffmann appears particularly vulnerable to criticism. Initially, his lordship maintained that the Alliance PEB was 'quite unrelated' to informing electoral choice. Then, in a curious retreat, he conceded that the Alliance's views were of interest to voters in Wales. However, noting the Alliance's low level of support in the 2001 general election in the Principality, he stated that its views were of concern to 'very few' Welsh voters, adding in the next sentence '[i]n any case, abortion is not in this country a party political issue'.[48] As such, there was nothing in the present application to suggest that PEBs should be exempt from ordinary taste and decency standards applicable to non-PEB output since these standards form:

---

44 See his uncritical adoption of the Electoral Commission's concerns expressed in its 2003 Report (at 36) that organizations might be encouraged to register as political parties and field sufficient candidates in order to gain access via the broadcast media to voters that would not otherwise be available (para. 69).

45 (1995) 83 DR 66.

46 (1995) 82A DR 98.

47 The Alliance, he stated, had no human right to be invited to the party, and it was not unreasonable for Parliament to ask it to behave.

48 *Ibid.*, at para. 68.

> … part of the country's cultural life and have created expectations on the part of viewers as to what they will and will not be shown on the screen in their homes.[49]

Having decided that the Alliance's PEB could properly be made subject to taste and decency requirements, Lord Hoffmann was unable to see anything in the BBC's refusal to screen the PEB in question to indicate that the broadcaster had acted unlawfully.

By way of comment, it may be thought that to allow 'cultural expectations' of viewers to inform the decision of whether to exempt PEBs from ordinary taste and decency conditions signally fails to mark out political expression as vitally important in a democracy, placing the limits of PEBs at the mercies of popular sentiment. Just as troubling is the reference made to low-level electoral support to reinforce the conclusion that the broadcaster's condition impacted on the democratic interest in an informed electorate in a minimal way only. Abortion, we learn, 'is not a party issue'. This is hardly credible. The presence alone of Alliance candidates on the list of candidates in Wales gives the lie to this assertion. Indeed, it is worth speculating whether the low level of electoral support ultimately secured by the Alliance (and used by Lord Hoffmann in part to justify his relaxed scrutiny standard) reflected the fact that it was unable to convey its message in the way it wished. This thought does not appear to have occurred to his lordship. More generally, it may be thought especially important in a democracy to allow the expression of views on an issue during an election in which the major political parties are not offering the electorate any policy choice.

Advocacy Advertising

Had the Alliance wished to publicize its views on television and radio outside of an election period, it would probably have fared little better. Advocacy advertising on the broadcast media by anyone/group wishing to raise public consciousness on an issue or cause remains prohibited under broadcasting laws. Section 8(2) of the 1990 *Broadcasting Act* imposes a total prohibition on 'political advertising' on commercial television. Section 92(2) achieves the same in respect of commercial radio. The term 'political advertising' was defined by the Court of Appeal in *R* v *Radio Authority ex parte Bull* to catch those advertisements which seek to bring about a change in the law or policy of this or any other country.[50] It follows that this set of restrictions operate not merely to prevent party political advertising but also any issue advocacy by pressure groups, corporations, trades unions and other elements of civil society. Two justifications for the ban were offered by Kennedy LJ in *R* v *Radio Authority ex parte Bull* in his ruling in the Queen's Bench Division. The first – and plainly less thought through – reason centred upon the claimed freedom of listeners 'from being virtually forced to listen to unsolicited information of a

49 *Ibid.*, at para. 70.

50 [1998] QB 294, deriving considerable support from Slade J in *McGovern* v *AG* [1982] Ch 321, 340.

contentious kind'.[51] More seriously however, the judge advanced a second reason for the ban namely 'the danger of the wealthy distorting the democratic process'.[52] This reflects a concern to prevent a powerful communicative tool (and the influence over public opinion it appears to holds out) being dominated by the economically-strong. After *Verein gegen Tierfabriken* v *Switzerland* however,[53] national authorities would be expected to demonstrate in any Article 10 challenge to the ban why, in any particular case, the advertiser possessed by virtue of their commercial power some form of influence or control over the output of the broadcaster. It is by no means clear that Amnesty or other pressure groups do in fact enjoy the level of influence attributed to them, although this might be true in respect of multinational corporations and other commercial organizations. Though unaddressed in *ex parte Bull*, a further justification for prohibition lies in the desire to prevent a political 'arms race' in which rival factions try to outspend each other in obtaining paid advertising space. This rationale is most obviously tied to arguments for controls on political parties' expenditure discussed in the following chapter. In 1998, the Neill Committee on Standards in Public Life urged retention of the advertising ban on this basis.[54] In *The Funding of Political Parties in the United Kingdom* the Government signalled its agreement with Neill.[55] As long as the ban is limited to broadcast media, it serves merely to displace a proportion of advertising expenditure into the print media. In any event, the objective of preventing an 'arms race' could be achieved by means of an expenditure ceiling, a device which would have the added attractions of limiting the scope for improper corporate/commercial influence on broadcasters as well as permitting a greater range of political views or opinions (such as from pressure groups) to be placed before the electorate. A genuine concern to promote the latter might even be thought to require a system of state subsidies to enable poorly financed interests to have their views heard. Even those who remain unpersuaded by the idea of state support might nonetheless concede that the present outright ban operates as a heavy-handed means of securing its intended objectives.

Other Restrictions on Expressive Political Activity

The Right to Vote

This right may be thought to enjoy an especially close link to political expression. Voters' preferences are formed to a greater or lesser extent after reflection on

51 A formulation that would catch much commercial advertising as well as political expression. It is not clear in any event that radio listeners are incapable of changing station when confronted with unsolicited advertisements they disapprove of. See A Scott (2003) 66 *MLR* 224, 234.

52 [1995] 4 All ER 481.

53 (2002) 34 EHRR 159.

54 Cm 4057 (1998) see Recommendation 94.

55 Home Office Cm 4413 (1999) at para. 9.2.

the parties' manifestos and other public communications. Although usually communicated by way of secret ballot to election officials only, the choice made by voters in turn is par excellence a statement of individual political preference. Were it not for the fact that the right to vote is usually accorded separate status in constitutional documents, it might be considered to be derived from the right to free expression. Unlike expression, which is typically conceived of as a 'negative' liberty, the right to vote entails some more obviously positive obligations on the part of the state. Consider, for example, Article 3 of Protocol 1 of the European Convention on Human Rights imposes an obligation on contracting states to

> … hold free elections at reasonable intervals by secret ballot, under conditions which will ensure the free expression of the opinion of the people in the choice of the legislature.

The right to vote may also be said to derive from the principle of political equality of citizens. As Justice Sachs of the South African Supreme Court remarked in a particularly poignant reflection,

> Universal adult suffrage on a common voters' roll is one of the foundational values of our entire constitutional order … The vote of each and every citizen is a badge of dignity and of personhood. Quite literally, it says that everybody counts. In a country of great disparities of wealth and power it declares that whoever we are, whether rich or poor, exalted or disgraced, we all belong to the same democratic South African nation.[56]

Likewise in *Mathieu-Mohin and Clerfayt* v *Belgium*, the reference in Article 3 of Protocol 1 ECHR to conditions necessary to ensure the free expression of the electorate was said to imply

> … apart from freedom of expression (already protected in Article 10 of the Convention) – the principle of equality of treatment of all citizens in the exercise of their right to vote and the right to stand for election.[57]

Conversely, a government that restricts voting entitlements to selected groups may be considered to have weakened its legitimacy by denying a truly representative democracy. Alongside a diminished authority to make laws, the punishment of those that contravene the law also becomes problematic.[58]

Aside from reflecting the values of political equality and expression, voting (and candidacy) rights are also ineluctably tied to the ideals of an inclusive, participatory and pluralistic democracy in which citizens can pursue different conceptions of the good society through engagement with electoral processes.[59] Respect for these rights would therefore appear crucial for the effective functioning of political democracies.

---

56 *August and another* v *Electoral Commission and others* [1999] ZACC 3.

57 (1988) 10 EHRR 1, 17.

58 See in this regard the remarks of the Canadian Supreme Court in *Sauvé* v *AG Canada* [2002] 3 SCR 519, para. 34.

59 *Ibid*., at para. 15.

As the European Court of Human Rights observed in *Mathieu-Mohin and Clerfayt* v *Belgium*, 'Since it enshrines a characteristic principle of democracy, Article 3 of Protocol No. 1 is accordingly of prime importance in the Convention system.'[60] On this view, it should follow that compelling reasons would need to be shown before any curtailment of these fundamental norms was considered constitutionally possible. This approach is evident in the Canadian Supreme Court majority's analysis of voting restrictions in *Sauvé* v *AG of Canada*.[61] There, the right to vote was stated to be fundamental to Charter guarantees of a participatory democracy and the rule of law.[62] 'Stringent examination' of limits placed on the right to vote was needed under s.1 of the Charter to ensure that the 'legislature's proffered justification was supported by logic and common sense'.[63] The ruling in *Sauvé* is discussed in greater detail at a later stage of this chapter.

A relatively demanding standard of judicial scrutiny of legislative regulation of the sort advocated in *Sauvé* is not, however, a universal feature of liberal democratic practice. In the especially contentious example of restrictions imposed on the voting rights of prisoners, courts in a number of jurisdictions have had to address the constitutional issues arising from a range of degrees of disenfranchisement. Not all have opted for a close look at legislative curtailment of voting rights, although a discernible trend towards both stricter judicial scrutiny and legislature-led relaxation of legal constraints is now evident across several jurisdictions. A central justification for judicial deference (where it occurs) is the varied pattern of restrictions encountered across liberal democracies and the different theoretical perspectives on the nature of voting upon which divergent legal rules are based. In more restrictive regimes, for example, voting is intimately connected to the promotion of good citizenship and the rule of law. Society may, on this view, make democratic participation conditional upon adherence to its core norms. Those found to have breached a norm that carries a penalty of imprisonment are said to have lost the moral authority to vote.[64] Denial of the vote to prison inmates[65] (which will for most be a temporary

60 (1988) 10 EHRR 1, 15.

61 [2002] 3 SCR 519.

62 A position which was emphasized by the fact that s.3 was exempted from s.33 – the Charter's legislative override clause.

63 [2002] 3 SCR 519, at para. 9, *per* McLachlin CJ.

64 See *Final Report of the Working Party on Electoral Procedures* (1999, Home Office) at para. 2.3.8 where this justification for disenfranchisement was accepted by the Working Party; for further discussion of theoretical perspectives invoked to support disenfranchisement see L Tribe 'Note: The Disenfranchisement of Ex-Felons: Citizenship, Criminality and the Purity of the Ballot Box' (1989) 102 *Harv L Rev* 1300. The European Commission in *Holland* v *Ireland* Application No. 24827/94 (1998) (unreported) declined to interfere with a domestic authority's failure to provide arrangements for inmates' postal voting on the ground in part that the 'dishonour' of being a convicted prisoner conferred on states a wide margin of appreciation in the extent to which the right to vote was curtailed. The case is discussed by H Lardy, 'Prisoner Disenfranchisement: Constitutional Rights and Wrongs' (2000) *PL* 524.

65 That is, convicted prisoners rather than those held on remand awaiting trial.

sanction) constitutes however not only a civil penalty for offenders, but also sends a wider deterrent message that serious criminal activity will not be tolerated by the community. The reference to the reinforcement of community values as a basis for denying voting rights can be seen to draw upon a particularly hard-line version of communitarian thinking. Even though there is interference with a core aspect of representative democracies, the overriding claims of the community to insist upon adherence to its values as expressed in disenfranchisement laws are considered to prevail over individual rights.

Less restrictive regimes, on the other hand, point *inter alia* to the rehabilitative potential of conferring an entitlement to vote, encouraging as it does both a constructive interest in political affairs and respect for democratic values. Disenfranchising individuals already at the margins of society is argued to make convicts even less able and/or willing to identify with membership of the community and its values. Others have pointed to the over-representation of minority groups in prisons (the obvious example being young black men) to raise concerns about the disproportionate impact of disenfranchisement rules on certain sections of the population.[66]

Given these conflicting rationales and the absence of hard empirical data to establish conclusively the effectiveness of either punitive or rehabilitative policies, the task of choosing from a range of reasonable, alternative policy stances is considered by some judges to be best left to the democratically elected representatives of the people. This was the position adopted by the minority of the Canadian Supreme Court in *Sauvé* v *AG of Canada*.[67] It also appears to have found an echo in the UK courts where, until 2004, all convicted prisoners were prevented from voting by s.3(1) of the *Representation of the People Act* 1983.[68] A challenge was taken to the bar in *Hirst* v *AG*.[69] Accepting that the UK Parliament could have adopted different (and presumably less draconian) rules to achieve its chosen policy objectives, Kennedy LJ in the Queen's Bench Division nonetheless declined to issue a declaration of incompatibility under s.4(2) of the *Human Rights Act* 1998, citing the 'broad spectrum' of approaches among democratic societies in support of allowing Parliament some

---

66 M J Gottlieb, 'Developments in the Law "One Person, No Vote: the Laws of Felon Disenfranchisement"' (2002) 115 *Harv L Rev* 1939. In the US state of Alabama, where convicted felons may not vote, it was estimated that, as of 2000, some 6.75 per cent of the voting-age population were ineligible to vote. Other estimates suggest that between 30 and 50 per cent of those disenfranchised were black.

67 See also in this regard the stance of the majority of the US Supreme Court in *Richardson* v *Ramirez* 418 US 24 (1974).

68 An even wider ban preventing voting by convicted but unsentenced prisoners, remand prisoners and mental patients was in force prior to February 2001. The ban was lifted in respect of remand prisoners and mental patients when the *Representation of the People Act* 2000 came into force.

69 [2002] ACD 26.

leeway in its rule-making.[70] At a supra-national level, the European Court of Human Rights has similarly applied a relatively relaxed standard of supervision in the past – a product no doubt in part of the 'broad spectrum' of policy stances that exists across Council of Europe member states and also in part of the structural feature of the Convention in which the Court sits as a supra-national body, overlooking the decisions of national authorities that have agreed to secure in the first place the enumerated rights and freedoms for persons under their jurisdiction. Viewed in this way, the finding in *Hirst* v *UK (No .2)*[71] that the UK Parliament's bar on voting by convicted prisoners violated the applicant's First Protocol entitlements may have come as something of a surprise. The reasons behind the ruling are explored in detail in the following section of materials.

Strasbourg

The interpretation of Article 3 of the First Protocol by the Strasbourg authorities as conferring upon individuals the right to vote and to stand for election represents an evolution in Convention thinking. The precise wording of Article 3 was the subject of much debate[72] and the formulation that was eventually agreed referred to obligations imposed on states rather than the individual rights-conferring constructions ('Everyone has the right' or 'No one shall') encountered throughout much of the rest of the Convention and its Protocols. Given these features, it is perhaps not surprising that early Commission cases stopped short of endorsing an individual rights-based interpretation. Early Commission cases recognized an 'institutional right' that free elections be held[73] and, later, the concept of universal suffrage.[74] The right to vote and stand for election was subsequently acknowledged by the Commission in *W, X, Y & Z* v *Belgium* in admissibility proceedings.[75] It took until the 1988 decision *Mathieu-Mohin and Clerfayt* v *Belgium* for the Court to confirm the implied individual rights to vote and stand for election.

It is, however, too simplistic a reading of Article 3 of the First Protocol to infer an entitlement on the part of all citizens to vote under all circumstances. The Court in

70 For discussion of domestic law see H Lardy, 'Prisoner Disenfranchisement: Constitutional Rights and Wrongs' (2000) *PL* 524.

71 *Application No. 74025/01* (2004) *The Times*, 8 April.

72 JG Merrills and AH Robertson, *Human Rights in Europe – A Study of the European Convention on Human Rights* (4th edn, 2001, Manchester University Press, Manchester) 248–9.

73 *X* v *Belgium Application No. 1028/61* (decision of 18 September 1961) *Yearbook of the European Convention on Human Rights* 4 (1961) 260 Martinus Nijhoff, The Hague, 1962. The Commission stated that the Article 3 obligation 'does not imply guaranteeing to every person the right to participate in such elections, which implies that the right to vote is not, as such, guaranteed by Article 3 …' at 268.

74 *X* v *Federal Republic of Germany Application No. 2728/66* (decision of 6 October 1966).

75 *Application Nos. 6745-6746/76* (decision of 30 May 1975).

Mathieu-Mohin and Clerfayt v *Belgium* held that, just as the rights to vote and stand had had to be implied from the initial guarantee, so too would limitations upon the rights. Contracting states could impose conditions upon the exercise of voting and candidacy rights within what the Court stated was a 'wide margin of appreciation'. Supervision by the Court would extend to an inquiry that national legal systems did not

> ... curtail the rights in question to such an extent as to impair their very essence and deprive them of their effectiveness; that they are imposed in pursuit of a legitimate aim and the means employed are not disproportionate.[76]

The latitude conferred on national authorities to run their own electoral systems poses a major obstacle in the way of those wishing to challenge national restrictions on voting/candidacy. In this context, the finding by a majority of the Grand Chamber in *Hirst* v *UK (No. 2)* that the UK's refusal to allow prisoners voting rights violated Article 3 of Protocol 1 may be thought somewhat surprising.[77] A central concern for the Court in *Hirst* was the blanket imposition of voting restrictions across all categories of convicted prisoners, irrespective of the length of sentence handed down by the court and the nature or gravity of the offence. This rendered s.3(1) of the 1983 Act a disproportionate interference with the right to vote. In earlier proceedings before the Chamber, the failure of domestic law to distinguish between different elements of a prisoner's custodial sentence had been criticized. Hirst, a discretionary life prisoner, had served the tariff element of his sentence (which related to the retributive and deterrent elements of his sentence) and was being kept in detention solely because the Parole Board adjudged him to pose a serious risk to members of the public. As the punitive element of his sentence had been completed, it was difficult to justify the retention of a bar on voting, when this was considered to constitute part of the punitive sanctions imposed on prisoners.[78]

Canadian and US Approaches

Outside of the Council of Europe, the fault lines detailed above between punitive and rehabilitative schools of thought recur in constitutional litigation contesting specific instances of disenfranchisement. Today, if a cross-jurisdictional trend can be identified, it points (as in *Hirst No. 2*) to closer judicial scrutiny of voting restrictions against a legislative backdrop in which arguments in favour of prisoners' voting rights based upon the abstract values of inclusiveness and equality have begun in

76 (1987) 10 EHRR 1 at para. 52.

77 *Application No. 74025/01* (2005) Judgment 6 October, available on the European Court of Human Rights portal. See also *Holland* v *Ireland* (1998) *Application No. 24827/94*, where a failure to provide postal voting facilities for prisoners was held not to breach Article 3 Protocol 1. For comment, see H Lardy, 'Prisoner Disenfranchisement: Constitutional Rights and Wrongs' (2002) *PL* 524.

78 See further J Broadhead, 'Votes for Prisoners' (2004) 154 *NLJ* 437.

any event to acquire momentum. In Canada, the Supreme Court has intervened to secure a gradual loosening of restrictions on prisoners' voting rights. Thus in 1993 it affirmed the decisions of the Ontario Court of Appeal in *Sauvé* v *AG of Canada* and the Federal Court of Appeal in *Belczowski* v *Canada* striking down a blanket ban on voting by inmates in any penal institution.[79] The ban was adjudged to constitute a disproportionate interference with s.3 of the *Canadian Charter of Rights and Freedoms* which states:

> Every citizen of Canada has the right to vote in an election of members of the House of Commons or of a legislative assembly and to be qualified for membership therein.

As a result, Canadian election law was revised to remove the disqualification where a prisoner was serving a sentence of less than two years.[80] In 2002, this narrowed disqualification was also invalidated by the Supreme Court in *Sauvé* v *AG of Canada*.[81] It will be recalled that the majority adopted a 'stringent' standard of review in this case to ascertain whether the infringement of s.3 of the Charter met the requirements of s.1 of the Charter. This provision allows curtailment of Charter rights to 'such reasonable limits prescribed by law as can be demonstrably justified in a free and democratic society'. The leading interpretation of s.1 is set out in *R* v *Oakes* which lays down a two-part test for limitations on Charter rights to be justified.[82] First, the objective behind a limitation must be considered of 'sufficient importance; that is, the limitation must be based upon pressing and substantial concerns in a democratic society. Second, the limitation must satisfy a three-limbed proportionality test; namely (i) rational connection to its objective; (ii) as minimal an impairment of the Charter right as is necessary to meet the objective; and (iii) the effect of the measures must not be out of all proportion to that which is gained by securing the objective.

In the present case, the government failed at the outset to show that the undoubted interference with inmates' s.3 rights was in response to a specific problem that was both pressing and substantial. The government's claimed objectives of enhancing civic responsibility and respect for the rule of law could be adduced for virtually every criminal law. Moreover, it had not been shown what additional purposes would be served by the voting ban (which the majority construed as an extra punishment) imposed on this class of prisoners that were not already being met by the sentences handed out to them. Even if the government's stated objectives had been considered pressing and substantial, it had further failed to show a rational connection between the measure and its intended purposes. Denying the vote to this admittedly smaller class of prisoners was likely to hinder rather than promote efforts at teaching

---

79 [1993] 2 SCR 438. The blanket ban was laid down in s.51(e) of the *Canadian Elections Act* RSC 1985.

80 SC 1993, c 19, s.23.

81 [2002] 3 SCR 519. Also joined to the action was *McCorrister and others* v *AG for Canada and others*.

82 [1986] 1 SCR 103.

prisoners democratic values and social responsibility.[83] It removed a route to social development and undermined efforts at rehabilitation. In a sideswipe at the measure's lack of proportionality, McLachlin CJ noted that the bar also struck indiscriminately at a wide variety of convicted persons, from motoring offenders at one end of the spectrum to serial murderers at the other. No distinction was made between inmates serving sentences of two years and those serving 20-year terms of imprisonment. The measure also struck *de facto* in an excessive manner at Aboriginal peoples who were over-represented in prison, a fact the Chief Justice attributed to some extent to higher rates of poverty and alienation from mainstream society. Disenfranchisement of this group meant that their unique perspectives and needs went unheard.

More generally, the Court declared that moral unworthiness could not act as a basis for disenfranchisement since it was inconsistent with notions of individual dignity which, according to Chief Justice McLachlin, lay 'at the heart of Canadian democracy and the Charter'.[84] Apart from the conflict with dignity, the measure could have 'no place in a democracy built upon principles of inclusiveness, equality and citizen participation'. It was significant in this regard that s.3 of the Charter is not subject to the legislative override in the s.33 'notwithstanding' clause which allows the Canadian Parliament and provincial legislatures to pass laws in other instances which would infringe Charter rights. Unpopular minorities who thus found their voting entitlements under legislative assault could seek redress in the courts without fear of legislative override. Having so found, there was no need to examine the appellant's separate submission that s.51(e) of the *Canada Elections Act* infringed the equality guarantee laid down in s.15(1) of the Charter.

By contrast with Canada, the US courts' approach to prisoner disenfranchisement displays a marked disinclination to interfere with community determinations of sanctions for criminal conduct. However, this is driven not so much by a desire to affirm the moral basis of commonly held local views underlying voting bars but rather by a technical reading of the constitutional text.[85] Thus in the 1974 Supreme Court ruling of *Richardson* v *Ramirez*, it was held that state legislatures enjoyed a broad discretion to determine the extent of voting rights lost by convicted felons, whether in custody or not.[86] The ruling was based on s.2 of the Fourteenth Amendment which empowers states to remove the franchise from citizens who participate in 'rebellion or other crime.' The Court's reliance upon the wide discretion conferred by the constitutional text upon states was criticized by some supporters of disenfranchisement as missing an opportunity to affirm commonly held moral sentiments underlying the voting bar.

83 Drawing here on the work of JS Mill, 'Thoughts on Parliamentary Reform' (1859) and contained in JM Robson (ed.), *Essays on Politics and Society Vol XIX* (1977, University of Toronto Press, Toronto) 311.

84 Citing with approval the South African Constitutional Court in *August* v *Electoral Commission and others* [1999] ZACC 3.

85 For comment criticizing the failure to endorse community norms, see CP Manfredi, *Judicial Power and the Charter* (2nd edn, 2001, OUP, Ontario) at 146.

86 418 US 24 (1974).

By 2002, however, a number of states had begun to liberalize their voting rules. Thus Virginia, which had in the past disenfranchised all its convicted felons for life, changed its laws to allow ex-felons to apply to circuit courts for restoration to the electoral roll after a five-year waiting period (for non-drugs-related offenders) or seven years (for drugs offenders).[87] With exceptions for certain crimes, Delaware, Nevada, New Mexico, Tennessee, Texas and Washington have also all enacted liberalizing measures in recent times.[88] These developments followed the Supreme Court's decision in *Hunter* v *Underwood*, affirming a Court of Appeal's ruling in 1985 that Alabama's disenfranchisement regime was enacted with discriminatory intent, thereby violating the Fourteenth Amendment's Equal Protection Clause.[89] The Alabama Constitutional Convention of 1901 had set out explicitly to enshrine the principle of white supremacy in the state constitution. The Court of Appeals for the Eleventh Circuit found that Article VIII 182 of the Alabama Constitution, which provided for the disenfranchisement of persons convicted of any crime 'involving moral turpitude', had been drafted with the intention of catching crimes of which black persons were frequently convicted, thereby denying black persons the vote. The Court invalidated Article VIII 182 under the Equal Protection Clause in a case involving appellants who had been convicted of presenting a worthless cheque (a crime apparently involving moral turpitude in Alabama).

In a clear contrast with Canadian Charter law as expounded in *Sauvé* v *AG of Canada*, the Equal Protection Clause cannot be used to challenge disenfranchisement *which happens in practice* (rather than intends, or is motivated in part by a desire) to exclude blacks and other minorities from the list of eligible voters. In these circumstances, s.2 of the *Voting Rights Act* 1965 might be thought to offer a more potent challenge to *de facto* racial disenfranchisement. This prohibits any voting practice or procedure that 'results in a denial or abridgement of the right of any citizen of the United States to vote on account of race or color'. Indeed, the strategy gained momentum with a ruling of the Second Circuit Court of Appeals in *Baker* v *Pataki* that while some, none or all of its felons might be disenfranchised for legitimate reasons, states could not disenfranchise using measures which had 'the effect, whether intentional or not, of disenfranchising felons because of their race'.[90] Yet, as the *Harvard Law Review* notes, the *Voting Rights Act* has failed to limit states' disenfranchisement powers. Courts have rejected an expansive reading of s.2 on the basis that the provision does not contain clear language to support a finding of

87 M J Gottlieb, 'Developments in the Law "One Person, No Vote: the Laws of Felon Disenfranchisement"' (2002) 115 *Harv L Rev* 1939.

88 *Ibid.*, at 1948–9.

89 471 US 222 (1985). The Fourteenth Amendment states 'Section 1: All persons born or naturalized in the United States, and subject to the jurisdiction thereof, are citizens of the United States and of the State wherein they reside. No State shall make or enforce any law which shall abridge the privileges or immunities of citizens of the United States; nor shall any State deprive any person of life, liberty, or property, without due process of law; nor deny to any person within its jurisdiction the equal protection of the laws.'

90 85 F.3d 919 (Second Cir. 1996).

Congressional intent to override longstanding state laws.[91] Even where s.2 has been applied to prisoners' loss of voting entitlements, legal challenges have foundered when no causal link between the practice of felon disenfranchisement and racial discrimination has been found.[92]

Prisoners' Voting Rights: A Conclusion

Unsurprisingly, judicial resort to normative principles of inclusivity, equality, dignity and citizenship which have informed the courts' more interventionist responses to the legislative restriction of prisoners' voting rights has attracted criticism. For some, such as constitutional interpretivists who insist that judicial review, to be legitimate, must be tied closely to the intention of the framers and the text of the Constitution, judicial discovery and application of abstract moral principles (referred to commonly as non-interpretivism) deny the respect that is owed to legislative majorities when they pass laws that do not obviously contradict the plain words of the constitutional text. On this account, the judgments of legislative and constitutional majorities must be preferred precisely because of their majoritarian credentials. Beyond this supposed defect, others such as Manfredi have pointed to the failure of non-interpretivism to 'take seriously the normative judgments embodied in majority rule'.[93] In the context of criminal disenfranchisement, those who subscribe to this view criticize the tendency of courts to cast aside all too easily value judgments made by the majority in the community about some or all criminals having forfeited temporarily the participation rights that come with membership of a democratic political community rights. It is not obvious that Supreme Court judges possess superior moral insights to ordinary citizens and their representatives and therefore we should be wary about vesting ultimate power in the courts to decide these largely moral questions.

A response to Manfredi's position might counter in the spirit of Alexander Bickel that, in the specific context of the treatment of prisoners, the temptation for legislatures and executives to act out of expediency rather than principle might prove difficult to resist. There are, after all, votes in most liberal democracies for being seen to take an uncompromising line with criminals. In such circumstances, judicial oversight may offer a valuable safeguard against short term, populist measures. In the UK, for example, the then Home Secretary Michael Howard based his decision in *Thompson & Venables* to set a tariff that was five years longer than that recommended by the Lord Chief Justice, after receiving representations from the *Sun* newspaper and its readers. The defendants were the notorious child murderers of a two-year-old

91 *Gregory* v *Ashcroft* 501 US 452, 460–61 (1991).

92 M J Gottlieb, 'Developments in the Law "One Person, No Vote: the Laws of Felon Disenfranchisement"' (2002) 115 *Harv L Rev* 1939, 1955–6. For an instance where the causal connection was established see *Farrakhan* v *Locke* 987 F.Supp. 1304 (E.D. Wash 1997).

93 At the same time, he also criticizes interpretivism for elevating the notion of majority rule for its own sake and ignoring the capacity of majorities to 'rule systematically in a principled way': *Judicial Power and the Charter* (2nd edn, 2001, OUP, Ontario) at 30–31.

toddler in Liverpool. The tabloid had published coupons demanding that Thompson and Venables be given whole tariffs. Readers were asked to fill in personal details and send to the Home Office. In the event, over 21,000 coupons were submitted. The House of Lords ruled in *R* v *Secretary of State for the Home Department ex parte Venables* that the Home Secretary's tariff was unlawful on account of the weight given by the Secretary of State to the tabloid campaign against the defendants.[94] If *Hirst* v *UK (No. 2)* is anything to go by, however, the era of deference towards national authorities and the wisdom of local majorities in Council of Europe states in this particular sphere might be on the wane.

The Right to Stand for Election and Engage in Other Party Political Activities

Alongside the right to vote, the right of each individual to seek elected political office has been described as 'the very embodiment of democracy'.[95] The guarantee that each citizen may put him/herself forward to be selected as a representative of voters affirms the equality of citizens and the inclusive, participatory nature of democracy. By standing, the candidate may become eligible to a range of benefits which facilitate the communication of his/her electoral message, thereby adding to the views and information placed before the electorate. In UK law these include free postage for one election communication and the use of schools and other public buildings without charge in order to hold election meetings.[96] It follows that limits on who may stand at election time can impact adversely on citizens' participation in political debate and the electorate's interest in receiving a broad range of materials that might be used to inform voting intentions.

Nonetheless, eligibility for elected political office in most democracies is limited. In the UK, for example, persons may be prevented from standing on grounds of age, mental health, bankruptcy or criminal convictions for corrupt and illegal practices.[97] Other offenders imprisoned for one year or more by a court (whether in the UK or not) are not eligible to be nominated as a candidate while they are detained.[98] A further and important set of disqualifications apply to public office holders such as civil servants, the judiciary,[99] police officers, members of the armed forces and the chairs and members of various administrative bodies listed in Parts 2–4 of Schedule 1 of the *House of Commons Disqualification Act* 1975.[100]

94 [1998] AC 407.

95 *Harvey* v *New Brunswick* [1996] 2 SCR 876 *per* LaForest J at para. 37.

96 *Representation of the People Act* 1983, ss.91 and 95.

97 For an account see A Bradley and K Ewing, *Constitutional and Administrative Law* (13th edn, 2003, Longman, Harlow) at 169–72.

98 *Representation of the People Act* 1981. If sentenced to a period of more than a year whilst unlawfully at large, an equivalent restriction applies.

99 Though lay magistrates are not barred from standing.

100 A Bradley and K Ewing, *Constitutional and Administrative Law* (13th edn, 2003, Longman, Harlow) at 170–71.

A controversial extension of restraints on the political activities of individuals domestically including (but not limited to) the right to stand for election is to be found in the *Local Government Officers (Political Restrictions) Regulations* 1990. Following recommendations from the Widdicombe Committee of Inquiry into Local Authority Business (designed to safeguard the political neutrality of senior local government officers and thereby confidence in public administration[101]), Parliament enacted the *Local Government and Housing Act* 1989. Section 1(5) of the Act conferred upon the Secretary of State for the Environment a power to make regulations to prescribe the political activities of persons holding a 'politically restricted post' in local government. The latter phrase was defined in the 1989 Act to include three classes of local authority employee: senior post-holders;[102] officers receiving in excess of a prescribed salary level whose posts are listed in the Regulations;[103] and officers paid less than the prescribed salary level but holding a listed post whose duties involve giving advice on a regular basis to the authority, its committees and sub-committees, or speaking on behalf of the authority on a regular basis to the media.[104] Local authorities were obliged to produce a list of posts within the second and third categories. An employee who wished to have his or her post removed from this list of posts could apply to an independent adjudicator.[105]

The types of political activity caught under the *Regulations* include standing as a candidate for election to the UK Parliament, the European Parliament, or any local authority. However, acting as an election agent and canvassing on behalf of a candidate is also forbidden. Holding any office or committee membership of a political party is proscribed if this would involve participating in the general management of the political party or representing the party in its dealings with others. Perhaps the most controversial aspect of the *Regulations* was the ban on speaking to the public or a section of the public or publishing any written or artistic work with the 'apparent intention of affecting public support for a political party'.[106]

After unsuccessfully seeking judicial review in the domestic courts,[107] four local government officers challenged the *Regulations* in Strasbourg, invoking the protection of Articles 10 and 11 of the main Convention and Article 3 of Protocol 1. The Commission looked first at the violation of Article 10. It concluded that,

101 Cmnd 9797 (1986). Widdicombe had argued that unless reform was undertaken, there was a 'very significant risk' that politically active officers whose duties involved advising elected councillors would be seen with suspicion by councillors representing other political parties.

102 Including the chief executive of a local authority, the director of social services, the chief education officer.

103 S.2(2)(a) and (b) of the 1989 Act. In 1998, this level was set at £25,746 p.a.

104 S.2(2)(c). Local authorities were obliged to produce a list of posts within the second and third categories.

105 S.3.

106 Schedule, Part II paras 6 and 7.

107 *R* v *Secretary of State for the Environment ex parte NALGO* (1993) 5 Admin Law Reports 785.

whilst the prohibitions could be viewed as pursuing a legitimate aim (namely the preservation of an effective political democracy), the Government had not shown that the various political activities which the applicants wished to pursue (including standing for election to a local authority and acting as office holders in local political parties) gave rise to concerns about their ability to carry out professional duties or would adversely impact on public confidence in the impartiality of local authority employees.[108] In view of the width of possible application of the restrictions, the limited class of exemptions and their imposition on previously agreed contracts of employment, the Commission declared that the 1990 *Regulations* constituted a disproportionate interference with the applicants' Article 10 rights. On referral to the Court, however, this finding was reversed in a 6–3 majority decision. In upholding the *Regulations* as corresponding to a pressing social need, emphasis was placed on the Widdicombe Committee's finding of specific instances where local authority officers had abused their power and the consensus among the Inquiry's consultees that the tradition of political neutrality in local government needed strengthening. Moreover, the categories of persons subject to restrictions had been 'carefully defined' and the exemption procedure was further evidence of the attempt to confine the *Regulations*' scope to a narrowly focused group of officers. Significance was also attached to the fact that the Government for its part had recently reviewed the *Regulations* and concluded that their retention was justified. States were to be allowed some margin of appreciation in the organization and functioning of local authorities since traditions varied across Council of Europe members. In any event, the *Regulations* did not prohibit all forms of political activity. They were targeted primarily on 'party political' activity that would link a restricted office holder in the mind of the public or council members to a particular party line. Those officers subject to the rules could nonetheless join any political party of their choosing.[109]

Academic reaction to the judgment was mainly critical. Vickers, for example, has argued that domestic law unduly restricts the free expression of a large number of public sector employees, even in areas not directly related to those in which the

---

108 *Ahmed* v *United Kingdom* (1997) Application No. 22954/93. For comment, see Gillian S Morris, 'Local Government Workers and Rights of Political Participation: Time for Change' (1998) *PL* 25.

109 For much the same reasons as were advanced in respect of Article 10, the Court found that there had been no violation of the applicants' Article 11 rights. For circumstances in which membership of a political party and political writings may provide sufficient grounds for dismissal from public sector employment, see *Kosiek* v *Germany* (1986) 9 EHRR 328. There, the applicant was dismissed from his post as a probationary civil servant when the state was made aware of the applicant's political activities and publications. The applicant was a prominent member of the neo-nazi National Democratic Party who had publicly praised the Third Reich. Adherence to the NPD's values meant that Kosiek could not, in the eyes of his employers, fulfil one of the requirements of probationers – to uphold consistently the free democratic system under the Basic Law. The Strasbourg Court declined to interfere with this determination.

employee is required to provide advice.[110] She concluded that, apart from a loss of individuals' participation rights, the democratic process itself is the weaker for being denied access to the opinions of a sizeable section of public servants.

Finally, in a separate aspect of the judgment, all members of the Court agreed that no breach of Article 3 of Protocol 1 had occurred. Any right to contest seats at elections could be subject to restrictions designed to secure the political impartiality of office holders who remained free to resign their posts in order to contest an election.

Conclusion

> We are in any case long past the point when interference with fundamental rights by public authorities can be justified by a bare demonstration of rationality or reasonableness. (Laws LJ, *R* v *BBC ex parte ProLife Alliance*[111])

The forms of expression considered in this chapter lie at the heart of what I have argued should be the most protected form of expression in a modern democracy – namely political expression. The ability of political parties to put their respective programmes to the electorate in the manner each chooses, the freedom of pressure groups to campaign for a change in the law, the rights of citizens to vote and stand in elections – all are intimately connected with notions of participative, democratic self-government. In Chapter 2, I argued that purely majoritarian systems of government are tempted to interfere with citizens' rights on an unprincipled basis. Within the field of freedom of political expression where the temptation may be strongest, examples of such interference include the suppression of minority opinion (such as anti-abortion campaigners) or, in relation to democratic rights, populist controls on prisoners' voting entitlements. Sometimes the intention that lies behind a restriction on political expression may be praiseworthy – as is the case in relation to the bar on civil servants' political activities where the aim of maintaining public confidence in state administration is entirely proper. However, even here it may be thought that good intentions have led to excessive curtailment of core political freedoms. In each of the liberal democracies considered in this chapter, it falls to the courts acting under the rule of law and *within their respective constitutional traditions and frameworks* to police acts of legislative and executive interference. Given the apathy that exists towards engagement with political processes in the UK and

---

110 L Vickers, *Freedom of Speech and Employment* (2002, OUP, Oxford) at 224. She suggests that the current ban may violate the International Labour Organization's Convention No. 111 – Discrimination (Employment and Occupation) (1958). This Convention was ratified by the UK in 1999. See further Vickers, Ch. 3. For a Canadian Supreme Court authority striking down a legislative restriction on civil servants' political conduct as disproportionate see *Osborne* v *Canada* [1991] 2 SCR 69. The restriction there affected a considerable number of civil servants who were not involved in discretionary tasks where political considerations might affect or appear to affect the exercise of discretion.

111 [2002] 3 WLR 1080, 1096–7.

elsewhere, strong constitutional protection for a diversity of political speech forms would seem to offer one means of ensuring an enriched public debate. Other, well-trailed advantages would also flow from heightened scrutiny, including enhanced accountability of public power and the greater acceptance by minority groups of decisions adverse to their interests.[112] Conversely, without close judicial oversight, the very notion of informed democratic debate and self-government is left at the mercy of temporary political majorities and administrative censors (such broadcast regulators) to impose their conception of majoritarian tastes and values.

112 *R* v *Secretary of State for the Home Department ex parte Simms* [2000] AC 115, 126, *per* Lord Steyn.

Chapter 4

Comparative Constitutional Issues Arising from the Regulation of Election Campaign Finance

Introduction

> Elections are won with television. You don't need endorsements, you don't need the press, you don't even need the truth. You need money.
>
> (*Timecop*, directed by Jean-Claude Van Damme, Universal Pictures 1994)

In Europe, concern has existed for some time that monetary contributions have bought legislative influence and damaged public confidence in elected office holders. Former French Prime Minister Alain Juppé was convicted in January 2004 of using municipal funds to create non-existent jobs to pay for his party supporters to work for him in the late 1980s and early 1990s. He was given an 18-month suspended prison sentence as well as a ban on holding elected office. In the previous decade, the high incidence of political corruption in a number of mature Western liberal democracies prompted a special issue of the journal *Political Studies* in which one contributor argued that, far from being an aberrant exception to the norm, overwhelming evidence existed that political corruption had taken root in many Western European nations.[1] Four years later, the Parliamentary Assembly of the Council of Europe was referring to 'a number of scandals linked to the financing of political parties in several Council of Europe member States'[2] and spoke of being 'seriously preoccupied' by instances of improper influence on political decisions which it said had caused a loss of confidence and interest in national politics on

1 P Heywood, 'Political Corruption; Problems and Perspectives' (1997) XLV *Political Studies* 417 *Special Issue*. For details of scandals in Italy, France, Germany and elsewhere, see Heywood and other contributors.

2 Those instances referred to included former German Chancellor Helmut Kohl's admission in 1999 that he kept secret accounts for contributions to his Christian Democratic Party. See further U von Alemann, 'Die Parteien und das Geld oder: Sind alle Politiker korr' (2000) *Gewerkschaftliche Monatscheft: Zeitschrift fur Theorie und Praxis* 51. In Belgium, the Walloon and Flemish socialist parties were found the previous year to have received large amounts of cash from Dassault (a French aerospace manufacturer) and Agusta (an Italian helicopter company) in return for the placing of military orders with the two companies. As a result of criminal proceedings, senior ministers were convicted of corrupt practices.

the part of electors. Recommendation 1516 (2001) called for the imposition of upper maximum limits on donations and expenditure.[3] The Assembly's proposals were taken up subsequently in a Recommendation of the Committee of Ministers to member states that was adopted in April 2003. This urged the adoption of common standards against corruption in political parties and electoral campaigns.[4] By this time, reform of UK domestic law had already occurred in the guise of the *Political Parties, Elections and Referendum Act* 2000 which brought a measure of greater transparency to the funding arrangements of political parties.

Given the important functions fulfilled by political parties in modern democracies, the task of restoring electors' confidence has rightly assumed considerable importance. In the previous chapter it was seen that parties constitute the units of action which transform electors into groups capable of political action. They generate competing sets of policies – an important facet of pluralism – which are then offered to voters at elections. The emergence of one party as outright victor settles the political direction of the state and allows for the implementation of the triumphant party's programme. Opposition parties for their part call the government to account for its policies and actions. Crucially, they present an alternative vision of how the affairs of the nation might be directed. Where, as a consequence in part of financial scandals, public confidence in both governing and opposition parties is low, it is to be expected that levels of voter apathy and disengagement from political debate will be commensurately high.

A separate issue to command attention within the field of electoral campaign finance relates to the fairness of elections in which one party is able to outspend its rivals. The extra communicative reach provided by additional expenditure is problematic for those who contend that the electorate ought to be given approximately equal access to the full range of political platforms on offer at election time. The inequalities between parties can be compounded where private organizations, corporations and trades unions pay for advertisements that advance directly or indirectly the campaign of their preferred party.

This chapter is not intended as a comprehensive statement of legal regulation in any of the jurisdictions discussed herein. Instead, it will set out to consider on a selective basis legislative reform of electoral finance laws and the outcome of constitutional challenges to such reforms. In the US, for example, Congress passed a set of measures aimed at eliminating perceived or real corruption among candidates for federal office in the *Bipartisan Campaign Reform Act* 2002 (hereafter *BCRA*). As would have been anticipated, the constitutional validity of *BCRA* was promptly challenged in the courts. In December 2003 the Supreme Court in *McConnell* v *Federal Election Commission* gave its verdict on the Act's key anti-corruption

3 Parliamentary Assembly Recommendation of 21 May 2001, Rec (2001) 1516. See further Venice Commission, *Guidelines and Report on the Financing of Political Parties* (2001) CDL-INF 8.

4 Council of Europe Committee of Ministers Recommendation of 8 April 2003, Rec (2003) 4.

measures.[5] The ruling of the Court had significant implications for the financing of the 2004 federal elections and is generally thought to have given the Republicans an advantage over their Democrat rivals. In Canada, judicial attention has focused on the question of expenditure limits during referendums and the extent to which citizens wishing to incur independent expenditures outside the two national committees expressly created to advance the case (including providing funds) for each option may challenge such limits under freedom of expression guarantees. On this side of the Atlantic, recent reforms to UK election law have sought to bring a measure of transparency to political donations as well as taking seriously the importance in referenda of facilitating the effective communication of each side's arguments via provisions for core state funding. Aspects of each jurisdiction's laws will be analysed in the following pages. Before this is attempted, a sketch of some issues of principle underpinning the topic of campaign finance is provided.

Issues of Principle

State regulation of donations and expenditure at election time raises some of the most acute problems for liberal democracies about permitted limits on political speech. The freedom of individuals and parties to campaign for election to public office, and the undoubted interest of the electorate in receiving information and opinion about candidates, parties and policies, would seem to call for the most vigilant watch against governmental interference.[6] Accepting that money allows more effective communication of political messages,[7] some have even argued that it is beneficial in a democracy for parties to have to compete with each other for the receipt of funds from private donors.[8] In expenditure terms, there is clearly an autonomy-based argument for letting individuals spend their wealth on persuading others to adopt their political preferences.

At the same time, a total absence of controls would seem to pose a different, though nonetheless significant, set of dangers that even more libertarian expression regimes must confront. A failure, for example, to limit corporate/individual contributions/expenditure in electoral campaigning (and the access to national media that this permits) might be thought to risk skewing the nature of the electoral debate in ways that drown out the views of less well resourced parties, thereby calling into question the overall fairness of any election result. A serious commitment to political equality in an inclusive community might entail the demand that the voices of the less affluent are also helped to be heard in political debate. Arguments in favour of limiting the impact of private wealth on the electoral process might be thought to connect with

5 124 S Ct 619 (2003).

6 Burger CJ in *Buckley* v *Valeo* 424 US 1, 235 (1976).

7 In *Bowman* v *UK* (1998) 26 EHRR 1, the European Court of Human Rights accepted that limits on third party expenditure on publications during an election time constituted an interference with freedom of expression, at para. 33.

8 See thus Neill, *Committee on Standards in Public Life* Cm 4057 (1998), Ch. 6.

the organizing principles of civic republicanism outlined earlier in this book. In the introductory chapter, it was noted that the idea of political equality forms a central strand of the civic republican strain of communitarian thinking. Concerned that economic wealth translates all too easily into political influence and power, scholars working within this tradition have urged a reduction in disparities of access to and influence upon political processes that stem from economic inequalities. Strategies for reducing unequal access/influence also accord with the civic republican goal of promoting a genuinely deliberative democracy, shorn of the distorting impact of private wealth. In advocating collective discussion and debate among political equals, they reject alternative systems that conceive of law-making as the reflection of the outcome of clashes between self-interested groups. Viewed from this perspective, the relevant issue is not *whether* to overcome the distorted patterns of access and influence but rather *how* this might be done. Thus the question arises of whether it is best to go down the route of imposing ceilings upon donations and expenditure or whether such a strategy produces harmful though unintended consequences which should force civic republicans to consider alternative, perhaps incentive-based approaches. One such might be the receipt of state funds on condition that the donee give an undertaking not to use privately raised funds or a system of public subsidies available to candidates to match all or a given percentage of the funds available to their privately funded opponents.[9] Alternatively, as others have urged, attention might be turned to non-financial methods of allowing less well endowed parties greater access to the electorate.[10]

The very idea of interfering with private wealth lawfully acquired to suit some wider societal interest in electoral fair play is of course anathema to the rival libertarian/pluralist conception of politics discussed previously. Government has no business setting constraints on the unfettered exchange of ideas between rival sets of private interests. The redistribution of private power to equalize (or make less unequal) communicative reach is entirely off-limits to the state. The most that can be tolerated is the imposition of rules to safeguard the integrity of the electoral process and accordingly retain public confidence in the same. Thus in *Buckley* v *Valeo* – the seminal First Amendment ruling on campaign finance – the US Supreme Court, whilst striking down statutory limits on expenditure limits on candidates and their political committees, nevertheless accepted that certain other limits could be justified in order to further the legitimate governmental interest in ensuring the electoral process remained free from actual or apparent corruption.[11]

In terms of recent legislative initiatives, several core objectives stand out. The most prominent among these is undoubtedly the desire to prevent real and apparent

9 C Sunstein, 'Political Equality and Unintended Consequences' (1994) 94 *Colum L Rev* 1390, although Sunstein admits there would difficult issues relating to who would receive federal funding.

10 D Oliver, in R Blackburn (ed.), *Constitutional Studies – Contemporary Issues and Controversies* (1992, Mansell Publishing, London).

11 424 US 1 (1976).

corruption in political parties. A second goal evident (in some jurisdictions at least) is the wish to make elections more 'equal'. Ringhand has argued that appeals to 'equality' mask a variety of different rationales for regulating campaign finance.[12] Nevertheless, she acknowledges that one commonly asserted basis for reforms of campaign finance law is the idea of equality of access to the marketplace of ideas.[13] On this view, there needs to be an approximately equal airing of competing political programmes in the public domain in order to allow listeners to make informed choices and hence further the interest of enlightened self-government. The basis of this appeal to equality is that free speech is linked inextricably and fundamentally to informed democratic self-control. Unregulated speech – in this context unlimited expenditure by parties and others such as corporations and trades unions – threatens informed decision-making because it skews voters' access to information about the full range of programmes on offer. The state is entitled to intervene via expenditure controls so as to prevent this distortion.

The premise in this argument that expenditure levels can affect voting outcomes is clearly accepted by the main political parties in Western liberal democracies (how else to explain the expenditure of millions of pounds during election campaigns?) but is it supported by empirical evidence? In Canada, the Lortie Commission concluded that differential spending levels in the 1988 federal election campaign did have a considerable impact on the election result.[14] At the time no controls existed to limit independent expenditure. Some $4.7 million was spent on advertising by independent third parties, the majority of which related to the issue of free trade. About four-fifths of advertising on this issue was pro-free trade and Lortie found that the imbalance had boosted electoral support for the Progressive Conservative Party as the only party openly to campaign for free trade. The argument that a causal link exists between money spent and votes cast is supported elsewhere in empirical studies. Writing in 1987, Johnston found that electoral performance and spending in constituencies were linked. Whilst careful not to claim that expenditure was a major or dominant factor in outcome, he concluded that:

12 L Ringhand, 'Concepts of Equality in British Election Financing Reform Proposals' (2002) 22 *OJLS* 253.

13 The other rationales she identifies are 'equality of arms' – preventing wealthier speakers having a greater influence on voting outcomes by means of a greater volume and/or better quality of publicity; and 'equality of influence' – preventing those with deep pockets from acquiring influence over elected officials. *Ibid.* It is questionable whether her 'equality of arms' notion is really distinct from the 'equality of access' rationale. Both assume distortions in electoral outcomes attributable to differential wealth levels among speakers.

14 Royal Commission on Electoral Reform and Party Financing, *Reforming Electoral Democracy: Final Report Vol 1* (1991, Minister of Supply and Services, Ottawa).

> ... in most aspects of British elections since 1950, and especially since 1969 when spending limits were raised, the results of constituency contests have been influenced by the campaign spending of the parties involved.[15]

The data gathered over nine general elections indicated that, especially in the 1970s and 1980s, 'one party could gain a vote advantage over its competitors by spending more'.[16] A later analysis of Liberal Democrat campaigning in the UK general election of 2001 by Cutts reached the same conclusion.[17]

If it is accepted that greater expenditure tends to result in enhanced electoral performance and, further, that left unregulated, some parties will significantly outspend their rivals, a system committed to preventing the distorting influence of wealth upon elections needs to confront some hard questions about state aid that are touched on briefly at the end of this chapter but, in truth, lie beyond the scope of this book.

UK Reforms

Domestically, the period before the 1997 general election was dominated by questions of sleaze as a succession of stories emerged about payments to individual MPs and contributions to political parties.[18] Lord Nolan's Committee on Standards in Public Life was set up by the Major Government in the wake of allegations of cash for political influence levelled at several Conservative MPs and confined itself to this question.[19] His successor, Lord Neill, enjoyed a broader remit to consider political parties' funding and soon found himself asked to rule on the propriety of a £1 million donation from the motor-racing tycoon Bernie Ecclestone to the Labour Party to help fund its general election campaign. The donation came to light shortly after Mr Ecclestone and the Prime Minister had met to discuss exempting motor-

---

15 R Johnston, *Money and Votes: Constituency Campaign Spending and Election Results* (1987, Croom Helm, London) at 179. The fact that, in this period, the Labour Party has enjoyed as much electoral success as their higher-spending Conservative rivals does not disprove a causal relationship between expenditure and votes. Labour might have had even greater electoral success had the party been able to match Conservative spending levels.

16 *Ibid.*, at 208. Johnston's book challenged the view taken by M Pinto-Duschinsky in *British Political Finance 1830–1980* (1981, American Enterprise Institute, Washington DC) that campaign expenditure is irrelevant to voting outcomes on the basis that it was not underpinned by detailed statistical analysis.

17 D Cutts, 'Did Local Activism Really Matter? Liberal Democrat Campaigning and the 2001 British General Election' (2004) *Political Studies Association* conference April 2004.

18 P Heywood, 'Political Corruption: Problems and Perspectives' (1997) XLV *Political Studies* 417.

19 *First Report Standards in Public Life* Cm 2850 (1995, HMSO, London).

racing from a ban on tobacco advertising at sporting events.[20] In the aftermath of the Neill Committee's report, Parliament passed the *Political Parties, Elections and Referendum Act* 2000 (hereafter *PPER*) which instituted a number of significant reforms. In the view of one leading commentator, the Act marked the transition from a period in which UK political parties were one of the least regulated in Europe to one in which they became one of the most highly regulated.[21] The Act created an Electoral Commission to oversee the conduct of elections in general[22] and, in relation to the issue of campaign finance, opted for a strategy that combined reporting and disclosure obligations, restrictions on who may donate (though not the amount that may be donated) and expenditure ceilings. Thus, all donations in excess of £5,000 (to the national party organization) and £1,000 (to the local equivalent) have to be reported to the Electoral Commission four times a year. The report must provide a number of details about donors, including names and addresses.[23] Lord Neill's Committee on Standards in Public Life had taken the view that, whilst unfashionable, privacy arguments in favour of the source and amount of donations to political parties remaining secret deserved serious consideration. The Committee accepted a number of legitimate reasons why donors might wish to resist identification including (i) not wanting to bring their giving to the attention of criminals; (ii) the risk of being pestered by causes; and (iii) in Northern Ireland, a continuing risk to persons publicly associated with particular parties.[24] It concluded that the strength of these privacy claims was such that disclosure of donor identity should only occur where a compelling public interest case was made out. This could be established where a donation was 'significant enough' to prompt questions about its purpose.[25] Neill had concluded that the suspicions which arise from large donations were 'commonly lacking in any justification'.[26] Nonetheless, he conceded that, in the case of anonymous large donations, it was:

20 See further Chapter 7. Lord Neill recommended that the donation be returned. His advice was followed. His report on funding is to be found at Cm 4507, 1998. See further M Linton, 'The Funding of Political Parties' in R Blackburn and R Plant (eds), *Constitutional Reform: The Labour Government's Constitutional Reform Agenda* (1999, Longman, Harlow). For an account of pre-Neill expenditure rules see K Ewing, *The Funding of Political Parties in Britain* (1987, CUP, Cambridge); M Pinto-Duschinsky, 'Trends in British Party Funding' (1988) 42 *Parliamentary Affairs* 197.

21 KD Ewing, 'Transparency, Accountability and Equality – The Political Parties, Elections and Referendums Act 2000' (2001) *PL* 542.

22 See Part 1 of the 2000 Act. The Commission also has a monitoring function in that it is to keep the practical operation of the Act under review. It is expected that expenditure limits in particular will be kept under close scrutiny. See further below.

23 *PPER* 2000, Schedule 6, para. 2.

24 *Fifth Report of the Committee on Standards in Public Life* Cm 4057 (1998, HMSO, London), paras 4.16–4.26.

25 *Ibid*., at para. 4.28

26 Cm 4507, at para. 4.5.

> … impossible to allay the suspicion that each large giver is actuated by some improper motive and that the recipient political party has accepted some tacit obligation to one or more such givers.[27]

Donations may only be made by a 'permissible donor', defined in the Act to include individuals registered in the electoral register, or a trade union or a company incorporated in the UK that 'carries on its business in the United Kingdom'.[28] The aim of this section is to prevent foreign interests from funding UK political parties.[29] There are no limits on the size of donations to political parties. This reflects the view in Neill that it was 'healthy' in a democracy for parties to be free to compete for donations and that the requirement to disclose sums of £5,000 or more would be sufficient to remove any 'illegitimate pressure' on parties which resulted from larger donations.[30] In a loophole to emerge during the 2005 general election campaign, however, the Electoral Commission launched an inquiry into allegations that the Conservative Party had received what *The Times* reported as a 'number of £1-million-plus loans'.[31] *PPER* does not require the identity of loan providers to be revealed under its reporting provisions where the funds are provided on commercial rates of interest.[32] Of course, where the loan is converted into a donation, then the donors would at some later stage be identified. Where a loan is not converted into a donation, a lack of transparency in a party's funding sources would plainly remain. Despite this lacuna, voters have been able during the 2005 general election campaign to access on the Electoral Commission's website the names of individual donors and the amounts donated.[33] The information was published on a week-by-week basis. We learnt, for example, in week two of the campaign that Sir Tom Cowie – a private individual – made a cash donation of £400,000 to the Conservative Party and that Lord Sushantha Bhattacharya, a Labour supporter, made both a cash donation of £100,000 and a gift of cars to the value of £19,822. This level of information has hitherto not been available to public scrutiny.

Until recently, whilst the expenditure of candidates at the local level was subject to strict limits (and still is),[34] no such constraints existed at the level of national

---

27 *Ibid.*, at para. 4.6.

28 *PPER* 2000, s.54(2).

29 This does not prevent all donations from abroad however. Expatriates of up to 20 years' standing were given the right to be entered on the electoral register under the *Representation of the People Act* 1985 (as amended). Section 141 of *PPER* Act reduces the maximum period of residence outside the UK to 15 years.

30 *Committee on Standards in Public Life* Cm 4057 (1998), Ch. 6.

31 *The Times* (2005) 21 April.

32 *PPER* s.50(2)(e).

33 The Electoral Commission's website may be found at http://www.electoralcommission.org.uk/regulatory-issues/registers.cfm.

34 *Representation of the People Act* 1983, s.76: the limits on candidates' expenditure depend on the number of electors in a constituency. In an average size constituency, a sum of £10,000 is thought to constitute the upper limit, see A Bradley and K Ewing, *Constitutional and Administrative Law* (13th ed., 2003, Longman, Harlow) 159. See also *R* v *Jones* [1999] 2

or regional expenditure.[35] Following a recommendation by Neill, *PPER* imposes limits on national party expenditure under a formula which ties expenditure to the number of constituencies which a party contests.[36] Neill described the arguments for expenditure limits as 'finely balanced'[37] and seems to have come down in support of constraints, partly because of fears about excessive spending and damaging pressures on parties to raise ever greater sums of money but also on account of its tentative conclusion that discrepancies in electoral spending may have affected the outcome of close post-war elections in 1950, 1951, 1964 and 1974 (in both February and October).[38]

Of course, the spending power of corporations and organized labour can also add significantly to the communicative reach of particular campaigns. The national campaigning expenditure of 'third parties' is also regulated under the Act. Pressure groups, trades unions and corporations may wish to campaign on specific sets of issues which would tend to favour the prospects of one party more than another in a general election. These 'third parties' may spend £10,000 in England and £5,000 in each of Scotland, Wales and Northern Ireland, provided notification is given to the Electoral Commission.[39] Should these limits prove insufficient, an application may be made to the Electoral Commission to be registered as a 'recognised third party'.[40] Where so registered, a third party may spend up to just under £1 million across the UK with maximum prescribed limits for England (£739,000), Scotland (108,000), Wales (£60,000) and Northern Ireland (27,000). Finally, at the local level, the limits on what may be spent by third parties in promoting or opposing a candidate have been raised to £500,[41] following the ruling of the European Court of Human Rights in *Bowman* v *UK* which declared that the previous £5 ceiling constituted a disproportionate interference with third parties' expression interests.[42] Apart from the specific proportionality point, *Bowman* will surely be seen as significant for the

Cr App R 253, 255, for judicial recognition of the importance of a level financial playing field between candidates locally. Neill did receive evidence of a tacit conspiracy among the main parties at Parliamentary by-elections to turn a blind eye to the overspending of each party. See Cm 4057 (1998) Ch. 10 at paras 8–10.

35 *R* v *Tronoh Mines Ltd* [1952] 1 All ER 697. In Scotland, see *Walker* v *UNISON* 1995 SLT 1226.

36 *Political Parties, Elections and Referendums Act* 2000, s.79 and see Sch. 9. For commentary on this and referendum limits, see KD Ewing, 'Transparency, Accountability and Equality – The Political Parties, Elections and Referendums Act 2000' (2001) *PL* 542.

37 Cm 4057 (1998) para. 10.24.

38 *Ibid.*, at para. 10.28.

39 These are the limits of 'controlled expenditure' defined in s.85 of the Act as 'expenses incurred in connection with the production or publication of election material which is made available to the public at large or any section of it'.

40 *PPER* 2000, ss. 88 and 94.

41 *Representation of the People Act* 1983, s.75. Breach of this rule constitutes a 'corrupt practice'. The rule does not apply however to the media.

42 (1998) 26 EHRR 1.

fact that the challenge to domestic election finance law was framed in terms of an unwarranted restriction on freedom of expression. Whether under the *Human Rights Act* 1998 Article 10 affords a basis for challenge of other aspects of UK electoral law remains to be seen. At the very least, the domestic courts will have to have regard to high status of political expression in Convention jurisprudence and the especially demanding scrutiny that the Strasbourg Court has brought to bear on restrictions targeting such expression.[43] All the same, the European consensus that exists around the importance of eliminating actual and apparent corruption in public life would seem to indicate that challenges say to the donor disclosure provisions of *PPER* on Article 8 privacy grounds would be given short shrift.

Referendums – UK and Canadian Perspectives

Referendums have become a regular feature of the UK political landscape. Employed in the late 1990s to ascertain the states of public opinion about Scottish and Welsh devolution, the Good Friday Agreement in Northern Ireland as well as a directly elected mayor and assembly in London, the referendum looks likely to remain a central mechanism for determining important constitutional questions. The Labour Party is committed to a further plebiscite in respect of further EU economic integration. The Neill Committee on Standards in Public Life accepted the case for a distinct regulatory framework for referendums including expenditure rules partly on the basis that, whilst parties are usually pitted against each other in ordinary elections, this does not necessarily hold for referendums when a party can be internally split or be wholly or partly in alliance with other parties (or elements of other parties).[44] Thus, in the 1975 referendum on continued EEC membership, the 'Yes' campaign is estimated to have spent ten times the amount incurred by the rival 'No' campaign.[45] More recently, the 'Just Say No' campaign against Welsh devolution was said by Neill to have been 'seriously underfunded' and reliant on a single wealthy benefactor.[46] The outcome, it will be recalled, was extremely close with just 50.3 per cent of those voting in favour of the proposed scheme of devolution and Neill speculated whether a more evenly funded set of campaigns would have produced a different result.[47] In

---

43 *Lingens* v *Austria* (1986) Series A, No 103; *Castells* v *Spain* (1992) Series A, No 236; although for a indication of a more relaxed standard of scrutiny see *R (on the applications of ProLife Alliance)* v *BBC* [2003] 2 WLR 1403 and commentary by Scott, '"A monstrous and unjustifiable infringement"? Political expression and the broadcasting ban on advocacy advertising' (2003) 66 MLR 224.

44 *Committee on Standards in Public Life*, Cm 4057 (1998), para. 12.21.

45 KD Ewing, 'Transparency, Accountability and Equality – The Political Parties, Elections and Referendums Act 2000' (2001) *PL* 542, 563.

46 The dangers associated with the apparent or real influence of wealthy donors over the political parties they fund clearly have little or no direct application to the context of a referendum campaign.

47 *Committee on Standards in Public Life*, Cm 4057 (1998), para. 12.32.

order to make sure that each side in a referendum has a fair opportunity to put across its views, Neill proposed that, depending on the circumstances, both sides should be given access to an amount of core funding 'sufficient to enable it to mount at least a minimal campaign and to make its views widely known'.[48] That said, Neill rejected the case for expenditure limits, pointing to the practical difficulties of devising adequate accounting procedures for the controlling the expenditures of individual and organizations, a number of whom would emerge solely for the purpose of influencing the result and cease to operate upon the close of the campaign.[49]

The rules settled on by Parliament in *PPER* Part VII adopt a number, though not all, of the Committee's recommendations. Thus, the Electoral Commission may grant one designated 'permitted participant'[50] from each side a sum of money not exceeding £600,000.[51] Further measures aimed at promoting access to the rival campaigns' arguments through public subsidy include provisions that permit the sending of one free referendum address, the use of rooms for meetings free of charge and political broadcasts.[52]

Contrary to another key recommendation of Neill, however, limits on referendum expenditure are also introduced in *PPER*. 'Permitted participants' (which can include political parties that have made a declaration to the Electoral Commission about the outcome for which they intend to campaign) may spend in excess of £10,000 in the referendum period.[53] Thereafter the maximum levels of expenditure vary according to the category of 'permitted participant' and, in the case of political parties, the amount of previously obtained popular support. Thus, each of the two designated campaign groups can spend up to £5 million. Political parties may, as permitted participants, spend up to £5 million if they obtained over 30 per cent of votes cast at the previous general election. For those parties polling at between 20 and 30 per cent, the limit is set at £4 million. Decreasing maximum totals are set for parties obtaining even lower levels of electoral support.[54] The third category of 'permitted participant' (which includes trade unions, companies and individuals) may spend a maximum of £500,000. The Act also sets out a series of reporting requirements ('returns') with which permitted participants must comply.[55] Public inspection of these returns is also provided for in the Act.[56]

---

48 *Ibid.*, Recommendation 84.

49 *Committee on Standards in Public Life,* Cm 4057 (1998), para. 12.46.

50 As defined in *PPER* 2000, s.105, this can be a registered party, individual resident in the UK or a body falling within s.54(2)(b) and (d)–(h).

51 *PPER* 2000, s.110(2). The grant may be made 'subject to such conditions as the Commission consider appropriate', s.110(3).

52 S.110(4) and Sch. 12 of the 2000 Act.

53 Of course where a party is seriously divided, it is unlikely to make such a declaration.

54 The figures are laid down in Sch. 14 of the 2000 Act.

55 *Ibid.*, at ss. 120–23, 2000 Act.

56 S.124, 2000 Act.

By way of comment it may be noted that the limits set out above fall short of guaranteeing equal levels of expenditure on each referendum option. Indeed, in precisely the sort of case where the need to hear an alternative set of arguments is arguably strongest – when the main political parties are in agreement and willing to spend at or near their maximum permitted levels – any rival campaign's expenditure level is likely to fall well short of the combined funds of the main parties, leading no doubt to the accusation of 'drowning out' of the rival message by the superior-resourced campaign. The core funding provisions which allow a maximum grant of £600,000 to the designated rival 'permitted participant' may not suffice to rebut this claim.

The constitutionality of third party spending limits during referendum campaigns was discussed by the Canadian Supreme Court in *Libman* v *Quebec*[57] when a challenge was taken to the limit of $600 placcd on 'unregulated' expenditure by persons who wished to remain unaffiliated to the national committees. Under s.404 of the *Quebec Referendum Act*,[58] this sum might only be spent on expenses incurred in organizing and holding a meeting.[59] The appellant Libman argued that this constituted an unjustified limit on his freedom of political expression and association with others who might also wish to join an unaffiliated campaign group.[60] The limit was struck down by the Supreme Court as failing the 'minimal impairment' limb of the test laid down in s.1 of the Charter as coming close to a total ban.[61] In passing, it should be noted that the objectives of restrictions – the promotion of (i) equality between the options and (ii) free and informed voting – were conceded by Libman to amount to a pressing and substantial importance in a democratic society. The Court for its part described as 'highly laudable' the egalitarian aims of preventing the most affluent members of society from exercising a disproportionate influence through independent expenditure on the referendum debate and allowing voters access to each position in the debate.[62] Notwithstanding this point, the *Referendum*

57 [1997] 3 SCR 569.

58 RSQ. C-64.

59 The national committees were able to incur 'regulated expenses' up to the equivalent of $1 per elector. Thus, in a province with 2 million persons, the national committee and its affiliated groups may not incur regulated expenses in excess of $2 million, regardless of the amount received in donations from financial supporters.

60 The unwillingness to join a national committee or affiliated group would extend beyond those wishing to participate as individuals in the referendum campaign to those who supported an option but could not join the national committee on account for example of a difference over strategy.

61 Section 1 requires the Court to ask first whether the restrictions on a Charter right correspond to a pressing and substantial concern in a democratic society and then whether the means chosen by the government are rationally connected to the objective(s), constitute a minimal impairment of the right or freedom in question and then whether there is proportionality between the objective and its deleterious effects and between the salutary and deleterious effects: *R* v *Oakes* [1986] 1 SCR 103, *Dagenais* v *CBC* [1994] 3 SCR 835.

62 Para. 42. Stricter limits on independent expenditure levels were also defensible on the ground that it could not be assumed that such spending would result in equal amounts being

Act's restriction on the appellant's and others' political expression demanded the closest degree of scrutiny from the Court *consistent* with the appropriate degree of deference to be shown to legislative policy-making in areas where the balancing of competing societal interests was required and the courts lacked the necessary expertise. On the minimal impairment aspect of the proportionality test, the role of the Court, according to the ruling in *Libman*, was to ask whether the means chosen to achieve the legitimate objectives were reasonable. The government would only fail on this point if there were measures that were 'clearly superior to the measures in force'.[63] A relevant factor here was the view of the 1991 Royal Commission on Electoral Reform and Party Financing which had recommended a higher limit of $1,000 for unpooled third party expenditure and had not laid down restrictions on how such sums might be spent.[64] In the Court's view, this mechanism intruded less into third parties' freedom of expression interests than s.404 whilst at the same time safeguarding the fairness of referendum campaigns.[65]

In a less hostile stance towards measures designed to ensure fairness at federal elections, the Ottawa Court upheld in *AG* v *Harper* various provisions of the *Canada Elections Act* 2000.[66] There the federal Parliament's limits of $3000 and $150,000 on third party election advertising at electoral district and national levels respectively were held to constitute a permissible limitation on freedom of expression. An accompanying ban on third party advertising on polling day was also upheld. For the majority, the absence of controls gave rise to the possibility that affluent individuals or groups that pooled their resources might

> … dominate the political discourse, depriving their opponents of a reasonable opportunity to speak and be heard, and undermining the voter's ability to be adequately informed of all views. Equality in the political discourse is thus necessary for meaningful participation in the electoral process and ultimately enhances the right to vote. This right, therefore, does not guarantee unimpeded and unlimited electoral debate or expression.[67]

The goal of maintaining equality in electoral discourse did not mean that each and every spending limit would be maintained. To be lawful, a limit would have to be:

---

devoted to each option in a referendum. For a different view which was disapproved by the Supreme Court see the Alberta Court of Appeal in *Somerville* v *Canada* (1996) 136 DLR (4th) 205 where comparatively low limits on independent expenditure on advertisements were deemed inconsistent with the Charter because they gave preferential treatment to parties and candidates.

63 Citing Wilson J in *Lavigne* v *Ontario Public Service Employees Union* [1991] 2 SCR 211, 296.

64 *Reforming Electoral Democracy: Final Report Vol 1.* (1991, Minister of Supply and Services, Ottawa) 350–56.

65 For a critical commentary, see C Manfredi, *Judicial Power and the Charter* (2nd edn, 2001, OUP, Oxford) at 151: '… if Libman announces any constitutional principle, it is that compliance with the Charter can be bought for $400.'

66 [2004] 1 SCR 827 at para. 72.

67 [2004] 1 SCR 827 at para. 73.

> … carefully tailored to ensure that candidates, political parties and third parties are able to convey their information to the voter; if overly restrictive, they may undermine the informational component of the right to vote.[68]

On the facts in *Harper*, the limits on local and national expenditure were sufficient to allow third parties to convey their messages to the electorate whilst at the same time safeguarding electoral discourse from being dominated by wealthy individuals and organizations.

Big Bucks and the First Amendment

The UK and Canada have not been alone in seeking to move away from light-touch regulation of political party funding to one of heightened statutory control. The US Congress has recently devoted considerable effort to plug gaps in the legislative framework devised in the mid 1970s. Unsurprisingly, in a jurisdiction where particularly strong constitutional protection is afforded to freedom of expression, this attempt to regulate the financing of political parties has encountered fierce legal resistance. A general question that the Court has had to address at the outset of such challenges concerns the appropriate level of intensity of judicial scrutiny brought to bear on legal regulation. How readily ought the courts to defer to legislative judgment about what is needed to safeguard the concededly legitimate state objectives of political integrity and prevent any misuse of corporate advantage? Deeper-level arguments of democratic theory and justifications for judicial review of legislative policy choices do not lie far from the surface of the case law and have, at times, openly featured in the litigation.

Those opposing recent efforts to regulate donation and expenditure rules argue for the application of strict scrutiny standards, pointing to interference with core political expression. They contend that the imposition of campaign donation/expenditure rules can serve to protect incumbents at the expense of new candidates, thereby curtailing electoral choice. Elected office holders, on this view, cannot be trusted to regulate the pre-conditions for political speech because of the tendency to fashion rules that favour existing office holders and make it difficult for outsiders to replace them. Within a tradition in which the state is not permitted to favour one side in political argument, it is to be expected that attempts to create a more level playing field in which the voices of the less affluent are amplified would incur strong opposition on content neutrality grounds. In *Buckley* v *Valeo*, the US Supreme Court stated that:

> The concept that the government may restrict the speech of some elements of our society in order to enhance the relative voice of others is wholly foreign to the First Amendment.[69]

---

68 *Ibid.*

69 424 US 1, 48–9 (1976). As Sunstein has pointed out, economic inequalities are not the only factors which hinder citizens' participation in political debate. A lack of education

Expenditure limits, for example, could even give rise to the suspicion of favouritism on the part of the state towards less affluent groups' political messages, and hostility to those emanating from the economically powerful. As such, this looks to be little different from viewpoint-based regulation of expression and, as such, presumptively unconstitutional.

Soft Money and Issue Advertising – The Road to the Bipartisan Campaign Reform Act 2002

Congress has long sought to tackle the reality and perception of corruption in political life. In 1924, one Senator referred to the apparent hold of businesses and other organizations upon political parties by virtue of large campaign contributions and declared it to be 'one of the great political evils of our time'.[70] Under the *Federal Election Campaign Act* 1971 (as amended, hereafter *FECA*),[71] Congress placed *inter alia* maximum limits on the contributions which individuals ($1,000) and political action committees (hereafter PACs) ($5,000) might donate to the campaign funds of candidates for federal election.[72] A separate limitation of $1,000 was imposed on independent expenditure by individuals or groups 'relative to a clearly identified candidate'.[73] The limits were intended to prevent wealthy donors exerting a significantly greater influence on the outcome of elections than other donors. In further provisions, contributions and expenditures exceeding lesser limits were subject to reporting and disclosure obligations.[74] Additionally, candidates were themselves subject to limits on what could be spent on self-promotion.

In *Buckley* v *Valeo*, a First Amendment challenge was taken to these various limits. Somewhat controversially, the Supreme Court upheld on the one hand the limits on direct contributions to candidates' campaign funds as well as the reporting and disclosure provisions but struck down on the other the independent expenditure

---

may also have this effect but even where educational inequalities were not present, economic inequalities would continue to limit opportunities for poorer speakers and deny audiences access to their opinions. See C Sunstein, 'Political Equality and Unintended Consequences' (1994) 94 *Colum L Rev* 1390.

70 65 *Congressional Record* 9507–9508 (1924) and cited by Stevens and O'Connor JJ in *McConnell*.

71 On the background to the1974 amendments which were prompted by the Watergate scandal see A Grant, 'The 1996 Elections and Campaign Finance in the United States' (1997) 10 *Talking Politics* 56.

72 The Act also provided federal funding for national party conventions and public finance to match levels of private donations raised in the Presidential nomination process.

73 PACs were not however limited in the aggregate amount of donations to all candidates.

74 Political committees and candidates became obliged to file quarterly reports detailing *inter alia* names and addresses of persons, businesses contributing more than $10 on any one occasion or $100 in one year.

limit and the ceiling on candidates' personal expenditure.[75] The Court found the contribution limits to be constitutionally justified under the 'closely drawn' (that is, not strict) standard of scrutiny as narrowly tailored to the legitimate governmental purpose of curbing the actuality and appearance of corruption which stemmed from large individual financial contributions. Having so found, the Court declined to consider whether, additionally, the goal of muting the voices of the affluent provided a further justification for the contribution limit.

In the case of the independent expenditure ceiling, the Court was prepared to construe the phrase 'relative to a clearly identified candidate' narrowly so as to be limited to the 'explicit advocacy of election or defeat of a candidate' as where a communication urged voters to 'Elect John Smith' or 'Vote against Jane Doe'. In this way the Court sought to draw a bright line between express advocacy, which might in theory be regulated by *FECA*, and issue advocacy, which could not. This by itself was, however, insufficient to save *FECA*'s expenditure limits provision. In finding that expenditure limits placed far greater restraints on the quality and diversity of speech than contribution limits (it necessarily impacted on the number of issues discussed, their depth of exploration and the size of audience reached), the Court, adopting a strict scrutiny standard, held that the limits (even as narrowed) did not prevent real and/or perceived corruption. Those determined to spend money in order to promote a candidate (and evade *FECA* limits) could do so by implicit advocacy.[76] Neither was the narrowed provision needed to catch those cases where the candidate controlled or coordinated the expenditure of an individual or group. *FECA* already treated such expenditures as 'contributions' and hence subject to the limits already upheld by the Court. It followed that the independent expenditure ceiling was unconstitutional. The Court further declared the limits on candidates' personal expenditure to be unconstitutional. The claimed governmental interest in equalizing the resources of candidates could not sustain this constraint. There could be no guarantee in any event that the limitation would secure financial equality since a candidate who was extremely successful in fundraising might not need to spend up to the limit on personal expenditure and yet still outspend another candidate. More

75 424 US 1 (1976). For an argument that expenditure and contribution rules ought to have been considered as conduct and not pure speech, see E Barendt, *Freedom of Speech* (1985, Clarendon Press, Oxford), 49–50. See also J Skelly Wright, 'Politics and the Constitution: Is Money Speech?' (1976) 85 *Yale LJ* 1001. It is right however to argue that *FECA*'s expenditure limits did have the effect of obstructing the unfettered exchange of ideas, at least in quantitative terms.

76 The quantity of communication affected by a limit on financial contributions on the other hand was said to interfere with the contributor's political communications at best only marginally. As for any interference with the recipient's speech, this would only be serious if the limits were set so low as to prevent candidates from amassing the resources needed for effective advocacy. In passing, it should be noted that the Court upheld rules elsewhere in the Act requiring parties to reveal sources of contributions exceeding $100 and to keep records of each contributor donating in excess of $10.

fundamentally, however, the First Amendment could not tolerate a restriction placed on a candidate's ability to speak on his own behalf.[77]

In upholding the Act's reporting and disclosure provisions, the Court pointed to the importance of publicity in deterring corruption, the value of the disclosed information to the electorate in evaluating candidates and, finally, the value of such data in detecting breaches of the Act's contribution limits. Here, the Court used the same narrowed construction of 'expenditure' that was employed in its analysis of the expenditure ceiling, with the result that the obligation to report details of persons making expenditure of more than $100 in any one year extended only as far as funds used for communications that expressly advocated the election or defeat of a particular candidate. It followed that reporting and disclosure of sums in excess of this figure would not be required where funds were expended on issue advocacy or implicit advocacy.

In conclusion, then, the Court treated contributions which enabled others to speak as lying further away from the core zone of protected political debate than direct expression which resulted from expenditure on putting across one's own political ideas. Stated thus, the differential levels of scrutiny promulgated by *Buckley* would not seem entirely without foundation. That is not to say, however, that the decision is wholly unproblematic. A central criticism made by commentators of the *Buckley* ruling was that it ignored the possibility that unlimited expenditure in support of a candidate could create much the same difficulties as those associated with large individual contributions.[78] Candidates, it was claimed, would learn of the identity of large spenders and in such circumstances the appearance, at least, of corruption could well arise. The statutory recognition of PACs in *FECA* and the fact that the $5000 contribution limit upheld in *Buckley* applied only to direct contributions to a particular candidate's official campaigning fund (so-called 'hard money') led many corporations and labour organizations to set up their own PACs with the aim of achieving a measure of influence over legislative policy by means of unregulated indirect contributions or 'soft money' as it became more generally known.[79] In 1974 Washington DC boasted some 608 PACs contributing $12.5 million to Democratic and Republican party funds. By 1994, there were almost 4,000 PACs contributing

77 For a notable dissent on this point see Marshall J who claimed that, alongside the limit on contributions, the ceiling on personal expenditure could be justified in preventing candidacy for public office becoming the exclusive province of the wealthy, 424 US 1, 288 (1976).

78 C Sunstein, *Democracy and the Problem of Free Speech* (1994, The Free Press, New York) Ch. 4, and see Blackmun J at 424 US 1, 290, who could not see any principled distinction between contributions and expenditures. On developments post-*Buckley* see KD Ewing, 'The Legal Regulation of Campaign Financing in American Federal Elections' (1988) 47 *CLJ* 370, and 'Legal Control of Party Political Finance' in I Loveland (ed.), *A Special Relationship – American Influences on Public Law in the UK* (1995, Clarendon Press, Oxford).

79 E Drew, *The Corruption of American Politics – What went Wrong and Why* (2000, Overlook Press, New York).

$179 million to party organizations.[80] These monies could be lawfully used for a party's general purposes fund (such as voter registration and political education initiatives). The fact that the top five corporate donors paid substantial soft money contributions to *both* major parties' national committees indicated that, rather than being an expression of their ideological preference, such contributions were made with a view to securing access to candidates and subsequently the legislative process.[81] There was also evidence to suggest that these donations were actively solicited by candidates. Just as controversially, 'soft money' was used to fund negative advertising against particular candidates. In 1995, the Federal Election Commission concluded that these monies could be used to finance 'legislative advocacy media advertisements' that mentioned the name of a federal candidate as long as there was no express advocacy of the candidate's election/defeat. In the case of negative advertising against a particular candidate, this expenditure could have been used to achieve the same end as regulated 'hard money'. One form of PAC – the Issue Advocacy group – became a particularly prominent vehicle for 'soft money' expenditure in political campaigning. In common with other PACs, not only did these groups fall outside *FECA*, they also avoided paying income tax on contributions.[82] According to Grant, the 1996 elections witnessed a huge growth in 'issue ads' attacking a legislator's record in office without specifically calling for the election of a rival candidate.[83] Until 2002, these advertisements were not limited at all under campaign finance laws, a loophole exploited by corporations and unions which were banned from making direct contributions to campaigns. According to the Supreme Court, corporations and unions spent hundreds of millions of dollars of their general funds to pay for issue ads. The fact that *FECA*'s disclosure rules did not apply to such ads also meant that the sponsors could conceal their true identities under misleading names. 'Citizens for Better Medicare', for example, was not a grassroots community-based health action group, rather it was a front name for an association of drug companies.

FECA did, however, limit the amount of financial assistance that the political parties could give in support of their candidates' campaigns to $5000. In a 1996 ruling, however, the Supreme Court ruled that these limits were unconstitutional so long as the political parties acted independently of the beneficiary candidates.[84] In so doing, the Court thus allowed unlimited spending by parties in support of candidates in much the same way as *Buckley* had lifted restraints upon independent individual and PAC expenditure. This proved extremely useful since *FECA* already allowed

80 D McKay, D Houghton and A Wroe, '*Controversies in American Politics and Society* (2001, Blackwell, Oxford) Ch. 4.

81 In 2000, 35 of the 50 largest soft money contributors gave money to both parties: 28 of the top 50 contributed more than $100,000 to both parties. These figures were cited by Stevens and O'Connor JJ in *McConnell* at fn.12 to their joint opinion.

82 Inland Revenue Code s.527. For commentary, see (2001) 114 *Harv L Rev* 2209.

83 (1997) 10 *Talking Politics* 56, 60.

84 *FEC* v *Colorado Federal Campaign Committee* 518 US 604 (1996).

individuals and PACs to contribute significantly more money to parties than might be given to the candidates.[85]

The Bipartisan Campaign Reform Act 2002

Of the various attempts to have been made over the years to bring soft money under regulatory control, perhaps the single most significant development in recent times has been the *Bipartisan Campaign Reform Act* 2002 (*BCRA*). Impetus for the 2002 reforms originated from the six-volume report of the Senate Committee on Governmental Affairs published in1998. The Senate Committee looked in particular at the effect of soft money on the federal elections of 1996 and concluded that *FECA*'s loopholes of soft money and issue advertising had prompted a 'meltdown' of the campaign finance system. In the 2002 Act, Congress gave legal status to a number of the Senate Committee's proposals. In particular, Title I of *BCRA* prohibited national party committees and their agents from 'soliciting, receiving, directing, or spending' any soft money.[86] Accompanying provisions reinforced these restrictions by preventing soft money being shifted to the state or local level for use in relation to activities that affect federal elections.[87] Political parties were also prohibited from donating funds to, or soliciting of funds for, tax-exempt organizations that engage in electioneering activities.[88] Federal candidates and office holders were separately prevented from receiving, spending or soliciting soft money in connection with federal elections.[89] Title II sought to prohibit the use of general treasury funds by trades unions and corporations for advertisements published in the weeks before a federal election that are intended to, or have the effect of influencing the outcome of that election.

In *McConnell* v *Federal Election Commission* a majority of the Court upheld the provisions of Titles I and II, appearing to endorse a central rationale of the new rules, namely that large political donations confer access to elected politicians and give rise to the potential for corruption.[90] Each part of the ruling will now be considered in turn.

Title I prohibitions At the outset, it should be noted that the Court treated the prohibitions on the soliciting, receipt or expenditure by national parties or their agents of soft money as subject to the looser standard of scrutiny applied by *Buckley*

85 Individuals might contribute up to $20,000 to a national political party (as compared to $1,000 to a candidate) whilst PACs might contribute up to $15,000 to a national party (as compared to $5,000 to a candidate)

86 S.323(a).

87 S.323(b).

88 S.323(d).

89 S.323(e).

90 124 S Ct 619 (2003).

to contributions.[91] The question for the Court on this set of prohibitions was whether, given the legitimate state interest of preventing actual and apparent instances of corruption of federal candidates and office holders, these restraints upon donations were constitutionally permissible. The Court noted that Congress had established an 'ample record' that the soft money loophole was exploited by donors with a view to create a debt on the part of particular office holders, as donors would ask the national party that their contribution be credited to specific candidates and that the office holder be made aware of the donor's identity. The record also showed that candidates also sought to receive soft money in order to increase their prospects of election. Indeed, the national party offices would often act as the willing conduit of such funds and were in fact themselves largely composed of federal office holders and candidates for federal office. National party committees could thus guarantee access to federal office holders in return for a sizeable donation. This intertwining of national party structures and office holders and candidates made the case for regulating soft money receipt and spending all the more compelling. These restrictions on national party activity would, however, become ineffective if the state or local party organization could remain a conduit for soft money donations. Accordingly, the supplementary ban on the use of non-federal funds for federal election activity was also upheld.[92] The ban on the raising and soliciting of soft money by federal candidates and office holders was likewise sustained as an additional anti-circumvention measure.[93] Donations at the request of a candidate/office holder gave rise to the same concerns about corruption as did donations made directly to candidates and office holders.

Title II non-candidate campaign expenditures In discarding *Buckley*'s bright line between express advocacy and issue advocacy, the Court accepted that this aspect of the 1976 ruling was responsible for many of the 'soft money' abuses to have marred previous federal election campaigns. *BCRA* amends the law by extending the ban on corporate and union expenditure out of general funds to cover all broadcast electioneering communications that mention a federal candidate or office holder within 30 days of a primary or 60 days of a general election and target that person's constituents. Congress had found a 'virtual torrent' of televised election-related advertisements during the periods immediately before federal elections and had concluded that reform was now needed. *BCRA* leaves corporations and unions (as well as individuals) free to set up segregated funds or PACs to pay for electioneering communications. Disclosure requirements in the case of disbursements

91 Even though the ban catches soft money expenditure by the national parties (and thus might have been made subject to *Buckley's* strict scrutiny standard), the Court concluded that Title I did not limit the total amount of money that parties could spend. They were still free to garner more hard money (*FECA*-regulated) contributions and spend these sums.

92 For exceptions to this ban, see s.323(b)(2) (known as the Levin Amendment) which allows certain activities to be funded with a mix of federal and non-federal funds.

93 Again *BCRA* did set out exceptions to this ban including where the soliciting benefits an organization whose primary purpose is not to engage in federal election activities and does not specify how the funds will be spent.

by corporations and unions towards the costs of producing and broadcasting electioneering communications require the identity of persons contributing $1,000 or more in any calendar year to be revealed to the Federal Election Commission.[94] Once more, the important state interest of preventing corruption (real or apparent), as well as providing the electorate with information about the real funding sources behind broadcast advertisements put out by groups such as 'Citizens for Better Medicare' and 'The Coalition-Americans Working for Real Change', inclined the Court to uphold the disclosure provisions' constitutionality.

Conclusion

Taking stock of the current rules in the jurisdictions considered in this chapter, a number of interesting comparisons are thrown up. Indeed, it is perhaps paradoxical that whilst each system starts out from a similar concern about the fundamental importance of maintaining confidence in elected politicians by tackling actual and apparent corruption, the rules adopted in the UK and US could fairly be described as virtual polar opposites. Thus, on the question of donations, the UK allows registered donors to make unlimited contributions and relies upon the obligation to disclose as sufficient to safeguard the goal of political integrity. In the US, by way of sharp contrast, whilst the maximum donation figure has been revised upwards, the principle of limits on direct contributions to federal candidates' campaign funds endorsed in *Buckley* remains valid today.[95]

More abstractly, the revised regulatory systems in the UK and US may be said to reflect a measure of consensus around the idea of reluctant interference with private wealth. In the UK, this is manifested in the absence of donation limits on the basis that individuals should be free to contribute what they choose to political parties. In the US, the First Amendment-led analysis of campaign finance rules has focused judicial attention on the deleterious impact of restraints upon expressive activity. Where the impact upon expression interests of speakers is judged to be greatest, namely expenditure limits, the Supreme Court has applied a stringent standard of scrutiny. In so doing, it has prioritized the interests of autonomous, wealthy individuals to advance their political views. Conversely, where the impact of legal curbs has been thought less severe on freedom of expression (for example contributions that allow other speakers more of the same speech), the Court has been more tolerant of Congressional efforts to eradicate corruption.

In respect of expenditure by political parties on the national campaign, *PPER* imposes a limit that is tied to the number of seats contested by a party. *BCRA* on the other hand – whilst closing soft money loopholes – does not put a ceiling on

94 In respect of disbursements made by individuals, the disclosure requirements apply to sums in excess of $10,000 and entail the identification of all persons sharing the costs of the disbursements.

95 The reporting and disclosure provisions in *FECA* were not considered sufficient in themselves to combat actual/apparent corruption.

national expenditure. After *McConnell*, Title I allows parties to accumulate *FECA*-regulated hard money contributions from their supporters across the nation and spend these sums. In practice, it is thought that this feature of the legislation benefits the Republican Party, who enjoy a wider base of individual contributors than their Democratic rivals although it would also seem likely that Democrats will now be prompted in their efforts to gather small donor contributions.[96] It will also be noted that, unlike their UK equivalents, US corporations and unions are not limited in their expenditure on electioneering communications provided this emanates from a segregated fund that meets *BCRA*'s disclosure requirements. The one major point of congruence is the emphasis upon transparency in reporting and disclosure provisions. Both sets of electorate, it seems, are entrusted to seek out and use donation and expenditure information to inform their political judgments. How much effort or attention voters actually pay to such information is, however, uncertain. Nevertheless, the UK system does manage at least to evince a concern with the distorting impact of unevenly funded campaigns. Although Neill stopped short of endorsing spending limits in these terms, the ceilings on political party and third party expenditures may work to lessen the distorting effect of private wealth on electoral outcomes.[97] As was seen above, the potential distorting effect of third party expenditure has also been recognized by the Canadian Supreme Court in *Harper* where the majority linked the idea of equality of resources to meaningful participation by voters in electoral decision making.

Notwithstanding this effort to instil greater 'equality' into domestic campaign finances law, might the national expenditure limits on parties and third parties be vulnerable to a *Buckley* v *Valeo* style challenge under Article 10 of the European Convention on Human Rights? In *Bowman* v *UK*, although the actual spending limit of £5 imposed on Bowman was deemed a disproportionate interference with her freedom of expression, the Court accepted that spending limits imposed on third parties that were intended to secure equality between candidates did pursue the legitimate aim of protecting the interests of candidates and the electorate.[98] The nature of the 'equality' interest at stake was not elucidated any further but it may plausibly be suggested that the Court was happy in principle to endorse expenditure limits that restricted the ability of wealthy persons/bodies to campaign for/against an individual candidate on informed democratic self-control grounds. In the absence of restraints, the UK had argued that political debate might be distorted by having political debate shift from matters of general concern onto more narrowly focused matters that lay closer to the interests of the speaker.[99] The basis for this suggestion is the Court's remark that,

---

96 For commentary, see *CRP Statement on McCain-Feingold Decision* – 10 December 2003 Press Release, Centre for Responsive Politics.

97 For a view pre-Neill that the two main parties' election expenditure has stifled the terms of domestic political debate, see D Oliver, in R Blackburn (ed.), *Constitutional Studies – Contemporary Issues and Controversies* (1992, Mansell Publishing, London).

98 (1998) 26 EHRR 1 at para. 38.

99 The UK had also argued that unlimited third party expenditure would force candidates with funds limited by law to devote some of those funds to combat the adverse effect of third

during elections, freedom of expression might have to be made subject to restrictions 'of a type not usually acceptable … in order to secure the "free expression of the people in the choice of the legislature"'.[100] Obviously, the Court was not referring here to ceilings on the spending of political parties campaigning on broader national issues which could not for that reason be susceptible to control on the grounds relied upon in the case of third parties. Instead, the most persuasive rationale for restriction would be the distorting effect of unlimited expenditure on the ability of the electors to access the full range of views and policies on offer at election time. Inevitably, much would hinge upon the proportionality of any impugned limit.

Expenditure ceilings do not, of course, guarantee equal spending and thus equal access to the electorate. Financially weak parties may fail to amass sums anywhere near the maximum permitted figure. To achieve something like parity of expenditure between major and minor parties, there would, as Ringhand suggests, have to be a cap on expenditure set at such a low level so that the least wealthy party could reach the spending ceiling or, alternatively, public funding to all minor parties to allow the less well endowed to spend up to the levels of the wealthiest. Neither scheme would appear to be without its own set of problems. The former would severely diminish the capacity of any party to communicate its view. The latter would make a massive demand on the public purse.[101] At present, apart from 'short money' made available to House of Commons' opposition parties in proportion to the number of seats won at the last general election,[102] there is currently little state aid for political parties in Britain despite the increasing number of post-devolution forums in which they are required to function.[103] Nonetheless, the ceilings may be treated as a nod in the direction of collective discussion and debate among political equals and brings out a final and significant contrast with US-style regulation where the government is the enemy of freedom of expression and the redistribution of private power is strictly off limits to the state. Moreover, in respect of referendum campaigns, the availability of 'core funding' from the Electoral Commission up to a maximum of £600,000 can only serve to promote voters' access to rival sets of arguments that might otherwise achieve lesser prominence.

---

party expenditure, *ibid.*, at para. 36.

100 *Ibid.*, at para. 43.

101 L Ringhand, 'Concepts of Equality in British Election Financing Reform Proposals' (2002) 22 *OJLS* 253, 260.

102 In 2004 this amounted to £12,094.63 plus £24.16 for every 200 votes the party obtains, see further R Kelly, *Short Money* (2004, Parliament and Constitution Centre, London). Neill was of the view that formula understated the costs of meeting actual demands on opposition parties, see Cm 4057–I (1998, HMSO, London) Ch. 9. The parties may use this money to fund their electoral campaigns although it must be declared to the Electoral Commission.

103 Other forms of limited assistance include free party political and election broadcasts, election mailshots and the use of rooms for meetings. See for background KD Ewing, *The Funding of Political Parties in Britain* (1987, CUP, Cambridge).

but the constitutional form of expression [illegible] or regulation [illegible]
[illegible] that free expression [illegible]
[illegible] the Court [illegible]
[illegible] political parties [illegible]
[illegible]
[illegible] third parties, in [illegible]
[illegible]
[illegible] laws and policies on [illegible]
[illegible] would [illegible] upon the proportion [illegible] of any [illegible]

[illegible]

[illegible]

[illegible]

Chapter 5

Wounding Words: The Constitutional Challenge Posed by Hate Speech in Modern Liberal Democracies

Introduction

This chapter addresses an issue which, since 11 September 2001, has commanded considerable legislative attention in the UK; namely, whether it is appropriate in a democracy committed to the fundamental importance of freedom of expression to criminalize expression which is intended to promote hatred on the basis of race, religion, ethnicity or national origin. Fearing a backlash against UK Muslim communities in the wake of the terrorist activities of members of Al Quaeda, the UK Government initially included a provision in the *Anti-Terrorism, Crime and Security Bill* 2001 which would have added a new offence of incitement to religious hatred alongside the existing prohibition on inciting racial hatred in Part III of the *Public Order Act* 1986.[1] This measure would have remedied the somewhat anomalous situation since *Mandla* v *Dowell Lee*[2] in which the followers of certain religions (Sikhs, for example) are considered to be members of an ethnic group and hence protected by incitement to racial hatred law whilst adherents of other religions (such as Muslims) are not.[3] Reform of domestic law was urged by the United Nations Human Rights Committee in the immediate aftermath of 11 September 2001. It expressed concern that, 'since recent terrorist attacks, persons have been the object of attack and harassment on the basis of religious beliefs ...'.[4] Clause 38

---

1 For a statement of the Government's position, see the remarks of Lord Goldsmith, the Attorney-General at (2001–2) HL Debs. Vol. 629, cc.1164–1167. In the case of Northern Ireland, such conduct is an offence, see the *Public Order (Northern Ireland) Order* 1987 Article 9(1) which also made it an offence to arouse fear of persons defined by reference to religious belief. On British race hate law in general, see I Loveland, 'The Criminalization of Racist Violence?' in I Loveland (ed.), *A Special Relationship? American Influences on Public Law in the UK* (1995, Clarendon Press, Oxford); I Hare, 'Legislating Against Hate – The Legal Response to Bias Crimes' (1997) 17 *OJLS* 415.

2 [1983] IRLR 209.

3 There is evidence to suggest that this loophole was being exploited by racists in London. See P Jepson, 'Tackling Religious Terminology that Stirs up Racial Hatred' (1999) 149 *NLJ* 554, 556.

4 United Nations Human Rights Committee – 73rd session (2001) CCPR/CO/73/UK. See also K Boyle, 'Religious Intolerance and the Incitement of Hatred' in S Coliver (ed.) *et*

of the *Anti-Terrorism, Crime and Security Bill* set out a new offence of racial or religious hatred, where 'religious hatred' was said to comprise hatred against a group of persons defined by reference to religious belief or lack of religious belief.[5] The measure was dropped after being voted down by the House of Lords on two separate occasions. As well as fears that some legitimate though robust religious and anti-religious expression would be caught or at least chilled by the clause,[6] concerns were also expressed about the appropriateness of including what was in essence a non-emergency measure within a larger emergency anti-terrorism bill which was being rushed through Parliament.[7] In its place, Parliament amended existing sentencing laws so that lengthier custodial penalties could be imposed in cases where specific offences were religiously aggravated.[8] The evident reluctance to create a free-standing offence may be traced in part to the belief that, whilst the victims of racially based hostile expression can do nothing to alter the fact of their racial identity, a person's religious affiliations are, to a greater or lesser extent, a matter of personal choice and thus less deserving of specific protection. After its re-election in May 2005, the Labour Government re-introduced the offence of religious hatred in its Racial and Religious Hatred Bill. Despite assurances that the measure would not prevent persons making rude or offensive remarks about Islam or other religions, the measures once again ran into serious parliamentary and extra parliamentary opposition. Following defeats in the House of Lords and House of Commons however, it was forced in early 2006 to accept a watered-down version of the offence.[9] As a result, intentional behaviour only is caught by the new offence (as opposed to recklessness is not sufficient) and the speech in question must be 'threatening' and not merely 'abusive or insulting' as the Government had originally wanted. Cast thus, the new offence creates criminal

---

al., *Striking a Balance – Hate Speech, Freedom of Expression and Non-discrimination* (1992, Article 19, London Human Rights Centre, University of Essex, Colchester). Writing in 1992, Boyle already noted the growth of hostility between different religions across the developing and developed world. Boyle makes the point that religious intolerance should not be equated purely with atheistic ideologies but is itself a feature of particular religious belief systems.

5 Research Paper 01/96, 16 November 2001, available electronically at http://www.parliament.uk/commons/lib/research/rp2001/rp01-096.pdf.

6 (2001–2) HL Debs. Vol. 629 at cc.1180 (Lord Peston), 1183 (Lord Desai), 1187 (Baroness Buscombe).

7 *Ibid.*, at col. 1169 (Lord Lester). The new law did however extend the ambit of the 1986 Act by removing the requirement that the racial group against whom any incitement to racial hatred is directed by a group of persons in Great Britain: *Anti-Terrorism, Crime and Security Act* 2001, Sch. 8(4) para. 1. The particular problem of racialist chanting at football matches was earlier made an offence by the *Football (Offences) Act* 1991, s.3. See further M Idriss, 'Religion and the Anti-Terrorism, Crime and Security Act' (2002) *Crim L R* 890.

8 *Anti-Terrorism, Crime and Security Act* 2001, s.39, amending the *Crime and Disorder Act* 1998 ss.28–32. The offences in respect of which religiously aggravated conduct now receives a longer custodial sentence include assault, criminal damage, various public order offences and harassment. For an early analysis of how the 1998 Act is working, see the report by E Burney and G Rose, *Home Office Research Study 244: Racist Offences – How is the Law Working?* (2002, Home Office Research, Development and Statistics Directorate, London).

9 (2005–6) HC Debs. Vol. 442, cc. 188-239.

liability in a narrower range of circumstances than the equivalent incitement to racial hatred offence.

North of the Border and against a highly distinctive historical/religious/cultural context, the Scottish Executive announced the formation of a cross-party working group to consider whether there was a need for new legislation to deal with the problem of religious hatred in Scotland. In *Tackling Religious Hatred*, the working group rejected arguments for a new offence of incitement to religious hatred, concluding that such a provision might inhibit open discussion of religious practices.[10] In line with the legal position prevailing in England and Wales, the group endorsed the current strategy of making religious hatred an aggravating factor in the commission of pre-existing crimes.[11] This was duly enacted in the *Criminal Justice Scotland Act* 2003.[12]

In international law, commitment to the fundamental and pervasive notions of equality and the inherent dignity of all human beings is well established, resulting in treaty-based and charter-based norms which impose severe constraints on the freedom to engage in various forms of hate expression. In the case of treaty-based norms, the International Covenant on Civil and Political Rights (ICCPR) provides in Article 19(2) that everyone has the right to seek, receive and impart information and ideas 'of all kinds'. The exercise of the rights in Article 19(2) may however be restricted by law when necessary for the respect of the rights or reputations of others,[13] or for the protection of national security, public order, public health or morals.[14] Article 20(2) further lays down that 'any advocacy of national, racial or religious hatred that constitutes incitement to discrimination, hostility or violence shall be prohibited by law'. In the 1996 case of *Robert Faurisson* v *France*, the ICCPR's implementing body – the Human Rights Committee – upheld the compatibility of France's Holocaust denial law with Article 19.[15] It will also be recalled that Article 4 of the International Convention on the Elimination of All Forms of Racial Discrimination (ICERD) requires signatory states to:

10 *Report of the Cross-Party Working Group on Religious Hatred* (2002) at para. 5.06, available electronically at http://www.scotland.gov.uk/views/views.asp.

11 Para. 5.04, although the failure of the Scottish courts to record on a routine basis the details of criminal cases where religious hatred was involved meant that the group could not draw any meaningful conclusions about the effectiveness of existing laws.

12 S.74(2) of the 2003 Act defines an offence as being aggravated by religious prejudice if '(a) at the time of committing the offence or immediately before or after doing so, the offender evinces towards the victim (if any) of the offence malice and ill-will based on the victim's membership (or presumed membership) of a religious group … or (b) the offence is motivated (wholly or partly) by malice or ill-will towards members of a religious group … based on membership of that group'.

13 Article 19(3)(a).

14 Article 19(3)(b).

15 Communication No 550/1993 reported at (1997) 18 *HRLJ* 40. See further D McGoldrick and T O'Donnell, 'Hate-speech Laws: Consistency with National and International Human Rights Law' (1998) 18 *Legal Studies* 453, 470–84.

> … declare an offence punishable by law all dissemination of ideas based on racial superiority or hatred, incitement to racial discrimination, as well as all acts of violence or incitement to such acts against any race or group of persons of another colour or ethnic origin … .[16]

The commitment of the international community to punish media incitement to genocide was demonstrated in December 2003 when the International Criminal Tribunal for Rwanda convicted two radio station executives and a journalist who urged members of the majority Hutu tribe to kill minority Tutsi tribe members. The station broadcast messages such as 'exterminate the cockroaches'. The executives received life sentences whilst the journalist was jailed for 35 years.[17] The convictions mark the first time since Nuremberg that broadcasters have been convicted for promoting crimes against humanity.

As for charter-based norms, the Preamble to the Charter of the United Nations speaks of 'the dignity and worth of the human person' whilst the Preamble to the Universal Declaration of Human Rights refers to the 'inherent dignity … and equal and inalienable rights of all members of the human family'. Article 1 of the Declaration states that 'All human beings are born free and equal in dignity and rights'. In 1993, the Commission on Human Rights appointed a Special Rapporteur on racism and xenophobia. The Rapporteur's annual reports have in turn provided the basis for the adoption of resolutions by the Commission. In April 2002 the Commission adopted a resolution in which it expressed its alarm

> … at the increase in racist violence and xenophobic ideas in many parts of the world, in political circles, in the sphere of public opinion and in society at large, as a result of resurgent activities of associations established on the basis of racist and xenophobic platforms and charters, and the persistent use of those platforms and charters to promote or incite racist ideologies.[18]

In the sphere of regional human rights instruments, the Council of Europe's Committee of Ministers adopted in 1997 *Recommendation No R (97) 20*. This urged member states to take 'appropriate steps' to combat hate speech based upon intolerance as part of a wider approach which tackled the social, economic and cultural causes of such expression. Consideration at the national level was to be given to civil (compensatory), criminal and administrative[19] measures to achieve this objective. At the same time, member states were cautioned to ensure that any interference with freedom of expression was 'narrowly circumscribed' and applied in a non-arbitrary manner. Specifically, in the case of criminal sanctions, the *Recommendation* reminded states of the need to maintain respect for the principle of proportionality.[20]

---

16 (1965) The Convention entered into force in 1969.

17 *The Times* (2003) 4 December.

18 Commission on Human Rights Resolution 2002/68.

19 For example the issuing of court orders to allow victims a right of reply or obliging a retraction of the offending expression, *Rec (97) 20* Principle 2.

20 *Ibid.*, Principle 5.

Subsequently, the *Cybercrimes Convention* and the *Additional Protocol to the Convention on Cybercrime* have sought the adoption of some common national standards in tackling hateful expression on the Internet.[21] At the same time, the Commission of the EU is seeking to harmonize laws on xenophobia, racism and Holocaust denial across all EU member states.[22]

The consensus in domestic and international law about the importance of eliminating forms of hateful expression may be contrasted with continuing judicial hostility in the US to state legislatures' attempts to curb the expressive activities of hateful speakers.[23] This is evidenced not only in the freedom accorded a quarter of a century ago to Nazi supporters in accompanying uniform and regalia to march through Skokie, a largely Jewish suburb of Chicago,[24] but also in the toleration of cross-burning used by the adherents of the Ku Klux Klan to communicate messages of white racial superiority and of intimidation and impending violence.[25] Apart from conferring full First Amendment protection upon the burning of crosses at exclusive gatherings of the Klan as symbolic, core political speech, the US Supreme Court moved in 1992 into even more controversial territory in *RAV* v *City of St Paul, Minnesota* when it declared invalid local ordinances which criminalized the

---

21 Article 3 of the *Additional Protocol to the Convention on Cybercrime, concerning the criminalisation of acts of a racist and xenophobic nature committed through computer systems* is headed 'Dissemination of racist and xenophobic material through computer systems' and states '1. Each Party shall adopt such legislative and other measures as may be necessary to establish as criminal offences under its domestic law, when committed intentionally and without right, the following conduct: distributing, or otherwise making available, racist and xenophobic material to the public through a computer system.' As of 30 September 2003 the Convention had been ratified by 3 states only (5 states needed before the Convention can enter into force). The Protocol which was opened for signature in January 2003 has yet to be ratified by a single state.

22 For comment see JUSTICE *Briefing on the European Commission Proposal for a Council Framework Decision on Racism and Xenophobia* (2002, London).

23 See A Nieuwenhuis, 'Freedom of Speech: *USA vs Germany and Europe*' (2000) 18 *Netherlands Quarterly of Human Rights* 195 especially 207–13.

24 Much has been written on this. See *inter alia* L Bollinger, *The Tolerant Society – Freedom of Speech and Extremist Speech in America* (1986, Clarendon Press, Oxford) 23–35; N Dorsen, 'Is There a Right to Stop Offensive Speech? The Case of the Nazis at Skokie' in L Gostin (ed.), *Civil Liberties in Conflict* (1988, Routledge, London); P Strum, *When the Nazis Came to Skokie: Freedom for Speech We Hate* (1999, University of Kansas Press, Lawrence KS).

25 In its first inception, the Klan was set up in 1866 to oppose Reconstruction after the Civil War. Its victims (blacks, Southern whites and 'carpetbagger' Northern whites) were whipped and threatened with being burnt at the stake. Some victims were murdered. By 1877, the Klan had been effectively suppressed, using powers conferred by an Act of Congress. No cross-burning appears to have been practised by the First Klan. However, from the moment of the Klan's rebirth in 1915, cross-burning was used to convey a message of racial superiority and threats of violence. See further D Chalmers, *Hooded Americanism: The First Century of the Ku Klux Klan 1865–1965* (1965, Doubleday & Company, Inc., New York).

burning by white youths of crosses inside the fenced yards of black families.[26] *RAV*'s dismantling of established First Amendment doctrine – which had hitherto been premised upon a tiered approach to the scrutiny of governmental restrictions upon speech types in which political speech forms were accorded greater protection than non-political equivalents – continues to the present day to have serious implications for local communities and elected politicians who seek to combat racially motivated intimidatory conduct. *RAV*'s remodelling of permitted/disallowed contents-based restraints on proscribable speech was applied by the Court to hate speech for first time in April 2003.[27] In what follows, I consider some arguments of principle for upholding/invalidating legislative restrictions on hateful expression before taking a closer look at a range of legal regimes where such communications are subject to a variety of controls. Contrast is then made with First Amendment doctrine. My argument is that the libertarian tone of recent US jurisprudence not only understates a countervailing constitutional value (equality) and mistakenly dismantles an earlier, settled reading of the hierarchy of speech values, it also requires of laws outlawing hateful expression an unrealistically onerous standard of harm that is unlikely to be demonstrated empirically. The fundamental question raised by this chapter is the extent to which, if any, law can play a constitutive role in the formation of communities' values on questions of individual worth and dignity or, in the alternative, whether the constitution ought to remain neutral on such questions and resist the temptation to engage in the fostering of 'good' beliefs.

Some General Considerations

Typically defined as speech targeted at an individual or group which seeks to promote hatred on the basis of the victim's race, religion, ethnic origin, gender or sexual orientation,[28] hate speech has been said to be 'deeply problematic' for liberal democratic societies.[29] On one hand, the high value placed on expression that challenges the political consensus would seem to require that special importance be attached to the free articulation and dissemination of unpopular or controversial viewpoints. Speakers and audience, individuals and society may all benefit when comfortable orthodoxies are held up to challenge. An enduring and distinctive feature of US First Amendment jurisprudence in this area is a libertarian distrust of the state's purposes in imposing viewpoint-based restrictions on speech intended as a

---

26 505 US 377 (1992).

27 *Virginia* v *Black* 262 Va.764, 553 S.E. 2d 738 affirmed in part, vacated in part (2003) available electronically at http://supct.law.cornell.edu/supct/html/01-1107.ZS.html.

28 This definition should be seen as under-inclusive, failing as it does to acknowledge abusive expression directed at disabled persons.

29 LW Sumner, 'Hate Propaganda and Charter Rights' in W J Waluchow (ed.), *Free Expression – Essays in Law and Philosophy* (1994, Clarendon Press, Oxford); and see also by the same author, 'Hate Crimes, Literature and Speech' in RG Frey and CH Wellman (eds), *A Companion to Applied Ethics* (2003, Blackwell, Malden MA).

contribution to public deliberation on some issue.[30] Selective treatment of particular topics and/or communications would raise the prospect that governments could remove certain disfavoured ideas from public discourse altogether.[31] We should resist the temptation to acquiesce in the official suppression of views with which we disagree/loathe because, on a subsequent occasion, it may be our speech or that belonging to persons with whom we agree that is targeted. The tenacity with which this view is held (particularly among liberal and left-leaning opinion in the US) may owe something to McCarthyism in the 1950s, when government officials and (later) film makers found themselves investigated by the House of Representatives' Committee on Un-American Activities.[32] More abstractly, others have pointed to the trait in human character that tends towards maintaining a sense of shared beliefs and values as a force for general intolerance and, consequently, the suppression of views outside, or in contradiction to, prevailing values. Judicial protection of forms of expression at this periphery against populist calls for regulation helps maintain a 'buffer zone' inside which more intrinsically valuable speech is insulated.[33] This insulation works by a conscious refusal to allow the value of any particular exercise of freedom of speech to be legally relevant to the question of whether it is constitutionally protected. Thus, in cases such as *Collin* v *Smith* can be found a refusal to allow the admitted worthlessness of claims to racial supremacy to weigh in the court's evaluation of whether the state can ban a march of members of the National Socialist Party of America (NSPA) through Skokie. Ruling that a local ordinance which prohibited the promotion or incitement of racial hatred violated the First Amendment, the US Court of Appeals for the Seventh Circuit declared:

> We would hopefully surprise no one by confessing personal views that NSPA's beliefs and goals are repugnant to the core values held generally by residents of this country, and, indeed, to much of what we cherish in civilization. As judges sworn to defend the Constitution, however, we cannot decide this or any case on that basis. Ideological tyranny, no matter how worthy its motivation, is forbidden as much to appointed judges as to elected legislators.[34]

Apart from its function of buffering more valuable forms of speech, toleration of objectionable speech has separately been advocated by Lee Bollinger in *The*

---

30 In Professor Bollinger's 'classical' and 'fortress' models of First Amendment jurisprudence, government poses a constant threat to free expression, tempted as it is to silence speech it disapproves of: L Bollinger, *The Tolerant Society* (1986, Clarendon Press, Oxford) Chs. 2 and 3.

31 *Simon & Schuster Inc.* v *Members of New York State Crime Victims Board* 502 US 105, 116 (1991).

32 E Schrecker, *The Age of McCarthyism* (2001, Palgrave, New York); S Whitfield, *The Culture of the Cold War* (2nd edn, 1996, Johns Hopkins University Press, Baltimore MD).

33 See further the fortress model of Professor Bollinger in *The Tolerant Society* (1986, Clarendon Press, Oxford), where he refers to the problematic 'impulse to excessive intolerance': 86–90 *et seq*.

34 578 F.2d 1197, 1200.

Tolerant Society on the ground that this type of expression is particularly suited to the inculcation of the virtues of self-discipline, restraint and open-mindedness.[35] Although necessarily tempered by a recognition of human frailty, freedom of speech for extremist viewpoints can be justified in terms of building up positive human characteristics. The limits of toleration are reached, however, on this view when the bonds that normally hold society together come under serious threat of destruction. This is a judgment for each society to make. Bollinger's own assessment of anti-Semitism in American society in 1978 as lacking the magnitude or pervasiveness that would transform an act of toleration into something that would bring about the dissolution of community bonds led him to conclude that the courts were right to allow Nazis to march through Skokie.[36] How much support did in fact exist for this particular act of toleration is unclear. One review essay of *The Tolerant Society* considered that even if Bollinger's assessment of the contemporary mood was accurate, the longer-term damaging effects of permitting such expression could not be disregarded. Not only was it a concern that Nazi views might proliferate where speakers became emboldened and the inhibitions of others were loosened but, additionally, self-restraint might regress into passive toleration upon prolonged exposure to vigorous manifestations of Nazi expression.[37]

Aside from improving self-restraint, there is, Bollinger suggests, an additional informational benefit to society in receiving such speech. By being made aware of the presence of this sort of discontent (and possibly its extent) we can then decide whether it merits a policy response in terms of improving educational, employment and housing conditions, and so on, in order to address grievances which may lie behind the expression. It is better for disruptive individuals/groups to operate in public – where a sense may be gained of the presence of disease within the body politic – rather than private – where conversely false beliefs might circulate more or less unchallenged. He is careful, however, to qualify this general proposition. A closer examination of individual instances of problematic speech may cast doubt on whether any of these benefits will really be forthcoming. Specifically he asks:

> Are the uninhibited activities of groups like the Nazis really that important to maintaining a vigorous belief that what they have to say is immoral and wrong? It seems an equally plausible theory as to some ideas, at least, that to regard them as unspeakable is the best method of rejection. Like all human activities, dialogue is not invariably useful under all conditions.[38]

---

35 (1986, Clarendon Press, Oxford). Precisely why self-restraint should be the pre-eminent justification for free speech when the type of expression it protects is likely to open up the prospect of inter-communal strife is a central question raised by this work.

36 For a similar view and a defence of the American Civil Liberties Union's involvement, see N Dorsen, 'Is There a Right to Stop Offensive Speech? The Case of the Nazis at Skokie' in L Gostin (ed.), *Civil Liberties in Conflict* (1988, Routledge, New York).

37 M Rosenfeld, '*Extremist Speech and the Paradox of Intolerance*' (1987) 100 *Harvard L Rev* 1457.

38 *The Tolerant Society* at 55–6.

It is also true that some members of minority groups on the receiving end of hateful expression want the speech of Nazis and other hate-mongers to be judicially protected. A broad principle of non-interference with expression on contents-based grounds offers these minorities the assurance that majority opinion cannot at a future date silence them in turn.[39] This may prove especially attractive and thus valuable to political activists who, having been inflamed by minority-hostile expression, wish to respond to their opponents in a direct and confrontational way.[40]

In the US, these rationales against regulation become manifest in the severe constitutional hurdles that the state must overcome when it wishes to restrict expression because of the message that is being conveyed. Indeed, such restrictions are said to be presumptively invalid[41] unless it can be shown that the speech falls outside First Amendment protection altogether.[42] In this way the decision about what views may be voiced is left largely to individual speakers. In the case of hate speech, unless intended and likely to produce imminent lawless action,[43] the speaker must not be fettered by the state, no matter how offensive the contents are considered to be by the recipient audience (or sections of it).[44] Of course, in passing it should be stated that discerning the point where lawful advocacy shades into unlawful incitement will not always be straightforward. To illustrate this point, Alan Dershowitz raises the example of an imam who urges the death in a fatwa of a specific individual or demands that a terrorist organization attack US institutions.[45] He suggests that these examples do not fit neatly into either advocacy or incitement categories. A fatwa or religious order goes beyond exhortation that listeners are free to accept or reject on its merits. At the same time, incitement is typically conceived of in terms of a face-to-face communication. Dershowitz concludes plausibly that the categorization in any particular case will be highly fact-specific in which factors such as the actual

39 A Neier, *Defending My Enemy: American Nazis in Skokie, Illinois and the Risks of Freedom* (1979, EP Dutton, New York).

40 K Greenawalt, *Fighting Words* (1995, Princeton University Press, Princeton NJ) at 145. It might nonetheless be observed that such toleration comes from a position of relative weakness in the political process, fearful of the future consequences of the dominant social group's censoring activities. As such, it is to be distinguished from the tolerance of a dominant social group that decides to refrain from using its legislative powers to quash an opinion it does not share. See M Rosenfeld, 'Extremist Speech and the Paradox of Intolerance' (1987) 100 *Harvard L Rev* 1457 – review of *The Tolerant Society*.

41 *RAV* v *City of St Paul, Minnesota* 505 US 377 (1992).

42 The 'slight social value' of obscene speech (*Miller* v *California* 413 US 15), defamatory speech about private figures (*New York Times Co* v *Sullivan* 376 US 254 (1964), *Gertz* v *Robert Welch Inc.* 418 US 323 (1974)) and 'fighting words' (*Chaplinsky* v *New Hampshire* 315 US 568 (1942)) means that these speech forms may be regulated on account of their constitutionally proscribable content. The phrase 'slight social value' is to be found in the opinion of Murphy J in *Chaplinsky*.

43 *Terminiello* v *Chicago* 337 US 1 (1949).

44 *Brandenburg v Ohio* 393 US 444 (1969).

45 Alan M Dershowitz, *Why Terrorism Works* (2002, Yale University Press, New Haven CT) 111–14.

words used or the proximity in time between the words and terrorist acts will be significant.

In a further argument against hate speech laws, opponents of restriction point to the practical uses to which such legislation is put. Writing in 1992, Coliver claimed that:

> … in most countries, hate speech laws have either been used to a substantial degree to suppress the rights of government critics and other minorities or else have been used arbitrarily or not at all.[46]

In support of the criticism of arbitrary or erratic application of such law, one need look no further than the conduct of the English trial judge Neil McKinnon QC in the 1978 case of *R* v *John Kingsley Reid*.[47] The defendant had made a public speech in which he referred to 'niggers, wogs and coons' and welcomed the murder of an Asian youth by remarking 'one down, a million to go'. He was charged with incitement to racial hatred. Judge McKinnon effectively directed the jury to acquit the defendant when, during his summing up, he recalled that there had to be 'toleration and freedom to the individual otherwise we are all caught in a vice of dictatorship, repression and slavery'. However, as will be shown later in this chapter, the criminal law was subsequently applied by the English courts in a way which complied more obviously with legislative intention.[48] To be fair, Coliver did concede that hate speech laws might improve the 'tone of civility in liberal democracies'. However, in her opinion this benefit was outweighed by their serious potential for abuse. Instead of suppression, the opponents of hate bans often argue that the proper response to hate speech is more speech from the targets of the speech and their supporters as a counterpoint.[49]

---

46 S Coliver, 'Hate Speech Laws: Do They Work? in S Coliver (ed.) *et al.*, *Striking a Balance – Hate Speech, Freedom of Expression and Non-discrimination* (1992, Article 19, London Human Rights Centre, University of Essex, Colchester).

47 (1978) 6 January, Central Criminal Court (unreported) noted by G Bindman, 'Incitement to Racial Hatred' (1982) *NLJ* 299. See further the application in practice of s.6 of the *Race Relations Act* 1965 as described by M Partington, '*Race Relations Act* 1965; a Too Restricted View' (1967) *Crim L R* 497; A Dickey, 'Prosecutions under the *Race Relations Act* 1965 s.6' (1968) *Crim L R* 489.

48 Nonetheless, the potential for juries to deliver verdicts that undermine legislative intent should not be ignored. An example of which may be the decision of the jury at Leeds Crown Court in the trial of British National Party Leader Nick Griffin and party member Mark Collett on incitement to racial hatred offences in February 2006. The defendants were acquitted on some charges despite being filmed by an undercover reporter at meetings stating *inter alia* that people in Bradford and Keighley were living in 'hell' because of rapes and muggings that were always committed by Asians against whites (Collett) and that white society had become a 'multi-racial hell-hole' as Asian Muslims were trying to take over Britain (Griffin). At the time of writing, the defendants face a retrial on the outstanding charges.

49 N Strossen, 'Balancing Rights to Freedom of Expression and Equality: A Civil Liberties Approach to Hate Speech on Campus' in S Coliver (ed.) *et al.*, *Striking a Balance*

Outside the US, libertarian distrust of state regulation is less commonly encountered.[50] In the UK, Canada and much of Europe, domestic authorities are given considerably greater latitude to regulate expression on contents grounds.[51] Far from being concerned that certain unpopular viewpoints will be excluded from public discourse, many liberal democracies have sought to silence speech considered to incite racial and even religious hatred. This is hardly surprising. The impetus for the protections enshrined in the Council of Europe's Convention on Human Rights may be located in the hatred and intolerance shown towards Jews, gypsies, homosexuals and others in the concentration camps of the Second World War. In interpreting Article 10 of the European Convention on Human Rights, the Strasbourg Court – whilst notionally tolerant of expression which shocks and offends[52] – has thus in practice readily subordinated the interests of offensive speakers to wider societal goals of tolerance and community harmony. Somewhat controversially in *Otto Preminger Institut* v *Austria*, expression that merely offended the sensibilities of a religious group (Roman Catholics) was adjudged by the Court to fall outside the protective ambit of Article 10.[53] In justifying these sorts of speech restrictions, the Court has invoked at various times the values of tolerance, and pluralism, equality and individual dignity which underpin the Convention. Writing in an extra-judicial capacity, the President of the European Court of Human Rights, Judge Luzius Wildhaber, has argued that the right to offend is

> … intended to guarantee the right of participation in democratic society through public debate of questions of general concern. The strength of the protection offered will depend on the extent to which the expression can be linked to the direct functioning of democratic society.[54]

The publication initially in Denmark and latterly Europe of cartoon images of the Prophet Muhammad has once again put centre stage the extent of freedom to cause offence to religious beliefs. One cartoon depicted the prophet with a lit bomb on his head in the shape of a turban. Re-publication of the images in a number of European newspapers led to angry protests in the Middle East and elsewhere as demonstrators

---

– *Hate Speech, Freedom of Expression and Non-discrimination* (1992, Article 19, London Human Rights Centre, University of Essex, Colchester).

50 An interesting comparative discussion is offered by M Rosenfeld, 'Hate Speech in Constitutional Jurisprudence: A Comparative Analysis' (2003) 24 *Cardozo L Rev* 1523.

51 For an indication of the type and range of legal techniques used in recent years in different jurisdictions see J Magnet, 'Hate Propaganda in Canada' in WJ Waluchow (ed.), *Free Expression* (1994, Clarendon Press, Oxford).

52 *Handyside* v *UK* (1979–80) 1 EHRR 737; *Oberschlick* v *Austria* (1995) 19 EHRR 389.

53 Note however the joint dissenting judgment of Judges Palm, Pekkanen and Makarczyk which maintained with some force '[t]here is no point in guaranteeing this freedom only as long as it is used in accordance with accepted opinion.' (1995) 19 EHRR 34, 61.

54 'The Right to Offend, Shock or Disturb? – Aspects of Freedom of Expression under the European Convention on Human Rights' (2001) 36 *Irish Jurist* 17, 19.

attacked Danish embassies. Some outside the Danish Embassy in London were seen to call for the 'beheading' or 'slaying' of the enemies of Islam. Perhaps the demonstrators might have been less anxious if they had appreciated the full scope of restrictions on religiously offensive speech under Convention jurisprudence. The deference shown by the Strasbourg Court towards national authorities' assessments of offensive religious expression may however be faulted for failing to distinguish between an attack on the tenets of a religion and verbally threatening attacks upon the followers of a religion that seeks to, or is likely to cause religious hatred. The failure to include the former within the protective ambit of Article 10 confers perversely an immunity upon religious beliefs and institutions that is denied to political beliefs and institutions.

In the context of expression on ethical matters more generally, the House of Lords has also accepted the notion of offence as a legitimate basis of restriction on expression. It declined to interfere with the BBC's refusal to show a party election broadcast which contained images of aborted foetuses.[55] The refusal was justified by reference to the broadcaster's 'best endeavours' obligation under the *Broadcasting Act* 1990 not to include in its programmes material which offends against good taste or decency. The obligation was deemed consistent with Article 10 of the Convention even though its impact was controversial in that political speech during an election was thereby curtailed. The ruling was considered in more detail in Chapter 3.

In respect of racist expression, speakers penalized under domestic law have not been able to establish interference with their Article 10 freedoms. As will be shown later in this chapter, this failure may be explained by reference to either the exclusion of racist expression from Article 10's protective ambit or, alternatively, on account of Article 17 of the Convention which affords the Court a basis for declaring as manifestly ill-founded Convention claims which are 'aimed at the destruction of any of the rights or freedoms set forth herein'.[56] The discussion later in this chapter will also look at the regulation of Holocaust denial/revision expression where both the Council of Europe and the EU have had to grapple with the difficult question of controlling expression purely on grounds of its content rather than any deleterious public order consequences.[57]

The Canadian Supreme Court – albeit reflecting a different historical and cultural background – has, like the European Court, drawn upon the values of equality and individual dignity as affording a constitutionally proper basis under the Charter for statutory restrictions on hate speech.[58] Canadian jurisprudence is considered in closer

---

55 *R (On the Application of ProLife Alliance)* v *BBC* [2003] EMLR 23.

56 *Glimmerveen & Hagenbeek* v *Netherlands* Application Nos. 8348/78 and 8406/78, 18 DR 187.

57 *Lehideux & Isorni* v *France* (1998) 5 BHRC 540. See further *H, W, P & K* v *Austria* Application No. 12774/87, 62 DR (1989) 216 and discussion by J Cooper and A M Williams, 'Hate Speech, Holocaust Denial and International Human Rights Law' (1999) 6 *EHRLR* 593.

58 *R* v *Keegstra* [1990] 3 SCR 697, 756 *per* Dickson CJ. Equality is enshrined as a constitutional value in s.15 of the *Canadian Charter of Rights and Freedoms* 1982. See also K Greenawalt, *Fighting Words: Individuals, Communities and Liberties of Speech* (1995, Princeton University Press, Princeton NJ) at 64–70. See further discussion *infra*.

detail below. In passing, however, it can be noted that the acceptance of restrictions owes much to Canada's willing embrace of norms in international human rights instruments.

Even within the US, the protection afforded by the First Amendment to hateful expression has not escaped criticism. Pointing to the Fourteenth Amendment's equality guarantee, Catharine Mackinnon has argued that the Supreme Court's free speech jurisprudence has signally failed to recognize any implications for First Amendment discourse of the constitution's commitment to the value of equality.[59] As she accurately points out, equality-promoting provisions on hate crimes 'tend to be attacked and defended solely in terms of the damage they do, or do not do, to speech'.[60] By contrast, defenders of race-hate curbs cite not only the 'silencing' effect of hate speech upon the expressive activities of victims of hateful speech, but also draw attention to other significant injuries and costs including the physiological symptoms and emotional distress (including post-traumatic stress disorder, hypertension and psychosis) experienced by the victims of race-hate speech.[61] There are tangible social and economic consequences too. Bollinger has drawn attention to the importance of the social context in which explicitly insulting speech occurs. Not only may others be persuaded to think less of individual group members,[62] but others will be watching to see how the target responds. This anticipation is sensed by the target who can never fully disconnect his/her own feelings towards him/herself from the feelings others have towards him/her.[63] Some are driven to reject their identity as a victim-group member. Mari Matsuda put it thus, 'to be hated, despised and alone is the ultimate fear of all human beings'.[64] Delgado and Stefancic have pointed to concrete economic disadvantages that flow from toleration of racist expression. A person who, as a result of encountering frequent racist abuse, is made resentful or tense is less likely to interact positively with colleagues in the workplace.[65] The authors cite a 1995 study by Steele and Aronson which demonstrates that African Americans who carry others' negative stereotyped images do not perform to the best of their abilities when they find themselves in competitive situations in which they

59 *Only Words* (1993, Harvard University Press, Harvard MA) 71 *et seq*. For a forthright rejection of the Fourteenth Amendment equality value in a First Amendment context, see Kennedy J in *Simon & Schuster Inc.* v *Members of New York State Crime Victims Board* 502 US 105, 116 (1991).

60 *Ibid.*, at 73.

61 *Ibid.*, at 73.

62 Using the example of Skokie, Bollinger notes that during the litigation, many Jewish residents in the community received threatening and anti-Semitic telephone calls.

63 'The interconnections between the individual self and social perceptions is true for groups as well as for individuals which, of course, is why racial and religious slurs are so hurtful.' *The Tolerant Society* (1986, Clarendon Press, Oxford) 66.

64 M J Matsuda, 'Public Response to Racist Speech: Considering the Victim's Story' (1989) 87 *Mich L Rev* 2320, at 2338.

65 R Delgado and J Stefancic, *Understanding Words That Wound* (2004, Westview Press, Oxford).

are reminded of a generally held belief that members of their group will fail.[66] As to patterns of hateful expression, FBI statistics make clear that the groups most likely to be the targets of hateful expression in the US are African Americans and other non-whites. Gay men and lesbians who make no effort to conceal their sexuality and obviously disabled persons (such as the blind or physically impaired) are also victims in their own right.[67] Indeed, the very real problems faced by some disabled persons in making a complaint suggests that reported levels of anti-disabled expression may seriously understate the extent of abuse actually experienced.[68]

Ultimately, the definition of the *community* itself is called into issue when hateful expression occurs. The response that dominant forces within a community give to hateful expression – their willingness to act against more overt forms of hatred – will assume a symbolic importance to beleaguered minorities. In this sense, the imposition of legal restraints can serve as the expression of a community position on the issues raised by the speaker and in so doing help to forge a social identity which uncompromisingly rejects as a value the unequal status of individuals urged by hateful speakers. Where, on the other hand, the will to protect individuals/groups is absent, a lessening of societal coherence may not be far behind. Even where the message is resisted by victims and well-meaning members of the dominant group, there are costs to inter-communal relations. Victim-group members may come to view all dominant group members with suspicion whilst the latter experience an ambivalent relief that they do not belong to the target group and thereby become distanced from victims.

Regulating Hateful Expression – Liberal and Civic Republican Perspectives

In the following pages, I turn to look at the differential impact of constitutional guarantees of equality upon the content of freedom of expression and attempt to provide reasons why modern liberal democracies can accord hateful expression such variable levels of protection.

In focusing on the legal and constitutional issues generated by hateful expression, I shall not consider in any detail attempts to combat expressions of racial (or other) superiority through school education or other non-legal means.[69] This should not be understood as dismissing the importance of such work. There is evidence for example to show a correlation between higher levels of education and lower levels

66 C M Steele and J Aronson, 'Stereotype Threat and the Intellectual Test Performance of African Americans' (1995) 69 *J Personality and Soc Psychol* 797.

67 FBI statistics for 1995 are available electronically at http://www.fbi.gov/ucr/hatecm.htm.

68 M Sherry, 'Don't Ask, Tell or Respond: Silent Acceptance of Disability Hate Crimes' at http:///www.farnorthernrc.org/mylifemychoice/Hate%20Crimes-Mark%Sherry.pdf, and see also I Cram, 'Hate Speech and Disabled People: Some Comparative Constitutional Thoughts' in A Lawson and C Gooding (eds), *Disability Rights in Europe: From Theory to Practice* (2005, Hart Publishing, Oxford).

69 A good example in this regard is Iceland. See further J Magnet, 'Hate Propaganda in Canada' in WJ Waluchow (ed.). *Free Expression* (1994, Clarendon Press, Oxford) at 227.

of anti-black and anti-Semitic opinion.[70] However, we cannot be sure that the best endeavours of education systems and citizenship programmes will by themselves eradicate all forms of hate speech. This suggests that the constitutional issue of how much speech to protect must still be confronted.

The essence of my argument is that the degree of protection manifested in any society will reflect a dominant underlying commitment either to the values of pluralism, communitarianism or its civic republican variant explored earlier in Chapter 2. It is quite clear, for example, that restrictions on hate speech will be more readily embraced in a state where a commitment to civic republican ideals is embraced than in its libertarian counterpart. The emphasis in civic republicanism upon deliberation among a society of politically equal individuals suggests a commitment to silencing the voices of powerful, majority voices and to affording additional opportunities for members of minority groups who under-participate in societal discussion and decision-making forums. The principle of citizenship undergirds this inclusive participative polity but is also valuable because, through a commitment to deliberation with others on an equal footing, we are more likely to develop the quality of empathy, an attribute so obviously lacking in the propagators of hate materials. Most controversially, however, the civic republican version of communitarianism holds out the prospect that the pursuit of the 'common good' (defined either by the community itself or by some external criteria) can justify the placing of legal restrictions on expressive activity where that activity hinders progress towards this ideal. Viewpoint restrictions of the sort encountered in the regulation of hateful expression can thus be supported because they suppress 'bad answers' to societal problems and deter minority groups from participating in community affairs as equal citizens. On this account, the freedom to engage in expressive activity is instrumental; it exists only in as much as it advances the common good. Speech that induces hatred of groups is only peripherally connected to the core reasons why freedom of expression is valuable. It is classically 'low-value' speech and as such its claims to constitutional protection are easily overridden by competing societal interests. Communitarians do not share liberals' faith that unencumbered reasoned discourse will undermine the claims of racist and other hateful speakers. They point to the successes of Nazi propaganda to show that at times of pressure and hardship, the individual can be 'swayed and even swept away by hysterical, emotional appeals'.[71] They further accuse liberals of understating the harms caused by the dissemination of extremist opinion.

Liberal thought, whilst often disavowing the sentiments that inform racist and other forms of hateful expression, objects at a fundamental level to viewpoint-based restrictions. The abandonment of state neutrality which viewpoint restrictions entail is considered dangerous, skewing as it does the deliberative processes by denying

70 R Selzer and GM Lopes, 'The Ku Klux Klan: Reasons for Support or Opposition among White Respondents' (1986) 17 *J of Black Studies* 91; RJ Byron and RL Lenton, 'The Distribution of Anti-Semitism in Canada in 1984' (1991) 16 *Canadian Journal of Sociology* 411, cited by Magnet, *ibid.*

71 Dickson CJ in *R* v *Keegstra* [1990] 3 SCR 697, 747.

citizens access to a set of non-orthodox, competing opinions in the arena of political expression. In the absence of a demonstrable and causally linked risk of physical harm to others, the state has no business telling people which opinions they may receive and those they may not. The centrality of the autonomous individual in liberal thought makes expression intrinsically valuable as opposed to the contribution it makes to societal goals. Racial and religious harmony is but one vision regarding the optimal organization of society. Individuals must be free to make up their own minds about whether they share this particular vision. Whilst the vast majority of liberals express their abhorrence at the sentiments found in hateful speech and wish it did not exist, they cannot support legal controls in the absence of a direct causal link between hate expression and physical assaults on members of minority groups. Instead they urge victims to respond with speech which counteracts the message of hate and, further, express confidence that hostile messages will be rejected.

In the sections that follow, some examples of national regulation of hate speech are provided. The purpose in describing these is to identify elements of liberal/communitarian thinking which underpin particular regulatory stances. At the beginning of this chapter we saw that much international law, including regional human rights instruments, qualifies expressive freedom in the name of equality and individual dignity. At the national level, the majority of liberal democratic constitutions seek to give effect to these international legal norms in provisions which advance the causes of racial/religious tolerance and impose limits on freedom of expression derived from 'common' values set down in the constitution. Most do not even require a causal nexus between hate speech and harm to others. The expression need not occur within the hearing or sight of the group members it targets. By contrast, the overriding individualist ethos that underpins First Amendment discourse in the US has proved resistant to attempts to mediate expressive freedom by values found elsewhere in the Constitution. There, much weight is placed on the absence of a clearly established causal connection between hateful expression and demonstrable harm to others. Other 'injuries' are said to lack empirical substantiation.

Constitutionally Permitted Regulation of Hateful Expression

Canada The Canadian Constitution offers a good example of a regulatory model in which the communal impact of hateful expression is paid considerable attention. The respective rights of speakers and audience to express and access racist thoughts, whilst within the scope of constitutionally protected expression, have been subordinated by the legislature and Supreme Court to competing constitutional values including multiculturalism, equality and dignity. Canada has been described as the 'most enthusiastic consumer of hate propaganda norms in the international community ...', ratifying everything and reserving nothing.[72]

72 See J Magnet, note 69 at 229.

Evidence of this commitment is to be found in s.319(2) of the *Canadian Criminal Code* which criminalizes the wilful promotion of hatred against any identifiable group. Defences to a person charged with a s.319(2) offence exist where the accused establishes that the statements were either (i) true; or (ii) expressions of opinion on a religious subject in good faith; or (iii) relevant to any subject of public interest, discussion of which was for public benefit and reasonably believed by the speaker to be true.[73] In *R* v *Keegstra*[74] and *R* v *Andrews*,[75] challenges were brought under the *Canadian Charter of Rights and Freedoms*. The Charter enjoys constitutional status by virtue of having been incorporated in the *Canada Act* 1982.[76] Under s.52(1) of that Act, any law which is inconsistent with the provisions of the Constitution is, 'to the extent of the inconsistency of no force or effect'. Responsibility for determining whether a breach of Charter rights and freedoms has occurred rests with a court of 'competent jurisdiction' under s.24(1) of the Charter.[77] Section 2 of the Charter states that 'Everyone has the following fundamental freedoms: … (b) freedom of thought, belief, opinion and expression, including freedom of the press and other media of communication'.

Importantly, s.1 of the Charter declares that the rights and freedoms enumerated in the Charter may be subject to such reasonable limits prescribed by law as can be demonstrably justified in a free and democratic society. This general qualifying provision reflects the fundamental tension in liberal society between individual rights and wider societal goals.[78] The leading judgment on s.1 is *R* v *Oakes*[79] which requires limits on Charter rights to have in the first place an objective of 'sufficient importance' that is based upon pressing and substantial

73 S.319(3)(a)–(c). A further defence is set out in s.319(3)(d) of pointing out in good faith 'for the purpose of removal, matters producing or tending to produce feelings of hatred towards an identifiable group in Canada.

74 [1990] 3 SCR 697.

75 [1990] 3 SCR 870.

76 For background see I Cram, *A Virtue Less Cloistered* (2002, Hart Publishing, Oxford) at 24–30.

77 On the meaning of a 'court of competent jurisdiction' see *R* v *Mills* [1986] 1 SCR 863.

78 See further S Woolman, 'Riding the Push-Me Pull-You; Constructing a Test that Reconciles the Conflicting Interests which Animate the Limitation Clause' (1994) 10 *South African Journal of Human Rights* 60; see also R Moon, 'Justified Limits on Freedom of Expression: The Collapse of the General Approach to Limits on Charter Rights' (2002) 40 *Osgoode Hall LJ* 337, for an argument that the Supreme Court's application of s.1 to freedom of expression cases reveals an insufficiently contextualised deference to legislative enactment. For a useful discussion of the protection of freedom of expression under the Charter, see R Burns, *An Overview of the Protection of Freedom of Expression under Canadian Constitutional Law and Section 2(b) of the Canadian Charter of Rights and Freedoms* (1996, Research Paper No. 3, Centre for Media, Communications and Information Technology Law, Melbourne University). Burns notes the debt owed by the framers of s.1 to international human rights instruments such as the International Convention on Civil and Political Rights and the European Convention on Human Rights.

79 [1986] 1 SCR 103.

concerns in a democratic society. Then, it has to be shown that the means chosen to advance the objective were rationally connected to the objective and impair the Charter right minimally. Finally, the adverse impact of the measure must not be out of all proportion to the benefits gained by advancing the objective.[80]

The circumstances in *Keegstra* concerned the conviction of the respondent, an Albertan high-school teacher under s.319(2) of the Code for making virulent anti-Semitic comments to students.[81] In *Andrews* the defendant was convicted under the same section for publishing and distributing white supremacist publications.[82] After divergent rulings from the Alberta and Ontario Courts of Appeal on the constitutionality of s.319(2), both cases went up to the Canadian Supreme Court where s.319(2) was narrowly held to be as a reasonable limit on freedom of expression. Writing the majority opinion, Dickson CJ pointed to the upsurge in levels of Canadian hate propaganda directed at Aboriginals, blacks, French persons, Jews and Roman Catholics, a proportion of which was distributed to Germany and other parts of Europe.[83] This upsurge harmed members of the target groups, causing emotional damage to their sense of self-worth in the form of feelings of humiliation and degradation which in turn inclined some victims to deny their racial or religious identities.[84] Beyond the victim group, hateful expression harmed society by recruiting fresh adherents and, by being tolerated as a matter of law, could gain credibility. Aided by clever presentation at times when particular socio-economic circumstances prevailed (such as economic recession), public susceptibility might increase significantly. In terms of the Charter, hate speech threatened the central constitutional values of equality and multiculturalism. Section 15 of the Charter committed the Canadian nation to the core principle of equality among citizens. Expression which denied that all members of society were equally deserving of concern,

80 The extent to which this final limb of the *Oakes* test adds anything of substance to its pre-existing elements is doubtful.

81 These included statements that Jews were 'treacherous', 'money-loving', 'subversive' and 'child killers'. Keegstra taught his students that Jews 'created the Holocaust to gain sympathy' and, in contrast to Christian people, were 'deceptive', 'secretive' and 'inherently evil'. He expected students to regurgitate these views and marked down the work of those who failed to do so.

82 The materials asserted *inter alia* that non-whites were responsible for increases in violent crime rates, that America was being 'swamped by coloureds who do not believe in democracy and harbour a hatred for white people' and that Zionists had fabricated the 'Holocaust Hoax'.

83 On the meaning of 'an identifiable group' for the purposes of s.319(2), see *R* v *Krymowski* [2005] SCC 7.

84 In the context of sexual 'banter', the Court had previously found that words by themselves were capable of harassment, *Janzen* v *Platy Enterprises Ltd* [1989] 1 SCR 1252.

respect and consideration was not consistent with this value.[85] Apart from s.15, the Charter also laid down a guarantee of multiculturalism in s.27 against which expressive activity must be measured. This commitment could not be 'preserved let alone enhanced if free rein is given to the promotion of hatred against identifiable cultural groups'.[86] It followed that the suppression of hateful expression offered a 'powerfully convincing legislative objective' as regards the first part of the test in *R* v *Oakes*.[87] The provision was also rationally connected to this objective since the suppression of hateful expression through the criminal law signalled not only collective disapprobation of hate-mongering but also the value which was attached to the worth and dignity of each human being. It was unlikely, according to Dickson CJ, that suppression would make the content of the suppressed speech more attractive.[88] As to whether resort to criminalization constituted a 'minimal impairment' of s.2(b), the majority approached this limb of the proportionality test bearing in mind the importance of the objective and the low value of the expression being regulated. Mindful also of the offence's stringent *mens rea* requirement, the range of defences open to an accused person (including truth and expression in the public interest), and the fact that private conversations were exempted from its scope, s.319(2) was deemed also to meet the minimal impairment test.[89] Recognizing that less restrictive means of advancing the goal of a tolerant society were open to the government (such as human rights legislation), the majority refused nonetheless to find resort to the criminal law disproportionate. Conferring a broad scope of discretion upon the government, the Court agreed that the criminal law could be an appropriate

85 The minority view on s.15 (and s.27) was that there was no discriminatory law or state action that could bring s.15 into play, see McLachlin J at [1990] 3 SCR 697, 833. A troubling implication of such an argument is that the construction of criminal law statutes could proceed without reference to the wider constitutional values.

86 [1990] 3 SCR 697, 758, citing with approval the remarks of Cory JA in *R* v *Andrews* (1988) 65 OR (2d) 161, 181, in the Ontario Court of Appeal.

87 A conclusion with which the minority agreed, see McLachlin J at 846–8.

88 Compare this with the minority position of McLachlin J, who doubted whether suppression did contribute to the cause of multiculturalism, at 851–4, noting the experience of pre-Hitler Germany where anti-hate laws were enforced with vigour and subsequently used by Nazi defendants in criminal proceedings to attract publicity to their cause.

89 In dissent, McLachlin J at 859–60 argued that the vagueness inherent in s.319(2) would chill some political speech on the part of those who might wish to speak out on issues of race/religion but who feared possible prosecution under the criminal law. See also *R* v *Zundel* [1992] 2 SCR 731 where a differently constituted Court struck down s.181 of the *Code* (creating the offence of wilful publication of false statement that is likely to cause injury or mischief to a public interest) on the ground *inter alia* that it was a disproportionate interference with freedom of expression. For judicial analysis of civil law restraints on discriminatory conduct, see *Canada (Human Rights Commission* v *Taylor* [1990] 3 SCR 892. For commentary, see J Manwaring, 'Legal Regulation of Hate Propaganda in Canada' in S Coliver (ed.) *et al.*, *Striking a Balance – Hate Speech, Freedom of Expression and Non-discrimination* (1992, Article 19, London Human Rights Centre, University of Essex, Colchester).

means of punishing recalcitrant hate-mongers and reinforcing Charter values. The remaining question was whether the deleterious effects of the measure on expressive freedom were out of all proportion to the state objectives which lay behind it. Having conceded the especial importance of the state's purpose in legislating and having found that hate expression was far removed from core freedom of expression values, the majority was never likely to find for the respondent on this final limb of the *Oakes* test.[90]

The Court's decision to uphold s.319(2) predictably spawned much debate about the impact of Canada's hate speech laws. One critic went so far as to characterize the law as a 'cheap, smug way of flattering ourselves that we have done the righteous thing'.[91] In practice, critics point to the fact that the law has been used against members of the very minority groups intended to be the beneficiaries of such laws, while much virulent racist expression has gone unpunished.[92] The opponents of hate speech laws (who include members of targeted communities) also fall back on the Millian-inspired free speech argument that if racist expression is suppressed, it hinders social mobilization of counter-racist forces and, further, treats the targets of hate speech as incapable of defending themselves.

Australia Michael Chesterman has argued that Australian laws aimed at curbing racist speech reflect a civic republican concern that the ideal of equality in a political community means that all members are equally eligible for inclusion in the community.[93] Racist expression undermines the ability of targeted groups to assert their right to equal treatment. Race-hate laws can thus be justified as serving to define rules of civility and, when enforced, play a 'significant role in constituting and maintaining the community as a society based on equality amongst its members'.[94] Of course, since the judicial development of an implied freedom to engage in political

---

90 Equally unsurprisingly, McLachlin J's dissent concluded that the questionable benefits of any hate speech ban were outweighed by the 'significant burden' on the s.2(b) freedom, *ibid.*, at 865.

91 J Magnet, 'Hate Propaganda in Canada' in WJ Waluchow (ed.), *Free Expression* (1994, Clarendon Press, Oxford) at 249.

92 J Magnet, *ibid.*, at 244–50, although hard empirical evidence to support these claims is not produced. Also, the small proportion of supposedly virulent material that is prosecuted may show that the s.319(2) is too narrowly drawn and in need of relaxing.

93 Borrowing from Robert Post's work in defamation law 'The Constitutional Concept of Public Discourse: Outrageous Opinion, Democratic Deliberation and *Hustler Magazine* v *Falwell*' (1990) 103 *Harv L Rev* 601.

94 *Freedom of Speech in Australian Law – A Delicate Plant* (2000, Ashgate, Aldershot) at 216. For a civility-based argument in the European context, see R Errera, 'Group Libel, Hate Speech, and other Fighting Words: Civility and the Uses of Law' in B Markesinis (ed.), *Law Making, Law Finding and Law Shaping: The Diverse Influences* (1997, OUP, Oxford).

communication in the early 1990s,[95] the constitutionality of any restraints on such expressive activity is a live issue.[96]

Australian civil and criminal legislation outlawing hate speech exists at both Commonwealth and state levels in a variety of forms.[97] In five jurisdictions – Australian Capital Territory, New South Wales, Queensland, South Australia, and Victoria – liability may be incurred under the civil and criminal law.[98] One state – Western Australia – has made hate speech a criminal offence only.[99] Commonwealth law, on the other hand, opts to impose civil liability across the land, supplementing omissions in Western Australia where no equivalent rules of civil liability have been developed.[100]

The leading model for combined criminal and civil liability at state level is the *Anti-Discrimination Act* 1977 (as amended) of New South Wales to which attention now turns. Vilification complaints which fall short of serious vilification are dealt with through a conciliation procedure at civil law. Those complaints that entail an allegation amounting to more serious vilification are dealt with through the criminal process.[101] Criminal liability exists for the offence of serious racial vilification as laid down in Section 20D. This occurs where a person by a public act incites:

---

95 *Nationwide News Pty Ltd* v *Wills* (1992) 177 CLR 1; *Australian Capital Television Pty Ltd* v *Commonwealth* (1992) 177 CLR 106; for a more recent statement of the implied freedom see *Lange* v *Australian Broadcasting Corporation* (1997) 189 CLR 520 and *Levy* v *Victoria* (1997) 189 CLR 579.

96 See K Gelber, 'Free Speech, Hate Speech and an Australian Bill of Rights' (2002) 2 *The Drawing Board: An Australian Review of Public Affairs* 107, who also compares Australian laws with South Africa's anti-hate speech laws contained within Article 16 of Constitution of the Republic of South Africa 1996. See also K Eastman, 'Racial Vilification: The Australian Experience' in S Coliver (ed.) *et al.*, *Striking a Balance – Hate Speech, Freedom of Expression and Non-discrimination* (1992, Article 19, London Human Rights Centre, University of Essex, Colchester).

97 A more detailed account of the various provisions is to be found in M Chesterman *Freedom of Speech in Australian Law – A Delicate Plant* (2000, Ashgate, Aldershot) at Ch. 5. See also L McNamara, *Regulating Racism: Racial Vilification Laws in Australia* (2002, Sydney Institute of Criminology, Sydney).

98 In the case of Victoria, a civil complaint was brought against two Christian pastors working for the 'Catch the Fire Ministries' under s.8(1) of the *Racial and Religious Tolerance Act* 2001 which prohibits engaging in conduct that incites hatred against or serious contempt for, or revulsion or severe ridicule of another person or class of persons on the ground of religious belief. The complaint was brought by the Islamic Council of Victoria in respect of seminars organized by the pastors in which the compatibility of Islam with Western notions of democracy was discussed. The pastors were found guilty of vilification in December 2004.

99 The legislation was a response to the activities of a white supremacist group, the Australian Nationalist Movement, whose members engaged in vandalism and intimidatory conduct of non-whites and displayed racist posters.

100 Apart from Western Australia, this includes Tasmania and the Northern Territory.

101 For an overview of the early operation of the 1977 Act, see N Hennessy and P Smith, 'Have We Got It Right? NSW Racial Vilification Laws Five Years On' (1994) *AJHR* 6.

(1) … hatred towards, serious contempt for or severe ridicule of, a person or group of persons on the ground of the race of the person or members of the group by means which include:

(a) threatening physical harm towards, or towards any property of, the person or group of persons, or

(b) inciting others to threaten physical harm towards, or towards any property of, the person or group of persons.

'Race' is defined as including 'colour, nationality, descent, and ethnic, ethno-religious or national origin'.[102] Subsequent legislation has added homosexual vilification,[103] HIV/AIDS vilification[104] and, in 1996, transgender vilification to the list of minority groups enjoying protection.[105] In 1999, the NSW Law Reform Commission considered and rejected proposals to extend the 1977 Act further to incorporate gender and disability vilification. In the case of gender vilification, the Commission concluded that, whilst violence against women might be unacceptably high in NSW and ought to be made subject to pre-existing criminal laws, it was not sure that misogynist speech presented a discrete problem worthy of specific legislation.[106] As for disability vilification, despite evidence from disability groups that their members have been subjected to vilifying statements which have disrupted their integration into society, the Commission declined to recommend protection of disabled persons as a class. The instances of vilification communicated to the Commission were confined to 'a few specific situations' and these were felt not to afford a basis for legislative reform.[107]

'Public act' is broadly defined to include any form of communication to the public (including speaking, writing or displaying notices and broadcasting); any conduct observable by members of the public (including the wearing of clothing, flags, emblems and insignia); and the distribution or dissemination of any matter to the public with the knowledge that the matter promotes or expresses hatred towards, serious contempt for, or severe ridicule of, a person or group of persons on the ground of the race of the person or members of the group.[108] Prosecutions may only be instituted with the consent of the Attorney General, offering some safeguard against arbitrary resort to the section.[109] However, the provisions of s.20D referring to physical harm and inciting others to threaten physical harm illustrate (rather than exhaust) the sorts of means by which hatred, serious contempt or severe ridicule might be inflicted. It is interesting to consider whether other means (that is, other

102 *Anti-Discrimination Act* 1977, s.4.

103 *Anti-Discrimination (Homosexual Vilification) Amendment Act* 1993 Sch. 1.

104 *Anti-Discrimination (Amendment) Act* 1994, Sch. 2.

105 *Transgender (Anti-Discrimination and Other Acts Amendment) Act* 1996.

106 *Report 92 – Review of the Anti-Discrimination Act 1977* (1999, Sydney, NSWLRC) para. 7.88.

107 *Ibid.*, at para. 7.92.

108 S.20B, *Anti-Discrimination Act* 1977.

109 S.20D(2).

expressive conduct) could also fall foul of the prohibition.[110] Severe ridicule, for example, could be caused by words/conduct which fall short of a threat of physical harm, as where, for example, a defendant throws bananas at a black target.[111] In practice, however, there has, at the time of writing, been no single prosecution for serious racial vilification in New South Wales. This is despite the fact that the President of the NSW Anti-Discrimination Board has referred a number of cases to the Attorney General for prosecution.[112] Hennessy and Smith have argued that the offence should be brought within the main *Crimes Act* 1900 in order to be a more effective means of combating vilificatory conduct.[113] They argue that this would signal the seriousness of the offence whilst enabling the police to investigate and arrest alleged breaches promptly. At the same time, it is recognized that concerns about existing police handling of incidents with a race component would necessitate a significant level of professional training before any legal reforms became effective in practice.

Less serious forms of vilification are dealt with under s.20C(1) of the 1977 Act. This also refers to the incitement of hatred towards, serious contempt for, or severe ridicule of, a person or group of persons on the ground of the race of the person or members of the group. However, it is different in two main respects from its criminal counterpart. First, the means by which the incitement of hatred and so on, may occur are not expressly indicated. Second, by s.20C(2), liability is lifted in respect of:

> (a) a fair report of a public act referred to in subsection (1), or
> (b) a communication or the distribution or dissemination of any matter comprising a publication … [that] is subject to a defence of absolute privilege in proceedings for defamation, or
> (c) a public act done reasonably and in good faith, for academic, artistic, scientific or research purposes or for other purposes in the public interest, including discussion or debate about and expositions of any act or matter.

---

110 Chesterman argues that the criminal provisions fall short of the requirements of Article 4(a) of ICERD and Article 20 of ICCPR. The former requires State Parties to declare 'an offence punishable by law all dissemination of ideas based on racial superiority or hatred, incitement to racial discrimination …', *Freedom of Speech in Australian Law – A Delicate Plant* (2000, Ashgate, Aldershot) 196–7. In this context, it is worth noting that the Australian Law Reform Commission's Report No. 57, *Multiculturalism and the Law*, did contain a minority recommendation to criminalize the publishing of 'anything that is based on ideas or theories of superiority of any race or group of persons of one colour or ethnic origin over another…' (1992, Sydney, ALRC) para. 7.48.

111 The New South Wales Law Reform Commission recognizes that 'serious contempt' and 'severe ridicule' constitute less stringent criteria for a prosecutor to establish: *Transgender (Anti-Discrimination and Other Acts Amendment) Act* 1996. *Report 92 – Review of the Anti-Discrimination 1977* (1999, Sydney, NSWLRC) para. 7.128.

112 For an analysis of the empirical evidence, see L McNamara, *Regulating Racism: Racial Vilification Laws in Australia* (2002, Sydney Institute of Criminology, Sydney).

113 N Hennessy and P Smith, 'Have We Got It Right? NSW Racial Vilification Laws Five Years On' (1994) *AJHR* 6.

This section acknowledges a wide set of exemptions from liability including, importantly, in (c), the discussion of matters of public interest.[114]

A conciliation procedure exists for dealing with vilification complaints at civil law. The complainant lodges his/her complaint to the President of the Anti-Discrimination Board who will investigate in cases where a contravention of vilification provisions is alleged. If appropriate, the President attempts to conciliate the complaint to achieve a mutually agreeable resolution of the problem. If this is not forthcoming, the complaint can be referred to the Equal Opportunity Tribunal for a hearing which can award damages[115] and/or order an apology/retraction. The vilifier can also be ordered not to repeat the statement which gave rise to the complaint. An appeal lies from decisions of the Equal Opportunity Tribunal's decisions to the Administrative Decisions Tribunal. An example of the manner in which the Administrative Decisions Tribunal applies the 1977 Act is provided by *Western Aboriginal Legal Service Ltd* v *Jones & another*. The tribunal upheld a complaint brought against a journalist for remarks he broadcast about the award of $6,000 to an Aboriginal woman against an estate agent by the Equal Opportunity Tribunal.[116] The journalist commented as follows:

> Now I think that is a joke … If I owned the only property on the real estate agent's list, the only property for letting, and a bloke walked through the door, and I don't care what colour he is, looking like a skunk and smelling like a skunk, with a sardine can on one foot and sandshoe on the other, and a half drunk bottle of beer under the arm, and he wanted to rent the final property available and it was mine, I'd expect the agent to say no without giving reasons. What discrimination would the agent be guilty of then?

The journalist's words were found to have incited in the ordinary, reasonable listener feelings of serious contempt for, and severe ridicule of, Aboriginal persons in New South Wales. He was ordered to broadcast an apology to the Aboriginal community in New South Wales, the terms of which were dictated by the tribunal and to forward a copy of the same to the complainant.[117]

In constitutional terms, the true scope of these various sets of restraints on vilificatory speech/conduct would be a central issue in any challenge to their validity under the implied freedom of political communication doctrine developed by the High Court. At the outset, the requirements in *Lange* v *Australian Broadcasting Corporation*[118] that the subject matter of the communication be relevant to the choices to be made by Commonwealth electors and facilitate the effective functioning of

---

114 For similarities with the defences in the law of defamation, see M Chesterman *Freedom of Speech in Australian Law – A Delicate Plant* (2000, Ashgate, Aldershot) 204–216.

115 In 1994, the maximum level of damages that could be awarded was $40,000.

116 [2000] NSWADT 102 (31 July 2000).

117 The equivalent provisions of Commonwealth law are found in the *Racial Discrimination Act* 1975.

118 (1997) 189 CLR 520.

responsible government would seem to offer a limited degree of protection. Plainly, the doctrine would apply to the speech of supporters of the One Nation Party which has criticized what it claims is the preferential treatment enjoyed by Aboriginal people. In the absence of any link to the Commonwealth electoral context, the version of the doctrine outlined in *Lange* is unlikely to offer protection to more general derogatory comments about the members of other racial groups. However, the narrowness of *Lange* on this point is unlikely to constitute the High Court's final word on the matter. Indeed, at much the same time as *Lange*, Gaudron and Toohey JJ in *Kruger* v *Commonwealth*[119] indicated their support for a more inclusive definition of 'political communication'. Justice Gaudron, for example, would have extended protection to 'information, ideas or opinions with respect to matters which may fall for consideration in the political process'.[120] So stated, it is to be doubted whether the articulation of claims to racial superiority would fall outside the ambit of the implied freedom. If, for the sake of argument, it is assumed that some forms of racial vilification do benefit from the implied freedom, the Commonwealth (or state) would then need to establish that legal restraints pursued a legitimate end and either were 'reasonably adapted to that end' (to use Brennan CJ's more relaxed scrutiny standard in *Levy* v *Victoria*[121]) or showed some 'overriding public purpose' or 'compelling justification' (the stricter scrutiny standard preferred by Gaudron and Toohey JJ in the same case).[122]

United Kingdom

At the beginning of this chapter, the initial lack of progress post-11 September 2001 towards a free-standing law against the incitement of religious hatred in Great Britain was discussed. In the case of Northern Ireland, however, the *Prevention of Incitement to Hatred Act* 1970 had already made it an offence to publish/distribute threatening, abusive or insulting material with intent to stir up religious hatred against or fear of others.[123] The Act was first used against the publishers of a book entitled *Orange Loyalist Songs* which appeared to endorse the murder of Catholics. The defendants

---

119 (1997) 190 CLR 1.

120 *Ibid.*, at 114. In the earlier decision of *Theophanous* v *The Herald & Weekly Times Ltd*, (1994) 182 CLR 104, Gaudron and Toohey JJ had endorsed Eric Barendt's definition of political speech as that which was 'relevant to the development of public opinion on the whole range of public issues which a citizen should think about': E Barendt, *Freedom of Speech* (1985, Clarendon Press, Oxford) 152.

121 (1997) 189 CLR 579, 596.

122 *Ibid.*, at 614.

123 Section 1. See A Twomey, 'Laws against Incitement to Racial Hatred in the United Kingdom' (1994) 1 *AJHR* 5, and T Murphy, 'Incitement to Hatred: Lessons from Northern Ireland' in S Coliver (ed.) *et al.*, *Striking a Balance: Hate Speech, Freedom of Expression and Non-discrimination* (1992, Article 19, London and Human Rights Centre, University of Essex, Colchester).

were acquitted after they claimed not to have intended to incite religious hatred. No prosecution was ever subsequently brought under this legislation though this was surely not on account of the absence of words intended to stir up sentiments of religious hatred. The 1970 Act's successor – the *Public Order (Northern Ireland) Order* 1987 – created several offences of using words/behaviour,[124] publishing or distributing written material,[125] and distributing, showing or playing a recording[126] with intent to stir up religious hatred. Somewhat surprisingly, there are no reported instances of prosecution of these offences.

As regards the enforcement of incitement to racial hatred laws on the mainland, the reported case law suggested that, in response to a rising tide of racist activity in the late 1970s, prosecutors began to focus upon anti-immigrant publications. A clutch of successful prosecutions were brought between 1979 and 1986 for incitement to racial hatred under s.5A of the *Public Order Act* 1936.[127] These targeted leaders of far right political parties such as John Tyndall, as well as lesser known propagandists.[128] More recently, attention has moved across to the troublesome matter of Holocaust denial, partly as a result of EU initiatives on the issue. In content terms, this encompasses a range of expression which contests the essential facts of the Holocaust. Such expression might take various forms including *inter alia* a denial that the extermination of the Jews was official Nazi policy, disputing the scale of deaths in concentration camps or denying that the gas chambers ever existed.[129] In terms of the tone of expression, Holocaust denial can take crude or sophisticated forms. The latter is to be found in publications that purport to be the product of academically rigorous historical research and has an impact that is considered especially insidious because of the attempt to pass itself off as revisionist history. The case for legislating against Holocaust denial is that it implies that the Holocaust was a myth created by Jews for their own ends, including to acquire international support and sympathy, to help secure the state of Israel and to make financial claims

---

124 Para. 9(1) states 'A person who uses threatening, abusive or insulting words or behaviour, or displays any written material which is threatening, abusive or insulting is guilty of an offence if – (a) he intends thereby to stir up hatred or arouse fear; or having regard to all the circumstances hatred is likely to be stirred up or fear is likely to be aroused thereby.' Paragraph 8 defines 'fear' as fear of a group of persons in Northern Ireland defined by reference to religious belief, colour, race, nationality (including citizenship) or ethnic or national origins. 'Hatred' is similarly defined by reference to religious belief, etc.

125 Para. 10(1).

126 Para. 11(1).

127 This section was repealed by the *Public Order Act* 1986, s.40(3) and Sch. 3. New offences of incitement to racial hatred were laid down in Part 3 of the 1986 Act.

128 *R* v *Morse;* R v *Tyndall* (1986) 8 Cr App R 369; *R* v *Edwards* (1983) 5 Cr App R 145; *R* v *Pearce* (1981) 72 Cr App R 295, and *R* v *Relf* (1979).

129 This distinguishes Holocaust denial from the work of scholars engaged in work that does not challenge the central facts. This would include research into the involvement of ordinary Germans in and knowledge of the Holocaust, the various roles played by key Nazi personnel in the execution of the policy and the timing of orders to exterminate the Jews.

on Germany and its allies. Errera has described such claims as 'an aggression against the dead, the survivors and society at large …'.[130] The negative image of the Jew carried by Holocaust deniers is designed to engender hatred and distrust of Jewish people in non-Jews. Moreover, as the Institute for Jewish Policy Research notes, denial causes Jews 'immeasurable offence and anger, and can cause those who are directly targeted by the material to feel fearful and intimidated'.[131]

ECHR and EU Norms

In the case of restrictions on racist speech, *Jersild* v *Denmark* informs us that national authorities may criminalize abusive racial expression without breaching Article 10.[132] The Court later affirmed in *Lehideux and Isorni* v *France* that where a speaker attempts to justify a pro-Nazi policy, protection of Article 10 could not be successfully claimed.[133] The basis of permissible legal controls lies in the values of tolerance, and pluralism, equality and individual dignity that underpin Convention rights and freedoms. This in turn suggests that abusive speech directed at people on other grounds such as gender, sexual orientation and disability might also be safely curtailed without infringing the Convention.[134] At the same time, *Jersild* reveals that media organizations have some latitude in the dissemination of the racist and hateful views of others as part of their role in facilitating debate on matters of public interest.[135] Nonetheless, as *Surek* v *Turkey (No. 1)* reveals, special care may still have to be exercised where a media outlet is at risk of being used for the propagation of inciteful expression in situations of political and/or armed conflict.[136]

---

130 'Group Libel, Hate Speech, and Other Fighting Words: Civility and the Uses of Law' in B Markesinis (ed.), *Law Making, Law Finding and Law Shaping: The Diverse Influences, Vol 2, The Clifford Chance Lectures* (1997, OUP, Oxford) at 50.

131 *Combating Holocaust Denial through Law in the United Kingdom* (2000, Institute for Jewish Policy Research, London).

132 (1995) 19 European Human Rights Reports 1. The broadcast remarks of members of the 'Greenjackets' included the statement, 'A nigger is not a human being, it's an animal, that goes for all the other foreign workers as well, Turks, Yugoslavs and whatever they are called.' The highly abusive nature of the anti-immigrant/anti-ethnic remarks were stated by the Court to be more than insulting to members of the targeted groups and outside the protection of Article 10. For background detail on Danish law, see P Justesen, 'Liberté d'Expression et Props Racistes au Danemark' (2001) 12 *Revue Trimestrielle des Droits de L'Homme* 343.

133 *Lehideux & Isorni* v *France* (1998) VII *Reports of Judgments and Decisions* 2864, 2886. See further *H, W, P & K* v *Austria* Application No. 12774/87, 62 DR (1989) 216, and discussion by J Cooper and A M Williams, 'Hate Speech, Holocaust Denial and International Human Rights Law' (1999) 6 *EHRLR* 593.

134 I Cram, 'Hate Speech and Disabled People – Some Comparative Constitutional Thoughts' in A Lawson and C Gooding (eds), *Disability Rights in Europe – From Theory to Practice* (2005, Hart Publishing, Oxford).

135 Committee of Ministers *Recommendation No. R (97) 20* Principles 4, 6 and 7.

136 *Application No. 26682/95 Judgment* of 8 July 1999.

The rarely invoked Article 17 might also be pleaded by member states to justify a proportionate restriction on hateful expressive forms. This provides that:

> Nothing in this Convention may be interpreted as implying for any state, group or person any right to engage in any activity aimed at the destruction of the rights and freedoms set forth herein or at their limitation to a greater extent than is provided for in the Convention.

In *Glimmerveen & Hagenbeek* v *Netherlands*, Article 17 was relied upon by the Strasbourg authorities against racist expression to dismiss, as 'manifestly ill-founded', an allegation of unlawful interference with Article 10 rights. The applicant, Glimmerveen, had been sentenced to two weeks' imprisonment for possession of leaflets likely to incite racial hatred, and was removed from a list of candidates seeking election to public office after openly calling for the repatriation of non-white immigrant workers. The Commission ruled that the applicant's words actively promoted racial discrimination in direct contradiction to norms set out in the Convention and elsewhere in international law and that, accordingly, they fell outside the protection of Article 10.[137] Article 17 has also been invoked by the Court to uphold laws outlawing Holocaust denial/revision. In *Lehideux* the Court declared that the negation or revision of clearly established historical facts was removed from the protection of Article 10 by the operation of Article 17.[138] In a separate concurring judgment, Judge Jambrek suggested that for Article 17 to apply there must be a desire on the part of the speaker to spread violence or hatred, to encourage others to use violence, or to pursue objectives that are racist or are likely to destroy the rights and freedoms of others.[139] There must, he maintained, be strict scrutiny of Article 17's requirements. Despite this clarification, concerns remain about the width of Article 17. Does it apply to sanction limits on freedom of expression regardless of whether a specific threat to the rights and freedoms of another person/group is actually made out on the facts?[140] Can it also have application to instances of genocide other than the Holocaust? How can we know what the 'essential' and 'clearly established' facts of a particular genocide are? What is the nature of the causal connection required by Article 17 and the damage/loss of others' rights and freedoms? Would merely

---

137 *Glimmerveen & Hagenbeek* v *Netherlands Application Nos. 8348/78* and *8406/78*, 18 DR 187.

138 (1998) VII *Reports of Judgments and Decisions* 2864, 2884, *Marais* v *France* (1996) *Application No. 31159/96.*

139 (1998) VII *Reports of Judgments and Decisions* 2864, 2891. See further *Norwood* v *United Kingdom* (2004) *Application No. 23131/03* in which it was held that a poster linking the attack on the twin towers of the World Trade Center with Muslims in Britain fell outside the protection of Article 10 by virtue of Article 17. This ruling has clear implications for the new offence in domestic law of incitement of religious hatred.

140 J Cooper and A M Williams, 'Hate Speech, Holocaust Denial and International Human Rights Law' (1999) 6 *EHRLR* 593, 606–7. The evidential issue raises questions as to the proportionality of any restriction on Holocaust denial.

causing others to think less highly of another group in society be sufficient to meet this test?

Notwithstanding these unresolved definitional questions, the EU Commission and Council of Ministers are leading moves to have denying or trivializing Nazi atrocities made into specific offences across EU countries.[141] At present, Austria, Belgium, France, Germany and Spain have laws which prohibit Holocaust denial.[142] Given prominence in the UK post-May 1997 by virtue of a Private Member's Bill to criminalize the denial of Nazi genocide,[143] and subsequently by the defamation action brought by David Irving against Deborah Lipstadt and Penguin Books,[144] Holocaust denial has become the focus of an intense debate about the purposes of, and permissible limits upon, freedom of expression. Existing incitement to racial hatred laws have no application where the expression in question does not threaten, abuse or insult. It is this lacuna which the supporters of a Holocaust denial law claim is exploited by more sophisticated anti-Semitic speakers to engender hostile attitudes towards, and cause offence/intimidation to, Jews and has led to calls for the amendment of UK law to capture non-inflammatory forms of Holocaust denial.[145] As the Institute for Jewish Policy Research notes, this would mark a significant shift away from previous measures such as those contained in public order legislation because it would make a speaker liable simply on account of expressive content rather than any deleterious public order consequences of that expression. Moreover, any measure which singled out the Holocaust for particular protection would also be controversial on account of signalling special treatment for Jewish persons. This might prove useful propaganda for anti-Semitic groups whilst leaving other speakers at liberty to deny atrocities inflicted on other racial/ethnic/religious groups.[146]

The upholding of restraints on hateful expression in ECHR law and the extension of domestic legal restrictions under EU prompting may point up underlying civic republican concerns in European Convention and EU jurisprudence that certain

---

141 J F Flauss, 'L'action de L'Union Européenne dans le Domaine de la Lutte contre le Racisme et la Xénophobie' (2001) 12 *Revue Trimestrielle des Droits de L'Homme* 487.

142 As do Switzerland and Israel. For a summary of various nations' legislation see *Combating Holocaust Denial through Law in the United Kingdom*, Appendix B, and discussion by G Bindman, 'Outlawing Holocaust Denial' (1997) 147 *NLJ* 466 and R Hofmann, 'Incitement to National and Racial Hatred: The Legal Position in Germany' in S Coliver (ed.) *et al.*, *Striking a Balance – Hate Speech, Freedom of Expression and Non-discrimination* (1992, Article 19, London Human Rights Centre, University of Essex, Colchester).

143 The *Holocaust Denial Bill* tabled by Mike Gapes MP (Labour) would have inserted an additional provision into Part 3 of the *Public Order Act* 1986. The Bill failed to progress beyond its Committee stage on account of insufficient parliamentary time.

144 D Lipstadt, *Denying the Holocaust: The Growing Assault on Truth* (1994, Plume, New York).

145 G Bindman, 'Outlawing Holocaust Denial' (1997) 147 *NLJ* 466. This would be achieved by deleting the words 'threatening, abusive or insulting' in s.17 of the *Public Order Act*.

146 Bindman's solution to this problem clearly avoids this difficulty, see *ibid*.

expressive activities offer 'bad solutions' to societal problems and may deter minority groups from participating in community affairs as equal citizens. This jurisprudence does not, it seems, share the faith of more libertarian schools of thought that reasoned discourse will always expose the vileness of hateful speakers and secure the triumph of non-hateful alternatives. Europe's history provides a forceful reminder that states' failure to signal their rejection of eugenic theories can, under the appropriate socio-economic conditions, have devastating human rights consequences. The assessment of whether a Holocaust denial law is now needed is probably best left to national authorities making informed choices based on accurate, empirical information. It would have to be shown, for example, that any additional restriction on freedom of expression was in response to a rising wave of anti-Semitic expression that threatened community cohesiveness in ways not treatable under existing laws and that the proposed restriction would counter these manifestations in a proportionate way, without impinging on other protected speech forms. However, the fact that Holocaust denial caused offence to Jewish persons ought not, by itself, to offer a sufficient basis for criminalization.

Constitutionally Barred Regulation of Hateful Expression in the US

First and Fourteenth Amendments of the US Constitution

The US has signed both the ICCPR and the ICERD but has failed to ratify either. As such, the US may not be monitored under international treaty-based organs. US experts were also closely involved in the drafting of the Council of Europe's Cybercrimes Convention although the US Government shows no inclination to accede to contents-based restrictions on Internet-based forms of hate expression.

The Fourteenth Amendment to the US Constitution directs that 'No State shall … deny to any person within its jurisdiction the equal protection of the laws.' It is accepted that the Amendment as originally conceived sought to prohibit racial discrimination against blacks. Beyond this, the outer limits of the guarantee have proved more controversial. One aspect of equal protection jurisprudence which has generated lively debate concerns its relationship to the First Amendment. Some have seen the equality principle as lying at the heart of the First Amendment's hostility towards contents-based speech restrictions. Karst, for example, cites the decision of *Police Department of the City of Chicago* v *Mosley* in support of his argument that equal protection or, more precisely, equal liberty from state interference is central to an understanding of the First Amendment.[147] The case concerned a challenge to an ordinance prohibiting picketing within 150 feet of a school during school hours. The ordinance did, however, exempt peaceful picketing of any school involved in a labour dispute. Striking down the ordinance, Marshall J giving the opinion of the

147 K Karst, 'Equality as a Central Principle of the First Amendment' (1975) 43 *Univ Chic L Rev* 20.

Court noted the ordinance's differential treatment of picketing according to subject matter and declared:

> Necessarily, then, under the Equal Protection Clause, not to mention the First Amendment itself, government may not grant the use of a forum to people whose views it finds acceptable but deny use to those wishing to express less favored or more controversial views.[148]

Thus stated, *Mosley* can be seen as espousing an essentially libertarian view of the constitution's speech and equality guarantees. On this account, the state is conceived of as a threat to the autonomy of individual speakers and listeners. Its interventions are characterized as having a distorting effect upon the marketplace of ideas in the form of suppressing unpopular ideas. In these circumstances, the courts have a responsibility to restore market equilibrium by striking down contents and viewpoint-based regulations.

One consequence of the position that all speakers and all points are entitled to be heard is to cast doubt upon the cogency of established First Amendment doctrine concerning the hierarchy of speech values which attach to different types of speech (such as political, commercial, artistic or obscene speech). *Mosley* suggests that attaching different social values to distinct speech forms and its corollary of different levels of judicial scrutiny falls foul of the ban on promoting/disfavouring speech on the basis of its contents. By placing certain speech types outside constitutional protection altogether, the court would appear to collude at times with the government's assessment of the utility of specific speech forms.[149] As shall be seen below, a version of this position was set out by the majority of the Court in *RAV* without express acknowledgement of the link to Karst's negative conception of equal protection.

Not all First Amendment scholars, however, share this pessimistic account of the dangers inherent in state regulation. For writers such as Owen Fiss and Cass Sunstein, who have argued for a civic republican perspective of the First Amendment in which the importance of participation in community affairs among equal citizens is stressed, state intervention in the marketplace may be judged in a more positive light where it serves the purpose of enriching public debate. Their starting point is the distinctive emphasis upon informed popular sovereignty in the US Constitution. This in turn requires a reading of the First Amendment that facilitates speech intended as a contribution to public debate. It follows that where the marketplace effectively excludes or drowns out certain ideas or speakers, the state may, in pursuit of the goal

---

148 408 US 92, 96 (1972). As Burger CJ pointed out in an otherwise concurring opinion, Marshall J's subsequent suggestion that government is never permitted to base regulation of expression upon content cannot be reconciled with the fighting words doctrine in *Chaplinsky* v *New Hampshire* 315 US 568 (1942) and other instances of contents-based regulation. See further below.

149 But see F Schauer, 'The Aim and the Target in Free Speech Methodology' (1989) 83 *Nw U L Rev* 562, 568, who argues that an assessment of the specific content of expression is necessary in First Amendment disputes to determine the value of the expression.

of having all views represented, regulate speech. According to Charles Lawrence, market distortion occurs through racist speech which devalues the speech of non-whites and decreases the likelihood of it reaching the marketplace.[150] Thus an idea that would be endorsed by large numbers of persons where it is offered by a white individual may be given less credence because it is advocated by a non-white speaker in a society where non-whites are stigmatized by racist beliefs. This may work in a subtle way where members of the audience are conscious of the need not to appear to let the racial identity of the speaker have any bearing on their responses. Lawrence cites examples of mayoral and gubernatorial elections in New York City and Virginia respectively where exit polls overstated the support among white voters for black candidates, a discrepancy attributed to an unwillingness on the part of white voters to admit even anonymously that they did not vote for the black candidate.[151]

How much silencing of racial and other minorities occurs is, of course, impossible to determine.[152] Once it is conceded that a silencing does occur, it may call for some fairly drastic state action to silence powerful private actors and empower the silenced. This, at any rate, is the position of Fiss.[153] Obviously, the arguments for such a course of action become more compelling when the speech of the more powerful players is pure invective, devoid of an appeal to the intellect, seeking instead to strike at the level of emotion. On this view, the Fourteenth Amendment's Equal Protection guarantee stands for something radically different from the negative conception discussed above.[154] For Fiss, the principle of equality has already required the state to interfere in social structures to outlaw discriminatory practices in housing, education

---

150 C Lawrence, 'If He Hollers Let Him Go: Regulating Racist Speech on Campus' (1990) *Duke L J* 431, 467–8. See also K Mahoney, 'Hate Speech: Affirmation or Contradiction of Freedom of Expression' (1996) *U Ill L Rev* 789, 792 – 'People who are targeted by hate propaganda respond to it by being fearful and withdrawing from full participation in society … They are silenced as their credibility is eroded.'

151 (1990) *Duke LJ* 431, 471 citing 'Broad Disparities in Votes and Polls Raising Questions', *New York Times* (1989) 9 November. See also in the context of the silencing of women, C Weiss and L Melling, 'The Legal Education of Twenty Women' (1988) 40 *Stan L Rev* 1299, 1336, where the authors' empirical study of graduate law students revealed aspects of gender-based silencing in higher education. 'There were times when women made points, and they were ignored or trivialized. Five minutes later, a man would make the same point, in three parts, and it was discussed.' The effect of this and other treatment was to make the women retreat to form their own community.

152 C Mackinnon, *Toward a Feminist Theory of the State* (1989, Harvard University Press, Harvard MA) 206.

153 *The Irony of Free Speech* (1996, Harvard University Press, Harvard MA) at 18. The Framers of the US Constitution also envisaged a positive role for the state in protecting citizens from the harms which might be inflicted by private power: S Holmes 'Liberal Constraints on Private Power? Reflections on the Origins and Rationale of Access Regulation' in J Lichtenberg (ed.), *Democracy and the Mass Media* (1990, CUP, Cambridge).

154 For a similar negative reading of the Fourteenth Amendment, see A Amar, 'The Case of the Missing Amendments' (1992) 106 *Harv L Rev* 124.

and other government programmes.[155] Why should First Amendment discourse not be mediated by this positive conception of equality?

Of course, the argument which asserts the need for an equalization of opportunities for minority groups' expression has much wider implications for the regulation of the media, some of which are touched on elsewhere in this book. A commitment to equal access would seem to require *inter alia* the revision of current rules on political parties' election expenditure, positive media access rights for minority groups as well as a right to reply for persons aggrieved by media coverage. Fiss's argument has met with criticism from those who say it rests upon an inappropriately passive conception of the citizen – that is someone who is unable to respond and participate in public debate.[156] In the particular context of cross-burning, however, it is not clear how a rebuttal of racist ideology is to be expected from the members of a black family who are woken in the night to find a gang of white youths burning a cross inside the family plot.

Instances where the Supreme Court has read the First Amendment in a manner that seeks expressly to incorporate the value of equality are hard to find. The closest it may have come was arguably *Beauharnais* v *Illinois* where on a 5–4 split the Supreme Court affirmed the constitutionality of a provision of the Illinois Criminal Code which prohibited the publication of material which

> … portrays depravity, criminality, unchastity, or lack of virtue of a class of citizens which exposes the citizens of any race, color, creed or religion to contempt, derision, or obloquy or which is productive of breach of the peace or riots.[157]

The defendant had distributed leaflets which asserted that white people, their property, neighbourhoods and persons were under assault from 'the Negro'. He went on to refer to the 'rapes, robberies, knives, guns and marijuana of the negro' and called upon white people to unite against the threat of being 'mongrelized by the negro'. Upon conviction in the municipal court of Chicago, Beauharnais appealed against his conviction on the ground that the Code violated his First Amendment rights. In upholding the impugned provision, Frankfurter J for the Court noted the history of racial tension and violence in Illinois and, whilst not certain that the legislature's preferred method of combating the problem would necessarily be successful, declared that the Constitution did not prevent the State punishing the libellous utterances of the defendant. Nonetheless, long before the ruling in *RAV*, the notion that *Beauharnais* rendered publishers of group libel beyond the protective ambit of the First Amendment had been discarded. In *New*

155 Most recently in *Grutter* v *Bollinger et al.* 288 F.3d 732 (2003), the use of racial preferences (alongside other factors) by the Law School at Michigan University was held by the Supreme Court to be narrowly tailored to furthering a compelling interest in obtaining the benefits which flow from a diverse student body. As such it did not violate the Equal Protection Clause.

156 See thus P Horwitz, 'Citizenship and Speech. A Review of Owen M Fiss' (1998) 43 *McGill LJ* 445.

157 343 US 250 (1952).

York Times v *Sullivan* the robust constitutional protection offered to the discussion of public issues (which extends to debates about racial matters) appeared to signal the demise of group libel as a basis for restraining racial invective.[158] After *RAV*, all doubts were removed. There, support for the negative or libertarian conception of equality emerges in the Court opinion given by Scalia J.[159] In sharp contrast, strands of civic republicanism are to be found in the separate opinion given by White J as well as the concurrence from Stevens J.

Re-writing the First Amendment – RAV *v* City of St Paul, Minnesota

Prior to this case, the Court still appeared committed to a tiered understanding of First Amendment freedoms which meant that regulation of political speech met with a more exacting form of judicial scrutiny than was applied to the regulation of commercial, artistic and non-obscene sexually explicit expression.[160] On this account, other categories of speech such as child pornography, obscenity and libellous statements about private individuals were wholly outside the First Amendment's protective ambit on account of the *de minimus* value to society of such expression. Also within this unprotected category were 'fighting words', defined in *Chaplinsky* v *New Hampshire* to mean those words 'which by their very utterance inflict injury or tend to incite an immediate breach of the peace'.[161] Chaplinsky had been convicted for calling a City Marshall a 'God-damned racketeer' and a 'damned fascist'. His remarks, whilst plainly of a political nature and addressed to a public official who might be reasonably expected to show a measure of self-restraint, were nonetheless outside the reach of the First Amendment. The extremely slight contribution to the exchange of ideas made by Chaplinsky's epithets and, conversely, the considerable danger of public disorder created by them meant that the conviction raised no constitutional problem.

In *RAV* v *City of St Paul, Minnesota* a unanimous Court struck down a city ordinance which purported to outlaw *inter alia* the burning of crosses which could reasonably be known to arouse anger, alarm or resentment in others on the basis of race, colour, creed, religion or gender.[162] Writing the Court opinion, Justice

158 376 US 254 (1964). But see K Lasson, 'Racial Defamation as Free Speech: Abusing the First Amendment' (1985) 17 *Colum Hum Rts L Rev* 11, and R Delgado, 'Words that Wound: A Tort Action for Racial Insults, Epithets and Name-Calling' (1982) 17 *Harv CR-CL Rev* 133 for the argument that *Beauharnais* might withstand a First Amendment challenge.

159 A Amar, 'The Case of the Missing Amendments' (1992) 106 *Harv L Rev* 124.

160 W Brennan, 'The Supreme Court and the Meiklejohn Interpretation of the First Amendment' (1965) 79 *Harv L Rev* 1, 11.

161 315 US 568 (1942).

162 505 US 377 (1992). In full, the ordinance stated, 'Whoever places on public or private property a symbol, object, appellation, characterization or graffiti, including but not limited to, a burning cross or Nazi swastika, which one knows or has reasonable grounds to know arouses anger, alarm or resentment in others on the basis of race, color, creed, religion or gender, commits disorderly conduct and shall be guilty of a misdemeanour'. The ordinance had been read down by the Minnesota Supreme Court to reach only those symbolic expressions of

Scalia[163] cast aside the idea that fighting words and other forms of *de minimus* expression were entirely invisible to the Constitution, laying down what one commentator called 'an ambitious reconceptualization and synthesis of First Amendment doctrine'.[164] Fighting words (that is, proscribable words), it seems, were entitled to First Amendment protection after all where, as here, the state was purporting to impose a contents-based restriction on expression. The city's selection of particular subsets of 'fighting words' meant that speakers who wished to air their views on disfavoured subjects could be caught by the ordinance whilst others who provoked anger, alarm or resentment on the bases of political affiliation, trade union membership or homosexuality were outside its sweep. Race-based fighting words (or symbolic acts) were to be treated differently from other sorts of fighting words. Moreover, the explicit examples cited in the ordinance (swastikas and cross-burning) suggested viewpoint discrimination might also be afoot. In any event, the selection of disfavoured subjects resulted in an under-inclusive set of speech curbs. The selection was not 'reasonably necessary' to advance the interests of groups whose members were the victims of discrimination. An ordinance not limited to the disfavoured subjects would have had the same effect. Somewhat paradoxically then, to have avoided a First Amendment challenge, the Court was obliging St Paul to have suppressed even more expressive activity. Here, as in *Mosley*, the Court required the state to be neutral as between topics which incited strong or virulently expressed views. Governmental intervention could only serve to distort the marketplace of ideas and intrude improperly upon the autonomy of individual speakers and listeners.[165]

The separate opinion given by White J and joined by Blackmun and Connor JJ (and for the most part by Stevens J) concurred in the conclusion that St Paul's ordinance was constitutionally invalid but chose to do so on overbreadth grounds,

---

hate speech which constituted fighting words. The US Supreme Court proceeded on the basis of this limiting construction.

163 Joined by Rehnquist CJ and Kennedy, Souter and Thomas JJ.

164 A R Amar, 'The Case of the Missing Amendments' (1992) 106 *Harv L Rev* 124, 127.

165 An interesting issue to arise shortly after *RAV* was whether statutes imposing enhanced penalties for crimes motivated by hatred against racial or religious groups also violated the First Amendment. In *Wisconsin* v *Mitchell* 508 US 476 (1993) the Supreme Court rejected this view. The ruling was controversial because in cases where there is a communicative element to the motives for the defendant's conduct (such as wishing to convey a message of physical superiority) the Court appeared to be allowing the state to mete out additional punishment to those advocating unpopular views. For support see I Hare, 'Legislating Against Hate – The Legal Response to Bias Crimes' (1997) 17 *OJLS* 415, 427–9. For criticism, see S Gey, 'What if *Wisconsin* v *Mitchell* had involved Martin Luther King Jr? The Constitutional Flaws of Hate Crime Enhancement Statutes' (1997) 65 *Geo Was L Rev* 1014. For a further defence, see C Sunstein, *Democracy and the Problem of Free Speech* (1993, The Free Press, New York) at 193–7, who argues that the enhancement penalty in the Wisconsin statute can be read as a contents-neutral restriction on conduct that is not 'ordinarily expressive'.

launching in the process a vigorous attack on the 'folly' of the Court's opinion in overturning settled First Amendment precepts.[166] Justice White situated his analysis of the ordinance within the historical context of cross-burning and referred to the harms suffered by the target group. He concluded that cross-burning done with the intent to intimidate on the basis of race constituted a form of 'fighting words' that was beyond the ambit of the First Amendment. However, St Paul still needed to show for the purposes of the Equal Protection Clause that its restriction advanced a compelling state interest in a reasonable manner. St Paul had judged that harms based on race, colour, creed, religion and gender were more pressing public concerns than harms caused by speech attacking others on the basis of trade union membership or political affiliation. For White J, '… in the light of our Nation's long and painful experience with discrimination, this determination is plainly reasonable'.[167] Stevens J made much the same point, noting that selective proscription of unprotected expression directed at particular groups could be constitutional if the state has *reasonably* determined that the harm caused by the regulated expression is more serious than the harm caused by the unregulated expression.[168] St Paul had made a reasonable determination. In some respects the ban was quite narrow. It did not outlaw all cross-burnings, only those which were threatening because they were directed at an individual or group. Neither did it prevent the espousal of views of racial superiority. So construed, it was difficult to maintain that St Paul was set on driving out speech about race or the advocacy of white supremacy altogether from the marketplace of ideas.[169] By contrast, the Court's revision of the categorical approach amounted to an 'adventure in doctrinal wonderland'.

Somewhat more tersely, Blackmun J commented that whilst

> … no First Amendment values … are compromised by a law that prohibits hoodlums from driving minorities out of their homes by burning crosses on their lawns … [there was] great harm in preventing the people of St Paul from specifically punishing the race-based fighting words that so prejudice their community.

Running through these separate opinions are strands of thinking that more obviously reflect civic republican concerns. References to the history and practice of cross-burning as a method of intimidating and silencing a section of the community (as well as other harms to society) and an inclination to read the ordinance as a legitimate means of lifting a barrier to black participation in societal affairs look to rest upon a conception of the common good in which the political equality of all citizens is highly valued and protected. The position of White, Stevens and Blackmun JJ may

166 For White J the ordinance was overbroad because it reached beyond 'fighting words' to impact on speech which merely caused hurt feelings or gave offence.

167 505 US 377, 402 (1992).

168 In *Ginsberg* v *New York* 390 US 629 (1968) the harms caused to minors by obtaining obscene publications justified a law prohibiting sale of such materials to minors.

169 The force of this point is missed by supporters of content neutrality.

thus be seen as underpinned by recognition of the benefits to deliberative democracy of increased participation of hitherto under-represented groups in political debate.

Virginia *v* Black – *Reaping* RAV's *Bitter Harvest?*

In its ambitious re-write of First Amendment doctrine, the Court in *RAV* did fashion a set of exceptions whereby a contents-based restraint on proscribable expression would not violate the First Amendment. One of these was said to exist where the basis of the restraint 'consists entirely of the very reason its entire class of speech is proscribable'. The example given in *RAV* related to the crime of threatening violence against the President. This was a contents-based ban on speech which was First Amendment-compliant. The reason for the offence (to protect an individual – the President – from fear and disruption induced by threats of violence) is the very reason the wider class of words threatening violence are unprotected. In *Virginia* v *Black* the scope of the exception was explored for the first time.[170] The Commonwealth of Virginia had enacted a statute which made cross-burning on private or public property with 'an intent to intimidate' a criminal offence. Unlike the St Paul ordinance, no reference was made to any disfavoured topics. The statute also provided that the burning of any cross 'shall be prima facie evidence of an intent to intimidate a person or a group or persons'. Three respondents were convicted separately of cross-burning and now questioned the constitutionality of the statute before the US Supreme Court. Two questions fell to be resolved. First, could a State, consistent with the First Amendment, ban cross-burning done with the intent to intimidate? Second, could the evidence provision as interpreted in the model jury instruction (and used to convict Black) survive First Amendment scrutiny?

On the first question, a majority of the Court held that a State could, without violating the First Amendment, ban cross-burning done with an intent to intimidate. The offence was akin to the federal ban on threatening violence against the President. The reason for Virginia's ban was to prohibit only those intimidatory forms most likely to cause fear in others of unlawful violence. It did not prohibit cross-burning done with an intention to intimidate selectively on the basis of colour, race, religion, etc. Cross-burning connected with all viewpoints was caught, provided it was done with an intention to intimidate. Accordingly, the Virginia statute did not violate the First Amendment.

A minority led by Souter J disputed the conclusion that the statute fell within the permitted exception under *RAV* to the general ban on contents-based restrictions. Threats against the President were not usually identified by reference to the content of any message accompanying the threat. Millions of statements were made about the President every day from every standpoint. The differential treatment of threats

170 262 Va.764, 553 S.E. 2d 738 (2003) affirmed in part, vacated in part available electronically at http://supct.law.cornell.edu/supct/html/01-1107.ZS.html. For comment see I Hare, 'Method and Objectivity in Free Speech Jurisprudence: Lessons from America' (2005) 54 *ICLQ* 49.

within this category was not related to any viewpoint expressed in the threat but rather the special risk they appeared to pose to the President's safety. By contrast, in the case of a selective ban on intimidatory cross-burning, it could not be entirely discounted that, given the history of cross-burning, the message of white supremacy was also being targeted, thus raising the spectre of viewpoint discrimination. For Souter J a content-neutral statute banning intimidatory conduct *per se* would have passed First Amendment scrutiny.[171] An obvious response to this claim is to note that non-intimidatory messages of white supremacy remained entirely unaffected by the statute and hence fears about distortion of the marketplace of ideas were somewhat misplaced.

On the second question, the evidence provision was held by a majority of 7–2 to create an unacceptable risk of the suppression of ideas. The provision skewed jury deliberations towards conviction in cases where the evidence of intimidation was weak or equivocal, and where the act of cross-burning was possibly consistent with the expression of political ideas. It had the effect of tending to bring non-threatening ideological cross-burning within the ambit of the offence.

By the time *Virginia* v *Black* reached the Supreme Court, the retirement of more civic republican-minded elements of the Court (White and Blackmun JJ)[172] meant that a counter-assault on the controversial re-write of First Amendment doctrine that occurred in *RAV* was far less likely.[173] *Chaplinsky* had offered local authorities the prospect that the selective regulation of expressive conduct which was based upon a realistic assessment about the intimidation of minority communities would lie beyond any First Amendment challenge. *RAV* shattered this possibility. Today, the Court is left in cases such as *Virginia* v *Black* to work through the implications of the *ad hoc* reasoning in *RAV*. As is apparent, the results may not always convince. The majority's conclusion that Virginia's contents-based statute fell within the same exceptional category as a statute dealing with threats against the President because both dealt with threats particularly likely to cause fear, disruption and injury in others stands uneasily alongside the outcome in *RAV*. St Paul's contents-based ordinance

171 See in support of this conclusion I Hare, 'Inflammatory Speech: Cross-Burning and the First Amendment' (2003) *PL* 408, 413.

172 For further evidence of civic republican strands in these judges' reasoning see *Smith* v *Collin* (the Skokie case) where Blackmun and White JJ disagreed with the majority's refusal to review the decision of the lower courts. They wished to examine the Skokie ordinances which prevented variously the dissemination of materials that promoted/incited racial hatred and the wearing of military-style uniforms. They favoured closer examination in part because of the 'potentially explosive and dangerous situation, inflamed by unforgettable recollections of traumatic experiences in the Second World War conflict … When citizens assert, not casually but with deep conviction, that the proposed demonstration is scheduled at a place and in a manner that is taunting and overwhelmingly offensive to the citizens of that place, that assertion . . . deserves to be examined.' Cert. denied 439 US 916 (1978), 918.

173 Of the original panel of Justices rejecting Scalia J's opinion in *RAV*, O'Connor J simply tried to apply its reasoning in *Virginia* v *Black*. Stevens J by contrast reiterated his view in *RAV* that threats of violence may be treated discriminately.

also looked to be based upon a judgment that harms caused by racial, religious and gender-based invective in St Paul were qualitatively different and more serious than harms caused by other forms of fighting words. One solution is to argue, like Hare, that the First Amendment required the striking down of the Virginia statute for viewpoint discrimination.[174] In this chapter, I have suggested that this position is premised on *RAV*'s misconceived dismantling of the hierarchical categories of protected expression previously established in the First Amendment. Restored to its rightful place, *Chaplinsky* offers a defensible starting point for contents-based regulation of expression intended or likely to engender group-based hatred.

Conclusion – Coerced Communities or Common Venture?

For the opponents of hate speech regulation outlined in this chapter, legal constraints on expressive activity are premised upon the misconceived notion that a polity has the potential to become a 'true' community of shared values and mutual bonding. The resort to law (including legal restraints on expressive activity) constitutes an improper attempt by the state to force dissenters to join (or at least suppress their outward dissent from) a community of shared values. The role of the state in defining community values, and thus defining the community itself, is then at the nub of the dispute. For many liberals, 'true' communities are unforced, freely chosen associations of autonomous individuals that come together spontaneously on account of their commonly held values such as empathy, tolerance and altruism. Law can have little or no role in constituting a polity into a community. Its function is simply to protect the possibility of community. Any wider role threatens individual autonomy and is to be resisted. Neuborne makes the distinction between this type of association and looser, group-based human endeavours designed to generate tangible benefits for individual participants which he labels 'common enterprises'.[175] The latter may require a measure of legal control to ensure everyone has fair access to resources and opportunities. On his view, the state is a common enterprise, albeit one on a giant scale that may require legal regulation to overcome individual objections to the participation of outsiders in the political system (for example, in seeking to deny others the vote). Neighbourhoods, it seems, are smaller-scale versions of common enterprises. The purpose behind the true community/common enterprise distinction is to place strict limits on what legal regulation may strive to achieve. As Neuborne himself asserts,

> [T]he distinction … is designed to eliminate bruised emotions as a justification for censorship and to force a would-be censor to demonstrate a tangible interference with something more concrete … An alleged bad tendency to cause a speculative harm to an entire group, however, can never be enough to justify censorship. Sociological theories,

174 'Inflammatory Speech: Cross-Burning and the First Amendment' (2003) *PL* 408.

175 B Neuborne, 'Ghosts in the Attic: Idealized Pluralism, Community and Hate Speech' (1992) 27 *Harv CR-CL L Rev* 371.

> even passionately held ones, about the adverse impact of unpopular speech on a category of hearers cannot justify censorship … .'[176]

Tangible harm might be evidenced by factual findings of *inter alia* the targeting of a specific individual, impaired participation by the target in the polity and the foreseeability and reasonableness of this adverse reaction. Unfortunately, Neuborne is not very forthcoming about the sorts of factual finding that might satisfy these indices of tangible harm. To take one criterion, it is by no means clear how he proposes to isolate and measure the 'impaired participation' of target groups in the polity that some claim springs from virulent anti-minority speech.

More fundamentally, the requirement of tangible harm may deflect attention away from the subtle ways in which hateful expression serves to oppress its targets. As academic contributors to the debate on pornography have similarly argued in respect of much sexually explicit material,[177] the toleration of hateful expression promotes an ideology that encourages and maintains disrespect and hostility towards minority groups and their members. Trying to prove that direct harm results from such speech is, as Kathleen Mahoney has remarked,

> … like trying to prove that alcohol causes traffic deaths… The links are suggestive but none of them are dispositive. The liberal requirement to prove 'clear and present danger' ignores these realities and analytically predetermines the issue …'[178]

Neuborne for his part would doubtless approve of the Supreme Court's ruling in *RAV* v *City of St Paul, Minnesota* since the ordinance there sought to prohibit expressive activity in order to coerce a community of shared values and mutual regard. Whilst the burning of a cross on a black family's private land at night ought to (and could) have been made subject to another, appropriately drafted criminal sanction without raising First Amendment issues,[179] Neuborne notes that the ordinance also would have swept up cross-burning in a vacant parking lot at a rally protesting at the family's arrival. In this instance, a legal response was not appropriate because of the absence of harm/loss of a tangible benefit to an identifiable person.[180]

By contrast with the natural, unforced communities that he sees at home, Neuborne paints a vivid picture of the coerced or 'ersatz' communities that he observes on foreign soil. In a striking section of prose, he claims that it is in these communities that hatred, fear and distrust are perpetuated. Warming to his theme, he continues by warning us that coerced communities:

---

176 *Ibid.*, at 393.

177 KE Mahoney, 'Destruction of Women's Rights through Mass Media' in KE Mahoney and P Mahoney (eds), *Human Rights in the Twenty First Century: A Global Challenge* (1995, Martinus Nijhoff, Dordrecht) and see Chapter 6 of this book.

178 *Ibid.*, at 766.

179 On the ground, for example, of inducing fear of physical harm.

180 To be fair, even the more communitarian-minded members of the Court accepted that this application of the ordinance rendered it overbroad.

> … use force to impose a false façade of unity, a process that has very often resulted in procrustean abuse and tyranny, without materially advancing the values of caring and humanity that make true community worth striving for.[181]

Leaving aside for one moment the unfortunate resort to offence to religious feelings in ECHR jurisprudence, this passage will strike many commentators outside the United States as startling and begs many questions. What support does he have for the claim of 'procrustean abuse and tyranny'? Few European citizens would recognize this description of their polities. Is he also claiming that legislation which proclaims non-toleration of vilificatory racial speech has contributed nothing to improved race relations but a false façade of unity? An alternative and preferable way of approaching the contrast between US and European regulatory systems is to inquire whether, to the extent that Europe's laws variously impede the expression of hateful expression, citizens on this side of the Atlantic are worse off (or more accurately are less well informed as electors and participants in the political affairs of their communities) by virtue of being denied certain opportunities to receive the outpourings of racist, xenophobic and other hateful speakers. It may further be asked whether members of minority communities are to some extent empowered in their daily lives upon encountering hateful expression by the knowledge of its official proscription.

Neuborne's opponents are, moreover, surely entitled to inquire whether the failure to suppress virulent forms of expression directed at minority groups in the US has contributed to a culture where members of those targeted groups participate less in their communities and are more obviously alienated from others. After all, the state is sending conflicting messages about the worth it attaches to minority groups – official promotion of equal opportunities at the workplace and in schools and universities accompanied by dumb silence in face of hate-mongering from members of the dominant community. Ultimately, the weakness in Neuborne's analysis is that it is unwilling to acknowledge the more subtle ways in which hateful expression sustains group-based enmity and the marginalization of individuals within minority groups. Another US First Amendment scholar, Alexander Bickel, was more alive to these concerns in his seminal work *The Morality of Consent*. Some speech, he argued, could amount to verbal violence. More than this, 'it may create a climate, an environment in which conduct and actions that were not possible before become possible ...'.[182]

Constitutions can, however, take a lead in signalling the equal worth of groups at the margins of community life. The South African Human Rights Commission made the point well when it spoke of law as a moral exemplar in that it sends out a clear message of acceptable and unacceptable behaviour in society. It plays a useful and constructive role if seen primarily as providing the social foundations needed

181 (1992) 27 *Harv CR-CL L Rev* 371, 379.

182 (1975, Yale University Press, New Haven CT) 72.

for altering deep-seated values, social attitudes and belief systems.[183] The goal of an inclusive society that recognizes and seeks to address actual inequalities among its communities demands that hateful expression be met with a proportionate legal response using the range of administrative, civil and criminal measures at the state's disposal.

183 *Hate Crimes and Hate Speech in South Africa* (2003, South African Human Rights Commission, Johannesburg).

Chapter 6

Sexually Explicit Expression and the Courts

Introduction

In earlier chapters, I have sought to argue that a unifying feature of advanced liberal democracies is the centrality of deliberative representative government. The commitment to deliberative democracy requires that strong protection be afforded to political speech forms, understood broadly to include intentional contributions to public debate on a range of matters in which citizens ought to be interested. Sexually explicit expression on the other hand appears to have little if any connection to a well-functioning deliberative democracy. The claims of pornography producers and their audiences to expressive freedom rest instead on arguments that connect to deeper-level libertarian arguments for individual autonomy and self-fulfilment. In the case of sexually explicit material about women, the opponents of regulation include some feminist scholars who argue that censorship is actually harmful to women's rights and safety. A past president of the American Civil Liberties Union – Nadine Strossen – has written:

> We adamantly oppose any effort to restrict sexual speech not only because it would violate our cherished First Amendment freedoms – our freedoms to read, think, speak, sing, write, paint, dance, dream, photograph, film and fantasize as we wish – but also because it would undermine our equality, status, our dignity and our autonomy.[1]

On this view, restrictions on pornography rest upon an unjustified paternalistic claim by the state to be acting in the best interests of each woman. Unacknowledged by Strossen however, there may be other, non-paternalist rationales for restriction. Thus, the societal interest in having inclusive forums of public decision-making could be said to support the curtailment of expressive activity that was shown to inhibit participation by a section of the population. As with race-hate expression, whilst conclusive empirical evidence might be nigh on impossible to produce, it might still be entirely reasonable to conclude that where dominant modes of discourse ascribe negative characteristics to particular groups in a society, the goal of attaining an inclusive deliberative democracy requires the state to remove barriers to fuller participation.

---

1 *Defending Pornography* (1996, Abacus, London) at 14.

The central inquiry of this book has been to consider the legitimacy of rights-based judicial intervention with the policy choices of democratically elected legislatures that impinge upon freedom of expression. This chapter looks at justifications offered by courts in their policing of legislatures' policy choices which have invariably sought to suppress the production of, and access to, sexually explicit materials about or directed to children and young persons. In Chapter 5, which looked at the constitutional treatment of hateful expression, I referred to the criticism of US First Amendment doctrine that legislative attempts to address problems of hateful anti-black expression tend to be analysed by the courts exclusively in terms of the damage inflicted (or not) on speech interests. The focus on harms done to speech either denies completely the relevance of harms done to countervailing constitutional values such as equality or privacy or understates the latter types of injury. Where the Fourteenth Amendment guarantee of equal treatment does feature in speech-related disputes, it is invariably cast in negative terms that prevent the state from advancing its view of desirable inter-community relations. Looming large in this essentially libertarian construct of freedom is the conception of the state as a threatening, coercive force that wishes to constitute ersatz communities through acts of censorship against disfavoured speech forms. From this perspective, in the absence of real, tangible harms, the state simply has no business telling people what to think, read, and so on. Similar concerns feature in the debates over the regulation of sexually explicit expression. Opponents of regulation argue that the autonomy of the individual to decide what to read/view justifies placing pornography within constitutional protection for freedom of expression and, moreover, that the courts should take legislative threats to curtail pornography just as seriously as they would limits on speech that dares to criticize the government. Supporters of legislative controls would counter that, to take one example, the limits recently imposed on computer-generated sexually explicit images of children invariably reflect the reasoned outcome of policy debates by legislatures after receiving expert testimony from child psychiatrists on the uses made by paedophiles of such materials.[2] To return to a theme first encountered at the beginning of this book, it is suggested that, for institutional reasons, courts are not best suited to resolve such complex policy questions.

My argument in this chapter is that, across each of the liberal democratic constitutions under consideration in this book, the freedom to produce and view/read non-political (including sexually explicit) materials lacks the central importance rightly conferred on the freedom to engage in political debate in representative systems of government. Instead, the value of sexually explicit speech seems to be linked more loosely to the intellectual growth and maturity of autonomous individuals. Furthermore, if self-fulfilment/autonomy is taken to include making

2 Such a position is not to be read as indicating support for a law-only approach to the problems of internet-based sexually explicit imagery. A multi-faceted approach involving educational strategies, parental supervision, software filtering and other tools of public policy would seem ultimately to offer greater prospects of success. This chapter is only concerned with judicial responses to legislative regulation of the problem.

the most out of oneself or making oneself as wise as possible, the rationale is rendered so open-ended as to fail to mark out speech *in particular* as worthy of protection.[3] Values such as equal respect, individual privacy, religious freedom and freedom of association are also self-evidently relevant to individual development and flourishing. If this argument is correct, it would follow that where a legislative restriction on speech interferes with individual self-fulfilment but is intended to further a conflicting constitutional value and regulates in a morally contested area, then constitutional courts would be justified in adopting a less hostile stance towards a clearly expressed policy choice of the legislature than would be appropriate in cases of majoritarian restrictions of political speech. Arguably, the greatest scope for legislative action ought to exist in respect of harmful sexually explicit materials. By 'harmful' is included materials that present (i) women as either enjoying coerced sexual relations or deserving of forms of physical abuse with a view to producing a state of sexual arousal in the viewer;[4] (ii) child/adult sexual relations as normal.

The principal focus of this chapter concerns the treatment of freedom of expression claims of the creators, distributors and possessors of sexually explicit imagery of children. Before developing my arguments on this topic, it is necessary to address some claims to expressive freedom made by the producers *et al.* of sexually explicit material depicting women. I take these materials to be capable of causing harm in the senses identified by the US legal philosopher Cass Sunstein of (a) causing injury to those women involved in the commercial production of pornography; (b) causing injury to those victims of sex crimes where the perpetrator has been motivated by access to violent sexually explicit materials; (c) contributing to the social conditioning that tolerates discrimination against women and makes it, if anything, less likely that their contributions to public debate and community life will be taken seriously.

Clearly, methodological problems exist in showing a direct causal link between the consumption of sexually explicit materials about women and sexual crimes against women. However, there is considerable empirical evidence to show that through exposure to sexually violent materials, some men become desensitized to the physical harms suffered by women in sexual assaults.[5] There is also victim testimony from the same empirical materials to show that a number of assailants in sexual assault cases were users of pornography.

3 J Lichtenberg (ed.), *Democracy and the Mass Media* (1990, CUP, Cambridge) at 108; G Gunther, *Constitutional Law* (1985, The Foundation Press Inc., New York) Ch. 11.

4 I rely here on elements of Cass Sunstein's approach in 'Pornography and the First Amendment' (1986) *Duke L J* 589.

5 D Zillmann and J Bryant, 'Pornography, Sexual Callousness, and the Trivialization of Rape' (1982) 32 *Journal of Communication* 10; E Donnerstein and D Linz, 'Mass Media Sexual Violence and Male Viewers: Current Theory and Research' (1986) 29 *American Behavioral Scientist* 601.

The more subtle effects of pornography in terms of the harms outlined in (c) above will not, however, register on the libertarian scale that requires a showing of direct, tangible harm. Neither, it might be argued, would harms in category (b), since it would doubtless be claimed that for every attacker who accesses sexually violent material, there are many men who 'enjoy' this type of publication without acting out the depicted scenes in their daily lives. As Mahoney has remarked, resort to the 'clear and present danger' standard 'analytically predetermines the issue in favo(u)r of pornographers'.[6] A commitment to political equality of the sort envisaged in civic republican writing set out in Chapter 1 on the other hand does offer a justification for restrictions on expression that currently plays a role in limiting women's participation in public life. A major difficulty here, though, arises from our inexact understanding of the extent to which much sexually explicit literature inhibits participation in public decision-making structures. Research in social science cannot isolate pornography from other influences and measure its inhibiting impact. This lack of knowledge in turn makes it difficult to gauge what types of restrictions might be needed to further the gaol of an inclusive community of political equals. Nonetheless, to the extent that certain sexually explicit materials play a contributory role in harms suffered by women, the inherent low value of these expressive forms ought to be recognized in constitutional challenges to restrictions imposed by democratically elected legislatures.

A counter-argument that has been aired in respect of materials falling within category (c) above is that, by definition, these materials do in fact express a view about male–female relationships and, as such, might be treated as making a contribution to discourse on social matters, lifting it out of the category of low value expression.[7] The flaw in this position is that the communication of any 'political' statement in pornography will hardly ever be an *intended* consequence of expression. The prime purposes behind publication are, on the part of the publisher, to sell a product and, in respect of purchasers, to achieve a state of sexual arousal. Neither party can plausibly be said to have an intention to further public debate on male–female sexual relations. To characterize men's magazines in this way, however, mistakenly elevates the speech to a status shared with expression that is critical of the government and goes further even than some of the more speech-indulgent members of the US Supreme Court. Take, for example, Justice Stevens in *City of Erie* v *Pap's AM tdba Kandyland* where, in a dissenting judgment, he concluded that the expressive element in nude dancing clubs allowed a successful challenge to an ordinance banning public nudity. In so doing, he nevertheless conceded that the protection enjoyed by nude dancing lay in the 'outer ambit' of

6 'Destruction of Women's Rights through Mass Media' in KE Mahoney and P Mahoney (eds), *Human Rights in the Twenty First Century: A Global Challenge* (1995, Martinus Nijhoff, Dordrecht) at 766.

7 D Feldman, *Human Rights and Civil Liberties in England and Wales* (2002, OUP, Oxford) at 927.

the First Amendment.[8] A further reason for denying men's magazines coordinate status with public interest expression is that the political case for revising attitudes towards sexual relations can be made without recourse to graphic imagery that reinforces notions of male dominance.

Turning to sexually explicit imagery of children, harms may be said to occur in the forms of (a) the actual sexual abuse of a child/young person; (b) the creation of a permanent record of that abuse; and (c) in respect of virtual and actual child pornography – its undoubted role in the conditioning of children and young persons to see paedophile activity as normal. An NSPCC-commissioned survey published in the UK in 2003 concluded that child pornography is used for sexual arousal purposes and to 'legitimate and normalise offenders' sexual activities with children' and as a tool for 'grooming, entrapment and blackmail'.[9] The authors concluded that child pornography 'must continue to be viewed as instrumental in the on-going abuse of children'.[10]

A final introductory point concerns reliance upon prevailing community norms to settle the boundaries of freedom of expression. In the case of sexually explicit materials depicting women and/or children, community standards (as reflected in legislative rule-making) may not reflect a wish to combat all/some of the harms listed above but may instead be religiously influenced and rely upon broad and vaguely defined notions of decency/offensiveness or obscenity. The view that offensiveness *per se* is an appropriate basis for restricting expressive activity cannot be considered an appropriate basis for grounding restrictions on sexually explicit materials, tying as it does in a vaguely defined way the amount of speech tolerated in any community/society to the values of the least tolerant segment of that community or society.

The Regulation of Sexually Explicit Materials About or Directed at Children and Young Persons

Children and younger persons enjoy claims to special protection from the expressive activity of others. This is because they lack the cognitive and judgmental skills that are required to make decisions which can impact greatly on their futures. Summarizing the social science findings, Wald noted that younger children are 'not able to think abstractly, have a limited future time sense and are limited in their ability to generalize and predict from experience'.[11] Clearly moral capacity develops over time (though at different rates) so we should not treat teenagers in the same way

8 529 US 277 (2000).

9 E Renold and S Creighton *et al.*, *Images of Abuse: A Review of the Evidence on Child Pornography* (2003, NSPCC Publications, London).

10 See further an Australian study by P Forde and A Patterson, *Paedophile Internet Activity* (Trends and Issues in Crime and Criminal Justice Paper No. 97) (1998, Australian Institute of Criminology, Canberra).

11 M Wald, 'Children's Rights: A Framework for Analysis' (1979) 12 *UC Davis L Rev* 255, 274.

as we treat toddlers. Neither, however, should we pretend that a 13-year-old has the capacity to make informed personal, moral judgments that most adults have.[12]

Unsurprisingly perhaps, legislative controls on access to sexually explicit materials have run into greatest constitutional difficulty in the US. The Supreme Court's treatment of a panoply of Congressional restrictions impacting directly on sexually explicit expression (as in the case of laws which prohibit both the dissemination of pornography to children or young persons and the production, distribution, sale or possession of actual or virtual child pornography) has demonstrated at times a preoccupation with the rights of adults to receive non-obscene indecent expression whilst managing to understate competing constitutional values. The overriding impression has been of a game of cat and mouse between the Supreme Court and Congress. In comparison (and within their different constitutional contexts), Canadian and UK regulation manage to signal much more clearly the low expressive value which attaches to virtual child pornography. All the same, the decision of the Canadian Supreme Court in *R* v *Sharpe* suggests that a US-influenced hostility to contents-based regulation may be prompting forms of judicial activism that sit uncomfortably with prevailing themes in Canadian political/constitutional culture. Meanwhile, on this side of the Atlantic, the legal regulation of computerized child pornography has typically centred around technical questions of statutory interpretation rather than grander issues of principle. Nonetheless, post-October 2000, it is to be expected that the proportionality of state interference with the right to respect for private life will feature in Convention-based challenges to the legality of the statutory offence of possession. Analysis of Canadian and UK approaches will follow discussion of the First Amendment materials.

Upholding the First Amendment? Some Problems Caused by Hostility to Contents-based Regulation of Sexually Explicit Material

As is well known, the US Supreme Court ruled in *Reno* v *ACLU* that two provisions of the *Communications Decency Act* 1996 (*CDA*) criminalized both the 'knowing' transmission of 'indecent' or 'patently offensive' materials on the Internet to recipients under 18 years and the allowing of minors to access such materials, and concluded that these constituted impermissibly vague and overbroad contents-based restrictions upon speech.[13] In response, Congress drafted a more tightly defined set of provisions in the *Child Online Protection Act* 1997 (*COPA*) which made it an offence for a person to transmit for commercial purposes material over the World Wide Web that is 'harmful to minors'.[14] This latter phrase is defined by reference to

12 A Etzioni, 'On Protecting Children from Speech' (2004) 79 *Uni Chicago-Kent Law Rev* 3.

13 521 US 844 (1997).

14 S.1405 of *COPA* also establishes a Commission to identify and report on technological or other means of reducing young persons' access to harmful material on the Internet.

the three-pronged obscenity test from *Miller* v *California*,[15] which requires jurors to apply a contemporary community standards test when assessing (with respect to minors) whether the material in question appeals to the prurient interest and whether it depicts or describes in a patently offensive way sexual conduct specifically defined by the applicable state law.[16] Excluded from the ambit of *COPA* are materials which, objectively judged, possess serious literary, artistic, political or scientific value. A defence was created for commercial publishers who restrict access to prohibited materials by requiring the use of a credit card or 'any other reasonable measures that are feasible under available technology'.

Web publishers challenged *inter alia* the application of the contemporary community standards test on overbreadth grounds claiming that, in the absence of technological means to control the geographic location of recipients, *COPA* effectively forced all Web speakers to abide by the most puritan community's standards, thereby curtailing some constitutionally protected speech. In May 2002, the Court in *Ashcroft* v *ACLU* upheld *COPA*'s reliance upon community standards with varying degrees of enthusiasm. The strongest defence of variable community standards is to be found in the plurality opinion of Thomas J.[17] He emphasized the relatively narrow class of materials prohibited by Congress, citing the fact that *COPA* applied to Web-based material communicated for commercial purposes only. *CDA* had, by contrast, caught all Internet material including e-mail messages and was not limited to those communications sent for purely commercial purposes. *COPA*'s narrow reach was also evident from the incorporation of both 'prurient interest' and 'serious value' prongs from Miller, neither of which had found their way into *CDA*. When these narrowing features were taken into account, the obligation on a speaker who wished to address a national audience to observe varying community standards could not, in itself, be said to violate the First Amendment.[18] As Thomas J. pointed out, the Court had already upheld resort to community standards in *Hamling* v *United States* in the context of statutes regulating the mailing of obscene material[19] and the use of telephones to make obscene or indecent communications for commercial purposes in *Sable Communications of California* v *FCC*.[20] O'Connor J, for her part, agreed that ACLU had failed to show on the facts that the variation in local community standards would be so great as to render *COPA* substantially overbroad.[21] However, she suggested that the technical burden placed on Internet speakers of controlling the geographic locations in which the speech is received might well permit a future litigant to make a more convincing case for substantial overbreadth. In these

15 413 US 15 (1973). The other prong of the test is that the material, taken as a whole, lacks serious literary, artistic, political or scientific value.

16 See further *Pope* v *Illinois* 481 US 497, 500 (1987).

17 Comprising Rehnquist CJ and Scalia J.

18 535 US 564 (2002).

19 418 US 87 (1974).

20 492 US 115 (1989).

21 Kennedy, Souter and Ginsburg JJ separately doubted that *ACLU* had established overbreadth.

circumstances, the Court should be prepared to consider the adoption of a national, uniform standard of 'patent offensiveness' and 'prurient interest'.[22] The speaker's lack of control over the recipients of speech meant that Justice Thomas's reliance upon *Hamling* and *Sable* was misplaced.[23]

At this stage of legal argument *Ashcroft* v *ACLU* was concerned with a narrow point about the constitutionality of the contemporary community standards test in web-based speech cases. Other issues of First Amendment compliance (principally *COPA*'s alleged vagueness and the application of strict scrutiny analysis) were not argued before the Supreme Court. On remand back to the Third Circuit Court of Appeals, the District Court's grant of a preliminary injunction preventing the enforcement of *COPA* was affirmed principally on the ground that *COPA* did not constitute the least restrictive means of stopping minors accessing sexually explicit materials on the Internet. On appeal to the Supreme Court in June 2004, the majority favoured letting the injunction stand until a full trial on the merits of the case took place.[24] The Government had not shown that it was likely to defeat ACLU's argument that blocking and filtering software represented a less restrictive and more effective means of securing the state's objective than *COPA*'s reliance on credit cards and other age-verification strategies. It was less restrictive because filtering did not criminalize any category of speech, thereby diminishing the potential chill on protected adult-to-adult speech. Furthermore, adults might access protected speech without having to give their credit card details. Filtering was also more effective than *COPA* because it caught all pornography posted on the Web, not just material uploaded from the US. Filters caught not just web-based materials but also e-mails and other forms of Internet communication. Evidence also existed that verification systems were prone to evasion and circumvention.

In separate legislative moves post-*Reno*, Congress also made federal subsidies for schools' and libraries' Internet access conditional upon the adoption of filtering software that screens out material deemed harmful to minors in the *Children's Internet Protection Act* 2000 (*CIPA*)[25] and, in an effort to curtail paedophiles' use

22 She envisaged juries across Maine, Mississippi, Las Vegas and New York City being asked to decide whether the 'nationwide community of adults' would find the charged material to appeal to the prurient interest and patently offensive. Whether as a matter of practice this would overcome the problem of imposing the least tolerant community's standards upon all persons within the jurisdiction is perhaps questionable.

23 See also Kennedy, Souter and Ginsburg JJ.

24 542 US 656 (2004).

25 If Congressional attempts to stem the flow of virtual child pornography via the criminal law have run into considerable First Amendment difficulties, the same cannot be said in respect of other federal legislation which makes federal funding programmes for Internet access in public libraries dependent upon the installation of blocking software. The lesson of *United States* v *American Library Association* 593 US 194 (2003) seems to be that if the legislature opts to use its considerable funding powers to promote on a contents-basis selective access to internet materials rather than going down the route of imposing criminal sanctions for disseminating and/or accessing non-obscene materials, the First Amendment

of internet images of children, passed the *Child Pornography Prevention Act* 1996 (*CPPA*). The latter measure prohibited the distribution, receipt or possession of an image that 'appears to be of a minor engaged in sexually explicit conduct'[26] or 'conveys' that impression.[27] In conflicting rulings from the lower courts, *CPPA* was held by First Circuit Court of Appeals not to infringe the First Amendment,[28] whilst the Ninth Circuit reached the contrary conclusion.[29] The Supreme Court has now pronounced upon the constitutionality of these criminal offences. An analysis of the Court's regulation of sexually explicit speech in respect of virtual child pornography follows later in this chapter.

Some Enduring First Amendment Themes and an Analytical Framework[30]

In Chapter 2, we saw that the abstract or open-textured nature of constitutional guarantees such as the First Amendment obliges each generation of Supreme Court judges to look beyond the terms of the written Constitution to have an understanding of the central themes or settled values which underpin the corpus of First Amendment jurisprudence and then to apply that understanding to the individual cases that come before them. Unsurprisingly, judicial and academic attempts to distil these themes/values have generated much controversy. Nonetheless, over time Supreme Court jurisprudence has yielded up a body of basic principles that can lay claim to general acceptance. One principle commanding widespread support maintains that not all speech forms enjoy the same level of protection from state interference.[31] On this view, the First Amendment is predicated upon a tiered system of speech forms in which 'political' speech is accorded greater protection than lower value speech forms such as pure commercial or artistic expression.[32] Significantly, however, in the context of sexually explicit expression, obscene speech and child pornography involving the use of actual children have all been cast outside the protective ambit of

---

offers little resistance. See I Cram, 'Unconstitutional conditions? – Public Libraries, Federal Subsidies and the Internet' (2004) 8 *Communications Law* 417, discussing *CIPA*.

26 S.2256(8)(B).

27 S.2256(8)(D).

28 *United States* v *Hilton* 167 F. 3d. 61 (First Cir. 1999).

29 *Free Speech Coalition* v *Reno* 68 *Law Week* 1381 (Ninth Cir. 2000).

30 An earlier version of this section appeared as 'Beyond Madison? The Supreme Court and the regulation of sexually explicit expression' (2002) *PL* 743.

31 See thus the Supreme Court rulings in *Chaplinsky* v *New Hampshire* 315 US 568 (1942); *Dennis* v *United States* 341 US 494 (1951); *Gertz* v *Robert Welch Inc.* 418 US 323 (1974); *Virginia Pharmacy Board* v *Virginia Consumer Council* 425 US 748 (1976); *Dun & Bradstreet Inc.* v *Greenmoss Builders Inc.* 472 US 749 (1985). See further C. Sunstein, *Democracy and the Problem of Free Speech* (1993, Free Press, New York); G. Stone, 'Content-Neutral Restrictions' (1987) 54 *Univ Chic L Rev* 46.

32 Line drawing between 'political' and 'commercial' or 'artistic' speech forms may not always be convincing or command universal agreement but this fact alone does not mean that the distinction should be discarded.

the First Amendment altogether on the basis that the value of the expressive conduct to society is *de minimus*.[33] This hierarchy of speech protection may be traced back to the Constitution's distinctive emphasis upon popular sovereignty. James Madison, the author of the First Amendment, famously contrasted the British system of government where sovereignty rested with the King in Parliament to that established under the US Constitution where 'the People, not the Government, possess the absolute sovereignty'.[34] To function effectively, popular sovereignty requires public access to information and opinions so as to make informed decisions. If this is granted, it would seem to follow that political speech – that is speech 'intended and received as a contribution to public deliberation about some issue'[35] – ought to be the central concern of the First Amendment and accorded the highest level of protection from governmental interference. The self-interested motives of government for suppressing such speech forms provide a supporting reason to uphold strict judicial oversight.[36] Accordingly, restrictions on political speech must satisfy an especially heavy burden of proof – namely clear and compelling evidence of substantial and imminent harm to a legitimate state interest.[37] Moreover, they must not be overbroad and strike at otherwise protected expression.[38]

Consistent with this view, speech falling outside the definition of political speech, such as commercial advertising, artistic expression or non-obscene sexually explicit speech, belongs to the lower tier of protected expression. However, even lower value speech is deemed worthy of some protection and may be regulated only where the restriction advances a substantial government interest in a proportionate manner and does not inadvertently chill political speech.[39] This degree of protection is usually justified on two grounds, although, as shall be argued, the second of these offers a comparatively weak basis for protecting speech claims against competing state and individual interests. The first defence of lower level speech claims can be traced

33 This is despite the fact that the categorization of obscene speech as morally offensive or corrosive is plainly contents-based. See respectively *Miller* v *California* 413 US 15 (1973) and *New York* v *Ferber* 458 US 747 (1982). Other examples of unprotected contents-based categories of expression include defamation of private figures (*Gertz* v *Robert Welch* 418 US 323 (1974)) and 'fighting words' (*Chaplinsky* v *New Hampshire* 315 US 568 (1942)).

34 Report on the Virginia Resolution, January 1800 *6 Papers of James Madison* 385.

35 This is the definition preferred by C. Sunstein, *Democracy and the Problem of Free Speech* (1993, Macmillan, New York) at 130.

36 See for example *New York Times* v *Sullivan* 376 US 254 (1964); *New York Times* v *United States* (Pentagon Papers case) 403 US 713 (1971). See the academic work of F Schauer, *Free Speech – a Philosophical Inquiry* (1982, CUP, Cambridge) and TM Scanlon, 'A Theory of Freedom of Expression' (1972) 1 *Philosophy and Public Affairs* 204, on this point.

37 See for example the test of 'clear and present danger of imminent and serious evil' adopted by the Court in *Bridges* v *California* 314 US 252 (1941) applied to restrictions on speech pertaining to court proceedings.

38 *Broadrick* v *Oklahoma* 413 US 601 (1973).

39 *Central Hudson Gas & Electricity* v *Public Service Commission* 447 US 557 (1980).

back to Madison. In essence, it argues that contents-based restrictions prompted by official disagreement with the message contained in the material are contrary to the Madisonian ideal of protecting speech at odds with the view of the state. Non-obscene sexually explicit speech, for example, whilst falling short of an intentional contribution to public deliberation about some issue, might nonetheless be considered to convey a message about forms of sexual conduct at odds with, and therefore challenging to, prevailing norms. On these lines, the Supreme Court, affirming the Seventh Circuit of Appeals, struck down an Indianapolis anti-pornography ordinance in *American Booksellers Association* v *Hudnut*,[40] on the basis that it attempted to establish and enforce an approved view of women and relations between the sexes violated the First Amendment. It is difficult to know what is more troubling about the reasoning in *Hudnut* – the ease with which the court is prepared to discover a contribution to societal debate in *Hustler* and *Mayfair* or the disinclination to accord respect to a determination made in good faith by politically accountable authorities about the harms caused to women in particular and society in general through the availability of pornography. The sentiment that virtually anything counts as a contribution to debate under the First Amendment was vividly demonstrated post-*Hudnut* when it was successfully invoked by the rap artist Dr Dre against a ban imposed by local authorities in Detroit and Auburn Hills on the showing of a video at his concerts. The video included scenes of a gunfight at a liquor store as well as shots of topless women. Without having to go to court, Dr Dre was apparently content for the two authorities to pay his legal fees and for the respective police forces to attend classes in First Amendment sensitivity training.[41]

Second, regulations which are motivated by a concern that people may be influenced or offended by the messages contained within communications undermine other core precepts in First Amendment thinking – the linked notions of listener autonomy and the self-fulfilment of individuals.[42] The emotional and intellectual maturation of individuals requires them to have access to a wide variety of ideas and information. The cogency of the connection between self-fulfilment and expressive freedom is, however, questionable. It is apparent for example that if, as most agree, autonomy is taken to include making the most of oneself, it is difficult to see why speech in particular ought to be singled out for especial protection. After all, values such as equal respect, individual privacy, religious freedom and freedom of association are also relevant to individual development and flourishing. In the case of child pornography, the weakness of the self-fulfilment rationale is compounded by the fact that arguments for restrictions on speech rest

40 475 US 1001 (1986).

41 See further: http://news.bbc.co.uk/hi/english/entertainment/music/newsid_1953000/1953026.stm.

42 See Brandeis J in *Whitney* v *California* 274 US 357, 374 (1927): 'Those who won our independence believed that the final end of the state was to make men free to develop their faculties… .' For an instance of offensive political speech see *Cohen* v *California* 403 US 15 (1971). See further TM Scanlon, 'A Theory of Freedom of Expression' (1972) 1 *Philosophy and Public Affairs* 204.

on broader claims to privacy and equal respect which enjoy constitutional status. Accordingly, in the case of legislative restrictions on speech intended to further a conflicting constitutional value, the Court might be justified in adopting a less hostile stance than might be appropriate in cases of other majoritarian restrictions of political speech. This deferential approach to federal and state restrictions on sexually explicit imagery of children commended itself to the Court in *New York* v *Ferber*. New York's compelling interest in the well-being of its youth and the particular vulnerability of children was held to confer some latitude on the state to regulate pornographic material.[43] Support for an attenuated standard of review in respect of the regulation of sexually explicit expression is additionally evident in the dissenting opinions in *United States* v *Playboy Entertainment Group Ltd.* A challenge was taken in respect of a statute designed to shield children from 'signal bleed' – the phenomenon whereby audio and/or visual portions of programmes scrambled for paying audiences may be heard/seen by non-payers.[44] Section 505 of the *Telecommunications Act* 1996 required cable television operators either to 'fully scramble or otherwise fully block' programming consisting of primarily sexually explicit material or to limit transmission of the same to the period between 10pm and 6am unless a subscriber asked to receive it. Most cable operators chose to limit the transmission to the late evening/early morning period. Given that some 30 to 50 per cent of all adult programming was apparently viewed in households before 10pm, a significant reduction in communicative activity (and, hence, Playboy's revenues) resulted from s.505. The majority applied a strict scrutiny standard to the 1996 Act and held that the state had failed to show that s.505 represented the least restrictive means of shielding children when parents could expressly request cable operators to be opted out of sexually explicit programming under s.504 of the same Act. In a dissenting opinion which can be read as essentially Madisonian in approach,[45] Breyer J faulted the majority's adoption of a strict scrutiny standard. Noting that the statute regulated commercial actors broadcasting 'virtually 100% sexually explicit material', and that it required cable operators to use better scrambling technology or confine broadcasting the period between 10pm and 6am (thereby not prohibiting sexually explicit expression altogether), he concluded that the narrow tailoring concerns presented in other cases were absent here. In particular, the material could not be said to have an obvious informational character (such as in *Reno* where non-commercial material, including birth control advice, was caught by the *Communications Decency Act* 1996). Nor, unlike *Reno*, did the statute purport to impose an absolute ban on the communicative activity. Viewed in this light, the proper question for the Court was whether, allowing a degree of discretion to the legislature in deciding among regulatory strategies, s.505 constituted an excessive means of ensuring that children did not have access to sexually explicit programmes. Finding that it did not, Breyer J relied on recent

43 458 US 747 (1982).

44 529 US 803 (2000).

45 Joined by Rehnquist CJ, O'Connor and Scalia JJ.

empirical evidence which showed that at least five million children were left at home without parental supervision each week. The opt-out provision in s.504 could not be construed to be a 'less restrictive but similarly practical and effective means' of pursuing the same objective because it only worked when several pre-conditions were in place; namely parental awareness of s.504 rights, parental knowledge or suspicion that their children were watching sexually explicit programmes and, finally, a prompt response from a cable operator to a blocking request.[46]

Virtual Child Pornography in the US

Recent legislative efforts to combat computerized forms of child pornography and Internet-based transmission of material judged harmful to minors for commercial purposes constitute more clearly contents-based regulations. Unsurprisingly then, the efforts of Congress have run into choppy constitutional waters. Despite being presented with opportunities to signal the lesser value which the Madisonian two-tier approach attaches to sexually explicit speech, the Court's intervention in *Ashcroft* v *Free Speech Coalition* may come to be seen as extending an unwarranted level of protection to sexually explicit speech, serving in the process to raise questions about the legitimacy of judicial intervention with legislative policy choices.

In *Ashcroft* v *Free Speech Coalition*, the Court considered the constitutionality of two provisions of the *Child Pornography Prevention Act* 1996 (*CPPA*).[47] The first of these prohibited any visual depiction, including computer-generated images, that 'is or appears to be of a minor engaged in sexually explicit conduct'.[48] The latter phrase was defined to include both actual and simulated sexual conduct. The Act also contained a separate prohibition on the production or distribution of material which conveys the impression it depicts a minor engaged in sexually explicit conduct (otherwise the 'pandering' provision).[49]

Writing the majority opinion, Justice Kennedy declared both provisions to be overbroad and unconstitutional. The reach of the first prohibition extended beyond the *Miller* obscenity standard (that is, materials that appealed to the prurient interest and were patently offensive and lacking in serious literary, artistic, political or scientific value).[50] The Court's earlier recognition in *Ferber* of the state's interest in the well-being of its youth could not be pleaded in support of the present restriction since the New York statute targeted expressive conduct which was intrinsically related to sexual abuse of children and which constituted a record of that abuse. Conversely, the present prohibition on virtual child pornography caught expressive

46 There was evidence before the Court that parents experienced difficulties in getting cable operators to act on blocking requests.

47 See further S Hanley Kosse, 'Virtual Child Pornography – a United States Update' (2004) 9 *Communications Law* 39.

48 18 USC s.2256(8)(B).

49 18 USC s.2256(8)(D).

50 413 US 15 (1973).

conduct which did not directly cause harm to children, even if the government maintained that virtual images played some subsequent role in the sexual abuse of children. According to Kennedy J:

> The argument that virtual child pornography whets paedophiles' appetites and encourages them to engage in illegal conduct is unavailing because the mere tendency of speech to encourage unlawful acts is not a sufficient reason for banning it, *Stanley* v *Georgia*, absent some showing of a direct connection between the speech and imminent illegal conduct, see [for example] *Brandenburg* v *Ohio*.[51]

Aside from computer-generated imagery of children, the provision's reference to simulated sexual activity was said by the majority to catch youthful-looking adult actors depicted as engaged in suggestive sexual activity. This might criminalize a production of Shakespeare's *Romeo and Juliet* and more recent cinematic works such as *Traffic* and *American Beauty*. This conclusion suggested a separate basis for upholding the finding of overbreadth since, once more, no children might actually be harmed in the production of the material. The 'pandering' provision also failed the overbreadth test. The reference to 'conveys the impression' meant that film titles and trailers which gave the false impression that the film's contents contained sexually explicit scenes involving young persons would be treated as child pornography with the result that possessors were in breach of the criminal law even if they did not actually intend to possess materials containing depictions of real minors engaged in sexually explicit activity.[52]

The failure of *CPPA*'s provisions to survive constitutional scrutiny is nonetheless controversial on a number of counts. The Court's intervention may be considered to lack a properly contextualized approach to review of legislative policy-making in what is a complex and fast-developing area. At issue here is the appropriate level of judicial protection for sexually explicit expression which, far from advancing a core constitutional value, contributes in an uncertain way to the self-fulfilment of individual possessors (in its most innocent form perhaps a masturbatory aid) – a rationale somewhat removed from the essential objectives of expressive freedom. In these circumstances, it is doubtful whether Kennedy J was right to apply the *Brandenburg* v *Ohio* standard requiring some direct connection between virtual child pornography and imminent illegal conduct.[53] *Brandenburg* was above all else a political speech case in which the speaker – a Ku Klux Klan leader – advocated

51 As confirmed in *American Booksellers Association* v *Hudnut* (*supra*) the tendency of published materials to give rise to 'bad' attitudes *per se* does not afford a basis for regulating such materials. By contrast, the Canadian Supreme Court has recently accepted that private viewing of child pornography may be regulated on the basis that it gives rise to a reasoned apprehension of harm to children by means of cognitive distortion, suggesting adult–child sexual relations as normal. *R* v *Sharpe* [2001] 1 SCR 45, see further below.

52 For the Congressional response to this reversal, see the *Prosecutorial Remedies and Tools Against the Exploitation of Children Today Act* 2003 and commentary by Hanley Kosse at (2004) 9 *Communications Law* 38, 41–4.

53 I refer to some difficulties of applying the *Brandenburg* test in the context of hate speech in Chapter 5.

the forcible repatriation of Jews and blacks and warned that 'there might have to be some revengeance taken' if the white Caucasian race continued to be suppressed. His conviction under an Ohio Criminal Syndicalism statute for advocating 'the duty, necessity, or propriety of crime, sabotage, violence, or unlawful methods of terrorism as a means of accomplishing industrial or political reform' was reversed as his speech did not incite imminent unlawful action. Apart from the fact that child pornography falls outside the definition of political speech (it is neither intended nor received as a contribution to public deliberation about some issue), it is doubtful whether 'imminence' is an appropriate standard in child pornography where the available expert evidence indicates that the material is used in part to whet the appetite of child abusers and in part to break down children's inhibitions over time and condition them to accept the normality of adult/child sex. A further factor pointing towards an attenuated standard of judicial scrutiny is the fact that the legislature's restrictions upon expression were intended to promote constitutionally recognized interests of a vulnerable section of society – namely the inherent dignity of each child. A more deferential approach to legislative policy choices in this arena is provided by the earlier ruling in *Ferber*. The leeway afforded to the state there upon recognition of its compelling interest in the well-being of the young could, it is suggested, have been stretched without too much difficulty across to the more recent category of virtual child pornography. Indeed, Justice O'Connor in her partial dissent found the expert evidence presented to Congress to support claims of appetite whetting and conditioning in conjunction with 'the rapid pace of advances in computer-graphics technology' sufficient to defer to Congressional judgment and rejected the claim of overbreadth in respect of the ban on virtual child pornography.[54] The majority's willingness to canvass unusual applications of the law in order to discover overbreadth would also appear to fly in the face of established jurisprudence. Recognized to be 'strong medicine' in its prevention of any enforcement of provisions impacting on constitutionally protected expression (even where the person challenging the statute cannot point to interference with his/her rights to expression), the doctrine of overbreadth has been employed sparingly by the Courts and only as a last resort.[55] Thus, overbreadth challenges have failed when a limiting construction has been

54 Citing Congressional findings at ss.121, 110 Stat. 3009-26. Joined by Rehnquist CJ and Scalia J. The existence of expert testimony on this point provides a means of distinguishing the Court's previous striking down of Georgia's obscenity laws in *Stanley* v *Georgia* 394 US 557 (1969). 'Georgia asserts that exposure to obscene materials may lead to deviant sexual behavior or crimes of sexual violence. There appears to be little empirical basis for that assertion … Given the present state of knowledge, the State may no more prohibit mere possession of obscene matter on the ground that it may lead to antisocial conduct than it may prohibit possession of chemistry books on the ground that they may lead to the manufacture of homemade spirits.'

55 *Broadrick* v *Oklahoma* 413 US 601 (1973). As Blackmun J observed in *Illinois Board of Elections* v *Socialist Workers Party* 440 US 173 at 188 (1979), all but the most unimaginative judges can find an alternative, slightly less restrictive rule in almost any situation which enables them to strike almost any legislation down.

or could be placed on the impugned statute which is consistent with its legislative purpose.[56] Equally, the Court has been reluctant in the past to strike down a statute on finding that there are a substantial number of situations to which it might validly be applied.[57] A survey of congressional debates during the passage of the *Child Pornography Prevention Act* reveals that the legislation's real target was an extension of an existing federal ban on actual child pornography across to the newer category of virtual child pornography. The new provisions did not seek to ban film portrayals of Shakespeare, rather they aimed instead at a narrow class of images, namely those visual depictions 'which are virtually indistinguishable to unsuspecting viewers from unretouched photographs of actual children engaging in identical sexual conduct'.[58]

Canadian Approaches to Sexually Explicit Expression – Towards Libertarianism?

In Chapter 2, it was argued that Canada's avowedly less individualistic political culture recognized the force of community claims as a moderating influence on individuals' rights talk. The Charter itself reflects this stance in the weight it accords to the pursuit of substantial community goals, both in terms of the procedural mechanisms designed to permit state interference with Charter rights and also judicial interpretation of the limits on freedom of expression. In these circumstances, the 2001 ruling of the Supreme Court in *R* v *Sharpe*[59] (concerning the constitutionality of penal restrictions inserted in the Criminal Code which criminalized the mere possession of child pornography) may mark a move in the direction of US-style strict scrutiny of sexually explicit expression fundamentally at odds with Canadian political culture. Whilst the relatively infrequent occasions on which federal and provincial statutes have been nullified in Charter-based challenges might yet indicate a cautious use of the Court's powers,[60] a more accurate gauge of the Court's activism needs to take account of its use of other means of intervention in public policy.[61] *Sharpe* itself provides an instance of the practice of 'reading in' exemptions to the Criminal Code in order to secure Charter compatibility. From a UK perspective, the outcome of a constitutional challenge to the possession offence will have been

56 *United States* v *Thirty-Seven Photographs* 402 US 363 (1971).

57 *Parker* v *Levy* 417 US 733 (1974).

58 Senate Reports No 104-358 pt. I, p.7 (1996). The Court has had regard to the legislative history of previous child pornography statutes which have been considered when construing the ambit of particular provisions, see *United States* v *X-Citement Video, Inc.* 513 US 64 (1994).

59 [2001] 1 SCR 45.

60 J Kelly, 'Charter Activism and Canadian Federalism: Rebalancing Liberal Constitutionalism in Canada 1982–1997', Ph.D Dissertation (1998, McGill University) records that 30 per cent of Charter-based requests to nullify were successful – cited in C Manfredi, *Judicial Power and the Charter* (2001, OUP, Ontario).

61 *Vriend* v *Alberta* [1998] 1 SCR 493.

watched with interest, given our child protection legislation and the more recent protection afforded to expression interests under our own *Human Rights Act* 1998.

As was noted in Chapters 3 and 4, the Ottawa Court has reserved a particularly stringent level of scrutiny in political expression cases. Recall, for example, in *Libman* v *Quebec (AG),* a unanimous Court spoke of the paramount importance for Canadian democracy of freedom of expression in the political realm before holding that the statutory ceiling on the referendum expenditure of non-affiliated groups violated s.2(b).[62] At the same time, the Court has accepted on previous occasions that self-fulfilment offers a less compelling rationale for speech protection.

Self-fulfilment, Low-value Expression and Judicial Deference

A number of the self-fulfilment cases to come before the Court may be treated as economic self-interest cases where the restriction under challenge is claimed to impact adversely on the challenger's economic well-being. As will be shown in this and the subsequent chapter on commercial expression, there is some evidence here of a more relaxed standard of review of legislative policy-making, extending at times even to penal rules. The deferential tone was established in cases such as *Ford* v *AG Quebec*,[63] and *AG Quebec* v *Irwin Toy Ltd.*[64] In the latter, provincial legislation prohibiting commercial advertising directed at persons under 13 years old was deemed by a majority to be a justified restriction of freedom of expression under s.1 of the Charter. Not only was the legislation held to have been prompted by a pressing and substantial concern – namely the protection of a group deemed especially susceptible to the persuasive techniques employed by commercial advertisers – it was also considered to be a proportionate response to this concern.[65] In justifying the relaxed level of scrutiny applied to this legislative prohibition, the Court drew a questionable distinction between instances where, on the one hand, a Charter dispute arose out of legislative mediation between the competing claims of different groups, and, on the other, constitutional conflicts in which the government might be characterized as the principal antagonist of the party whose right had been infringed. An example of the latter category of case would be the enforcement of the criminal law where the state acted as the representative of societal interests in prosecuting those alleged to have breached community standards. In the former, due respect for the legislature's representative function meant that the Courts should be slow to intervene in legislative policy-making where it was alleged that the impairment of a Charter right was more than minimal. The case for judicial restraint was especially strong where the beneficiaries of the policy stance were considered

62 [1997] 3 SCR 569. The Court did agree however that some limit on campaign expenditure was necessary to ensure equality and fairness in elections, see further Chapter 4.

63 [1988] 2 SCR 712.

64 [1989] 1 SCR 927.

65 Advertisers were, after all, still free to direct their advertising at parents and other adult carers of children.

especially vulnerable.[66] After all, policy-making in this context frequently involved an assessment of conflicting scientific evidence and competing, though justifiable demands on scarce resources. By contrast, in determining the constitutionality of a rights-infringing provision of the criminal law, the courts might more confidently assess whether the 'least drastic means' for achieving the state's particular objective had been chosen.

Whatever the conceptual merits of this distinction, it has palpably not endured. Just one year on from *Irwin Toy* the deferential approach was applied to a set of criminal prohibitions on expression in *Reference re ss.193 & 195.1(1)(c) of the Criminal Code (Manitoba)* where a plurality opinion sustained the constitutionality of a provision of the Criminal Code which prohibited prostitutes from soliciting in public places.[67] The Court began by noting the peripheral nature of the expression interest implicated in the challenge. Whilst there was an undisputed infringement with expressive activity, the particular context of the case – communications about sex for money – 'could hardly be said … (to) lie at or even near, the core of the guarantee of freedom of expression'.[68] This fact made judicial intervention less, not more, likely. Significantly, in a separate opinion concurring with the plurality, Lamer J offered an alternative basis for conferring a margin of appreciation to legislative policy-making. According to Lamer J, the legislature enjoyed a broader sphere of discretion when making contentious and morally laden policy choices:

> Parliament was faced with a myriad of views and options from which to choose in respect of dealing with the problem of street solicitation for the purpose of prostitution. The role of this Court is not to second-guess the wisdom of policy choices made by the legislators. Prostitution, and specifically, the solicitation for the purpose thereof, is an especially contentious and at times morally laden issue, requiring the weighing of competing political pressures. The issue for this Court to determine is not whether Parliament has weighed those interests and pressures wisely but rather whether the limit they have imposed on a Charter right or freedom is reasonable and just.[69]

In *R* v *Butler*,[70] the Court similarly applied a less demanding standard of scrutiny to criminal legislation dealing with a moral issue, this time in the context of obscenity provisions of the Criminal Code. Once more, the Court's starting point was the low value to be attached to publications whose dominant characteristic was the 'undue exploitation of sex'. It noted that:

---

66 The majority relied upon the remarks of Dickson CJ in *Edwards Books & Art Ltd* v *The Queen* [1986] 2 SCR 713, 779: 'In interpreting and applying the Charter I believe that the courts must be cautious to ensure that it does not simply become an instrument of better situated individuals to roll back legislation which has as its object the improvement of the condition of less advantaged persons.'

67 [1990] 1 SCR 1123.

68 Dickson CJ, LaForest and Sopinka JJ, *ibid.*, at 1136.

69 *Ibid.*, at 1199.

70 [1992] 1 SCR 452.

> [T]he kind of expression which is sought to be advanced does not stand on an equal footing with other kinds of expression which directly engage the 'core' of freedom of expression values.[71]

Parliament had reasonably concluded that certain sexually explicit material reinforced unhealthy tendencies in Canadian society by attempting to present degradation, humiliation and violence in human relationships as normal.[72] A society committed to the fundamental values of equal respect and non-violence was entitled through its legislature to prohibit materials which undermined these values. Granting Parliament a relatively wide margin of appreciation, the Court found that the absence of conclusive social science evidence linking the consumption of 'hard-core' material to anti-social conduct did not invalidate the imposition of criminal restrictions on the creation and distribution of the material. It was sufficient for the Crown to show instead a 'reasoned apprehension of harm'.[73]

A sea change in Supreme Court attitudes towards legislative restrictions on non-political expression did however occur subsequently in *RJR McDonald Inc.* v *Canada*,[74] concerning penal restrictions on tobacco advertising imposed by federal statute and prompted by the government's desire to protect the public from health risks associated with tobacco. The issues thrown up by this commercial speech ruling are discussed in more detail in the proceeding chapter. For present purposes, it can simply be noted that the majority led by McLachlin J sought to avoid what they saw as excessive deference to legislative interference with Charter rights. Applying strict scrutiny to the ban, the majority held that the government had failed to show that the less intrusive measure of a partial ban or attributed health warnings might equally have met its legitimate goal of preventing people from being persuaded to use tobacco products.

After *RJR McDonald*, it remained to be seen whether the demanding level of judicial scrutiny preferred by the majority would be carried over into cases outside a commercial context where a legislative incursion on expression was challenged on the basis of a self-fulfilment type claim for s.2(b) protection. The resolution of *R* v *Sharpe* has now revealed the Court's preferred stance in the context of a challenge to provisions of the Criminal Code outlawing the possession of child pornography.

---

71 *Ibid.*, at 500.

72 According to Sopinka J, provided the target of the legislation was the anti-social, anti-Charter value attitudes linked to 'hard-core' materials, rather than an attempt to impose a particular conception of public morality, then the obscenity provisions of the Code would have a 'pressing and substantial' objective.

73 'We have not, of course, found that the images people are exposed to are a greater cause of sexual violence than all or even many other possible causes, the investigation of which has been beyond our mandate. Nevertheless, it would be strange indeed if graphic representations of a form of behavior as desirable, did not at least have some effect on patterns of behavior.' *Per* Sopinka J [1992] 1 SCR 452 at 502.

74 [1995] 3 SCR 199.

Sharpe – *Misguided Judicial Activism in Defence of Weak Speech Claims?*

The respondent was charged with two counts of possessing child pornography (s.163.1(4) of the Criminal Code) and with two counts of possession for the purposes of distribution or sale (s.163.1(3)). He brought a preliminary motion prior to his trial in which he argued that the offence of mere possession violated his constitutional entitlement to freedom of expression under s.2(b). Under s.163.1(1) of the Code, 'child pornography' was defined to include:

> … visual representations that show a person who is or who is depicted as under the age of 18 years and is engaged in or is depicted as engaged in explicit sexual activity and visual representations the dominant characteristic of which is the depiction for a sexual purpose, of a sexual organ or the anal region of a person under the age of 18 years.

Section 163.1(6) provided defences for material with artistic merit and that which served an educational, scientific or medical purpose. A public good defence was also inserted into the Code.[75]

In the respondent's possession were found computer disks which contained material entitled 'Sam Paloc's Boyabuse – Flogging, Fun and Fortitude: A Collection of Kiddiekink Classics', as well as photographs showing boys kissing each other, masturbating and performing fellatio. The respondent had also written a collection of stories which the Court heard were extremely violent in nature and involved children usually under the age of 10 in sadomasochistic acts with other children and adults. A theme in the writing was that children enjoy being beaten, sexually assaulted and actually seek out this treatment.

In the British Columbia Court of Appeal, a majority of 2–1 held that the mere possession offence violated the respondent's Charter right to free expression, albeit on different grounds.[76] Southam JA found that a criminal prohibition on the mere possession of child pornography could never constitute a reasonable limit on freedom of expression in a free and democratic society. For his part, Rowles JA held that the offence as presently constructed was overbroad, catching more material than was demanded by the legislative purpose underlying it and thereby was not a proportionate limit on the s.2(b) right. In his dissenting judgment, McEachern CJ disregarded what he characterized as remote applications of the impugned provision and declared it to be within the range of lawful restrictions on freedom of expression under s.1 of the Charter.

In the Supreme Court, a majority of 6–3 led by Chief Justice McLachlin ruled that the s.163.1(4) offence violated the respondent's Charter right to expression and was not saved under the s.1 'reasonable limits' clause. At the outset, the majority accepted that the aim of reducing harm to children was a pressing and substantial objective. It was also conceded that the legislature could cite a number of arguments

75 S.163.1(7).

76 At first instance, the trial judge had also found that the offence was not justified in a free and democratic society.

to support a rational connection between the objective and the means used to advance the objective. Specifically, private viewing of child pornography gave rise to a reasoned apprehension that viewers might come to see sexual relations with children as normal.[77] It was also reasonable to assume that possession served to fuel the fantasies of paedophiles, even though there was a lack of unanimity among scientific opinion on this point. Criminalizing mere possession would also assist in tracking down those involved in the production and distribution of child pornography and so provided further evidence of a rational connection to the aim of reducing harm to children. Clamping down on possession additionally reduced the market for child pornography and the abuse of children that this market entailed. The Court noted here the lifelong trauma and violation of individual dignity caused by the creation of a permanent record of degrading images. Finally, there was clear and uncontradicted evidence that the possession of such materials was used by paedophiles to groom and seduce children into taking part in sexual activity.

As for the second and third prongs of the proportionality test, the majority doubted, however, whether the Canadian Parliament had tailored the prohibition sufficiently narrowly, concluding that the detrimental impact upon lawful activity would be out of proportion to its beneficial effects. McLachlin CJ reasoned as follows: whilst in practice the vast majority of situations in which the prohibition would be invoked would not pose a constitutional problem, as currently drafted it extended to two problematic areas; namely (i) the possession of written materials/visual representations created and held by an accused person and intended solely for his/her personal use, and (ii) visual recordings created by or depicting the accused that do not depict unlawful sexual activity held by the accused solely for private use.[78] So applied, the ban caught a teenager's sexually explicit recordings of himself/herself either alone or engaged in lawful sexual activity with another person under 18 years.[79] For McLachlin CJ, these admittedly peripheral applications of the law imposed significant costs to teenagers' self-fulfilment/self-actualization interests and had only a tenuous connection to the legitimate aim of reducing harm to children. Accordingly, the majority re-wrote the Code to incorporate exceptions into s.163.1 of the Code for (i) self-created expressive material intended for private use, and (ii) private recordings of lawful sexual activity created by the accused and held by the accused purely for private use of the accused and the parties depicted therein.[80]

---

77 The application of the 'reasoned apprehension' standard meant that the Crown did not have to meet the more stringent 'scientific proof of actual harm' standard.

78 McLachlin CJ did concede a 'small risk' that this material could come into the hands of someone who would use it to harm children.

79 In Canadian law, young persons may consent to sex from the age of 14 years.

80 Once legislation is in breach of the Charter, there are five remedies which are available under s.52(1). These are namely: striking down the offending legislation; severing the offending provision; striking down or severing together with a temporary suspension of the invalidity finding; reading down an offending provision; reading in a constitutionally compliant provision. For guidance on judicial resort to these remedial powers, see *Schachter* v *Canada* [1992] 2 SCR 679 and, extra-judicially, Justice Iacobucci in D Beatty (ed.), *Human*

The dissenting opinion in *Sharpe* drew more explicitly upon legislative context in its adoption of a more deferential stance towards the legislature's preferred policy, concluding that the mere possession charge was saved under s.1 of the Charter. In particular, emphasis was placed on the fact that the legislation sought to further other constitutional values such as respect for the inherent dignity of each person, non-violence and privacy.[81] These values were reinforced by international legal norms on the protection of children[82] which, of late, had focused specifically on the issue of child pornography.[83] These norms were relevant to the interpretation of domestic constitutional provisions.[84] At the level of domestic legal systems, the dissent noted that a number of states had moved against the mere possession of child pornography. In the UK, for example, s.7 of the *Protection of Children Act* 1978 (as amended) creates an offence of private possession of photographs and pseudo-photographs of persons who are or appear to be under 16 years of age.[85] Where material existed in electronic form, this posed a heightened risk that a possessor could become a disseminator. Clamping down on possession would hinder dissemination in such circumstances. Balanced against these factors, the slight nature of the particular expression claim at issue here (in most cases – the right of adults who seek personal fulfilment through possession of child pornography)[86] and its link to harm to children suggested that the new provisions were within the range of lawful policy stances that Parliament could adopt. The peripheral cost to teenagers who produce permanent records of their own lawful sexual activity did not amount to a disproportionate loss when viewed against the gain of reduced harm to children. In any event, such 'diary' material could remain out of the courts upon the adoption of sensible prosecution guidelines.

The re-write of the Criminal Code that occurred in *Sharpe* might be claimed as a further chapter in the cooperative venture that is the dialogue between the courts and legislatures. Indeed, it might be reasoned what the judges are doing

---

Rights and Judicial Review – A Comparative Perspective (1994, Kluwer Academic Publishers, Dordrecht) Ch. 3.

81 It was pointed out here that the self-fulfilment interests of children were furthered by the legislation.

82 *Universal Declaration of Human Rights*, Article 25(2) GA Res 217 A (III), UN Doc A/810 (1948); *Convention on the Rights of the Child.*

83 *Sale of Children, Child Prostitution and Child Pornography: Note by the Secretary General*, UN Doc A/49/478 (1994) at paras 196–7. See also moves by the Council of the EU to combat what it called 'a particularly serious form of sexual exploitation of children' occurring on the Internet. Council decision of 29 May 2000. OJ L 138, 9 June 2000 and Article 9 of the Council of Europe's *Convention on Cybercrime* (adopted by the Committee of Ministers on 8 November 2001 and opened for signature on 23 November 2001).

84 *Baker* v *Canada (Minister of Citizenship and Immigration)* [1999] 2 SCR 817.

85 As amended by *Criminal Justice and Public Order Act* 1994, s.84(3)(c).

86 In its most benign form, mere possession could be said to assist an adult's sexual fantasizing about children, thus reducing the expression claim to one in which the material serves as a masturbatory aid.

in cases such as *Sharpe* is extending a helping hand to the legislature to produce Charter-compliant laws. *Sharpe*, however, may be thought to lend support to earlier criticism of the notion of 'dialogue' in Chapter 2 that, where dialogue does occur, it does so on terms laid down by the Supreme Court, rather than as part of a negotiated relationship between equals. The legislature is not at liberty to articulate an alternative version of policy which departs from the constraints laid down by the judges. It is clear now that the failure to differentiate between the relative importance of the respective rationales for expression detected earlier in *RJR McDonald* and carried over in *Sharpe* has led to a distorted view of the appropriate level of constitutional protection for the possession of sexually explicit imagery of children, the value of which to the least persuasive rationale for expression is at best marginal. Whilst the 'reading-in' response of the majority in *Sharpe* cannot be claimed to be a particularly dramatic judicial intervention, it remains the case that the Court has once more interfered in an area of complex and morally-contested social policy.

A United Kingdom Perspective

In sharp contrast with respective legal arguments in the US and Canada, the regulation of pornography in the UK has been distinctive on account of the absence of principled debate about the boundaries of freedom of expression and the constitutional basis of legitimate state interference with speech. Instead, as will be shown below, technical issues have been to the fore. In the section below, some of the key provisions which may be used to regulate virtual pornography are described.[87] After which, some possible *Human Rights Act* implications for existing domestic laws will be considered.

The Children Act *1978 and Specific Offences*

Under the heading 'Indecent photographs of children', s.1 of the Act states that:

> (1) It is an offence for a person:
> (a) to take, or permit to be taken or to make, any indecent photograph or pseudo-photograph of a child; or
> (b) to distribute or show such indecent photographs or pseudo-photographs; or
> (c) to have in his possession such indecent photographs or pseudo-photographs, with a view to their being distributed or shown by himself or others; or
> (d) to publish or cause to be published any advertisement likely to be understood as conveying that the advertiser distributes or shows such indecent photographs or pseudo-photographs, or intends to do so.

87 See also Y Akdeniz, 'Child pornography' in Y Akdeniz, C Walker and D Wall (eds), *The Internet, Law and Society* (2000, Longman, Harlow). Akdeniz discusses issues of enforcement and regulatory techniques that are not considered in this book.

The offence created in s.1(1)(a) is an absolute one, admitting of no defences. By contrast, in respect of offences in s.1(1)(b) and (c), a defendant may avoid criminal liability if he can prove that a 'legitimate reason' existed for distributing, showing or possessing the photographs or pseudo-photographs. Alternatively, the defendant may show that he had not seen the photographs/pseudo-photographs and did not know, nor had any cause to suspect, them to be indecent.

An early indication of the purposive approach adopted by the English courts to the regulation of sexually explicit imagery of children is evident in *R* v *Fellows & Arnold*.[88] The first defendant used his employer's computing facilities to store data which allowed the display, printing and Internet distribution of indecent pictures of children. The second defendant supplied similar data to the first defendant in return for which access was given to the first defendant's image database.[89] The latter was charged under s.1(1)(c) with four counts of having in his possession indecent photographs of children with a view to their being distributed or shown by himself to others. The second defendant was charged with three counts of distributing or showing indecent photographs of children contrary to s.1(1)(b). Upon conviction,[90] they challenged the trial judge's ruling that the database did not consist of 'photographs' as understood in the 1978 Act. Argument centred around the meaning of s.7(2) which states:

> References to an indecent photograph include an indecent film, a copy of an indecent photograph or film, and an indecent photograph ... comprised in a film.

In particular, a central point of disagreement was whether data stored on disk was capable of being a 'copy of an indecent photograph'. For the appellants, much emphasis was placed on the fact that Parliament had later introduced amendments into the *Children Act*. Specifically, the s.7 definition of a photograph was amended by the *Criminal Justice and Public Order Act* 1994 to include 'data stored on computer disk or by other electronic means which is capable of conversion into a photograph'.[91]

---

88 [1997] 1 Cr App R 244.

89 In a period of about 12 months in 1993–94, the first defendant amassed in one sub-directory entitled 'Young/Minors' data relating to approximately 1875 pictures of children engaged in sexual activities or poses. His computer also held hundreds of pornographic pictures obtained from bulletin boards in Denmark and the US. The second defendant supplied the first defendant with data relating to between 20 and 30 photographs.

90 For analysis of the trial judge's ruling, see C Manchester, 'More about Computer Pornography' [1996] *Crim L R* 645.

91 *Criminal Justice and Public Order Act* 1994, s.84 states:

(3) In section 7 (interpretation):

(a) ...

(b) for subsection (4) there shall be substituted the following subsection:

'(4) References to a photograph include:

(a) the negative as well as the positive version; and

(b) data stored on a computer disc or by other electronic means which is capable of conversion into a photograph'.

Whilst the amendment would have been directly relevant to the facts of the case had it been in force at the time of the alleged offences, the appellants argued that the 1994 amendment indicated that Parliament in 1994 had not considered the original version of s.7 to cover the appellants' activities. Rejecting this argument, the Court of Appeal held that once it had been shown that the clear words of the 1978 Act were sufficiently wide to cover subsequent technological innovations, the fact that a particular device was not in the contemplation of Parliament would not be relevant.[92] As to the meaning of a 'copy of an indecent photograph', the Court noted that the 1978 Act did not require that the 'copy' should itself be a photograph. Instead, it concluded that the original definition was broad enough to capture data (representing the photograph in a different form) which was capable of being converted into (i) a screen image and/or (ii) a print which exactly reproduced the original photograph. As Manchester has commented, this part of the ruling is significant because the Act is being read to apply to intangible objects (electronic data) which are incapable of being viewed without some further action being taken.[93]

On the subsequent question of whether these photographs were held by the first appellant with a view to being 'distributed or shown by himself', the Court accepted the need for the prosecution to demonstrate some 'active' conduct on the part of the appellant but found that the steps taken by him to store the indecent photographs and to make them available on the Internet, as well as the e-mail correspondence with those who wished to access his collection, furnished the necessary evidence of active conduct.[94]

'Making' an indecent photo/pseudo-photograph Until 1994, s.1(1)(a) of the 1978 *Children Act* did not refer to the 'making' of indecent photographs or pseudo-photographs. The amendments introduced by s.84 of the *Criminal Justice and Public Order Act* 1994 sought to reflect wider public concern about the creation, distribution and proliferation of computerized child pornography. That the courts have been interpreting this legislation with this concern in mind is apparent in the purposive interpretation of the amended 1978 Act. In *R* v *Bowden* the defendant had downloaded indecent material from the Internet onto his computer screen, then printing or storing them on his hard disk for later use.[95] In the Court of Appeal, it was held that a person who stores images onto disk or prints them off is 'making' them. Subsequently, a stipendiary magistrate in *Atkins* v *DPP*[96] ruled that the mere storage of images of children on hard disk did not amount to 'making' those images since 'making' required an act of creation. According to the magistrate, any other conclusion would cause injustice by criminalizing the conduct of innocent parties (for example, those

92 Citing *AG's Reference* (No. 5 of 1980) (1981) 72 Cr. App. R. 71.

93 C Manchester, 'More about Computer Pornography' [1996] *Crim L R* 645, 646.

94 The second appellant did not contest the trial judge's conviction for 'distributing' indecent photographs.

95 [2000] 2 All ER 418.

96 [2000] 2 Cr App R 248.

seeking to make copies for the purpose of collecting evidence) since the s.1(1)(a) offence was absolute in nature. Although the Queen's Bench Division recognized the force of this point and suggested that the section be construed narrowly to avoid this result,[97] it followed *Bowden* to conclude that 'making' meant 'to cause to exist; to produce by action; to bring about'. Accordingly, the defendant should have been convicted in respect of materials downloaded and stored on his computer's hard drive. *Atkins* v *DPP* further decided that copies made unknowingly on the cache created automatically by the computer's Internet browser constituted 'unintentional copying' since the Court could not be sure that defendant knew that the computer would retain upon its hard disk information sent to it at the user's request and that the offence of 'making' did not occur in respect of such 'unintentional copying'.

Opening e-mail attachments or viewing indecent images on screen The issue of the 'making' of an indecent photograph was further discussed in *R* v *Smith & Jayson*[98] where the Court of Appeal had to decide the application of the 1978 Act to the opening of e-mail attachments and the viewing of indecent images on screen. In the case of *Smith*, which concerned e-mail attachments, the Court found that the mental element of the s.1(1)(a) 'making' offence would be present if, on opening the attachment, the user had been aware that the attachment contained or was likely to contain an indecent photograph or pseudo-photograph of a child. Lack of such knowledge would be fatal to the prosecution's case. As to the automatic storing of any photograph in the cache caused by the browser, the user would lack the necessary *mens rea* to make an indecent photograph if he/she had no knowledge of the automatic downloading process onto the cache.

Jayson on the other hand centred upon the viewing of an indecent image on screen. The Court of Appeal held that the voluntary downloading of an indecent Internet image onto a computer monitor did fall within the definition of making a photograph or pseudo-photograph. The Court reasoned that by downloading from the webpage onto the screen, the user was causing the image to exist on the screen. One commentator has welcomed the finding, claiming that it may help avoid the 'technical morass' entailed in analysing *mens rea* issues surrounding the creation of computer caches.[99]

---

97 The consent of the Director of Public Prosecutions is needed for a prosecution under s.1 of the 1978 Act and so this unfortunate occurrence is perhaps unlikely.

98 [2002] EWCA Crim 683.

99 G Smith, *Internet Law and Regulation* (2002, 3rd edn, Sweet & Maxwell, London) at 12-079. Specifically, in the case of a network connection, the user may have done nothing to create the copy of an attachment which arrives via an unsolicited e-mail other than by configuring his computer to receive e-mails when they are routed to him. Does the user have the necessary *mens rea* when he decides to open the e-mail? If so, hasn't the act of 'making' already been completed, meaning that an offence cannot be committed in relation to that copy? Smith suggests that the only way around this is to suggest that 'making' can consist in some continuing act of storage.

The Criminal Justice Act *1988 – Mere Possession*

In circumstances where the available evidence falls short of establishing an intention to show or distribute to others,[100] a prosecution for mere possession may be brought under s.160 of the *Criminal Justice Act* 1988 (as amended).[101] Subsection 1 states:

> It is an offence for a person to have any indecent photograph or pseudo-photograph of a child[102] in his possession.
> Where a person is charged with an offence under subsection (1) above, it shall be a defence for him to prove:
> (a) that he had a legitimate reason for having the photograph or pseudo-photograph in his possession; or
> (b) that he had not himself seen the photograph or pseudo-photograph and did not know, nor had any cause to suspect, it to be indecent; or
> (c) that the photograph or pseudo-photograph was sent to him without any prior request made by him or on his behalf and that he did not keep it for an unreasonable time.

It is an essential component of a s.160(1) offence that the prosecution show that the defendant knows (or from the circumstances must have known) of the photograph's existence.[103] Thus, where a defendant is unaware of the storage of photographs on a computer's cache caused automatically by browser, an essential element of the offence is not present.[104] By contrast, the user's act of downloading information or documents in the computer's hard drive will be firm evidence of knowledge of possession.

Some guidance on the defence of 'legitimate reason' in s.160(2)(a) is provided by the Queen's Bench Division in *Atkins* v *DPP* and *Goodland* v *DPP*.[105] In directing trial courts to scrutinize any 'legitimate reason' defence closely, Simon Brown LJ

100 On the need under s.1(1)(c) of the *Children Act* 1978 for another party to be shown the material, see *R* v *ET* [1999] Crim LR 749 where the defendant was caught in possession of a ciné film which depicted sexual acts between a female child and adult male. The prosecution did not seek to show that the defendant intended to show it to others, relying on an admission that he intended to watch the film by himself. A conviction at the trial court on a count of possession with a view to showing under s.1(1)(c) was quashed on appeal. 'Showing' meant giving access to others. See generally, A Gillespie, 'Child Pornography: Balancing Substantive and Evidential Law to Safeguard Children Effectively from Abuse' (2005) 9 *International Journal of Evidence and Proof* 29.

101 By s.84(4) of the *Criminal Justice and Public Order Act* 1994 whereby references to 'pseudo-photographs' were inserted into subsections (1) and (2). Note also that the DPP's consent to the bringing of a prosecution is needed, s.160(4). For judicial criticism of the ease with which this consent is given, see the remarks of Simon Brown LJ in *Atkins* v *DPP; Goodland* v *DPP* [2000] 2 Cr App R 248, 264–5.

102 That is, a person under the age of 16 years.

103 *Atkins* v *DPP; Goodland* v *DPP* [2000] 2 Cr App R 248; *R* v *Collier* [2005] 1 Cr App R 9.

104 *Ibid.*

105 [2000] 2 Cr. App.R. 248, 257.

stated that the central question of fact for magistrates or juries to determine will be whether the defendant is

> … essentially a person of unhealthy interests in possession of indecent photographs in the pretence of undertaking research or by contrast a genuine researcher with no alternative but to have this sort of unpleasant material in his possession. In other cases, there will be other categories of 'legitimate reason' advanced. They will each have to be considered on their own facts. Courts are plainly entitled to bring a measure of scepticism to bear upon such an enquiry; they should not too readily conclude that the defence has been made out.

On the facts in *Atkins*, the appellant claimed that his possession of the photographs was motivated from reasons for academic research. After considering the available evidence, this claim was rejected by the magistrate, a conclusion with which the Queen's Bench Division on appeal did not interfere.[106]

The Obscene Publications Act *1959 (as Amended)*

In the case of materials which, to use Lord Parker's terminology, are at the upper end of the scale of offensiveness, it may be possible to prosecute under the *Obscene Publications Act* 1959. It is an offence under this Act to publish an obscene article, whether for gain or not.[107] Publication occurs in the case of an article containing matter to be looked at when a person 'shows, plays or projects it'.[108] Once more, in the few reported proceedings involving electronically available material, much legal argument has focused on the application of the 1959 statute to computer pornography. In *R* v *Fellows & Arnold*[109] where, having already taken a broad interpretation of the *Protection of Children Act* 1978 to hold that data held on a computer was capable of constituting a copy of an indecent photograph, it also found that a computer disk was an 'article' for the purposes of the 1959 Act and that the article was 'shown, played or projected' to those who gained access to the first appellant's archive. The lower court's conviction for publishing an obscene article was upheld.

An attempt to avoid the jurisdiction of the English courts was unsuccessful in *R* v *Waddon*[110] where obscene images had been posted by the appellant (who was resident in England) on a Web server in America. He argued that the materials had therefore not been published in England. This contention was rejected by the Court of Appeal. The appellant had published the material in England when he uploaded

---

106 For an indication of current sentencing policy, see *R* v *Thompson* [2004] 2 Cr App R 16 and A Gillespie, 'Sentences for Offences Involving Child Pornography' (2003) *Crim L R* 81.

107 *Obscene Publications Act* 1959, s.2(1).

108 *Obscene Publications Act* 1959, s.1(3)(b).

109 [1997] 1 Cr App R 244.

110 (2000) 6 April Westlaw Transcript Service.

material to the website and, again, when he was involved in its re-transmission back to this country.

ECHR and Child Pornography[111]

It is surely time for the English courts to abandon their rather technical and unprincipled approach to the interpretation of child pornography laws and adopt a more obviously rights-based analysis of the competing interests implicated in the regulation of this field. If the arguably least serious offence is considered for illustrative purposes – that of mere possession of an indecent pseudo-photograph under s.160(1) of the *Criminal Justice Act* 1988 – defendants are likely to argue that this constitutes a disproportionate interference with their Convention rights both to respect for private life (Article 8) and expression (Article 10). An issue to be settled in any such litigation would be whether the defences of legitimate reason, ignorance of the fact of possession or unsolicited receipt were sufficiently extensive as to render domestic law Convention-compliant. Of course, as described above, the English judiciary's unwillingness to engage in strained interpretation so as to achieve compatibility would appear to rule out imaginative attempts to read in new provisions or read down existing provisions with the result that, in cases where the plain reading of the statute was held to infringe a Convention right, the most a defendant might expect is a declaration of incompatibility and a remedial order laid before Parliament to remove the incompatibility.[112] Such an order would not, of course, alter the fact of conviction and would constitute at best a pyrrhic triumph. A finding of incompatibility would not in any event be a foregone conclusion. The Council of Europe's *Convention on Cybercrimes* (2001) which has now entered into force, prompts member states to strengthen existing domestic laws on harmful Internet content (including those relating to virtual child pornography) and thus points towards greater restriction of sexually explicit imagery of children at state level.[113]

---

111 I do not discuss here EU initiatives in controlling virtual child pornography. For detail see http://europa.eu.int/information_society/activities/sip/index_en.htm.

112 *Human Rights Act* 1998, ss.10, 20(1).

113 *Convention on Cybercrimes* (2001) CETS No. 185 Title 3 – Content-related offences:

> Article 9 – Offences related to child pornography
>
> 1. Each Party shall adopt such legislative and other measures as may be necessary to establish as criminal offences under its domestic law, when committed intentionally and without right, the following conduct:
>
> (a) producing child pornography for the purpose of its distribution through a computer system;
>
> (b) offering or making available child pornography through a computer system;
>
> (c) distributing or transmitting child pornography through a computer system;
>
> (d) procuring child pornography through a computer system for oneself or for another;

As far as the jurisprudence of the Strasbourg Court is concerned, national authorities' far-ranging restrictions on the production, dissemination and possession of sexually explicit material have almost without exception been upheld. Starting from *Handyside*, in which the UK's obscenity laws were deemed to fall within the 'protection of morals' exception to freedom of expression,[114] the Court has accorded a broad margin of appreciation to domestic courts and legislatures to determine what action is required to safeguard moral standards. This reflects variations across member states in prevailing moral standards.[115] The seizure and forfeiture of offending materials have all been considered proportionate responses to counter the threat to moral standards. In *Handyside*, this conclusion owed much to the fact that the publication was targeted at children as young as 12. The right of religious persons not to be insulted or offended has also figured as a legitimate basis for curtailing sexually explicit expression under the 'rights of others' head of Article 10(2). In *Wingrove* v *UK* the Court refused to interfere with the decision of a video licensing body to refuse a distribution certificate to the applicant's film, *Visions of Ecstasy*, which depicted alleged sexual relations between St Teresa of Avila and Jesus Christ.[116] Once more, by virtue of their 'direct and continuous contact with the vital forces of their countries', national authorities were considered better placed than the Strasbourg Court to draw the line between permitted and unlawful expression.[117] Moreover, even though the refusal to grant a certificate amounted in effect to a total ban, this was said to be 'understandable' in the light of the view of the competent authorities that the film was blasphemous.[118]

The purpose of alluding to the decisions above is not to be drawn into analysis of their persuasiveness or otherwise, it is rather to identify some over-arching norms that inform the Strasbourg Court's approach to child pornography. That involving the use of real, as opposed to virtual, images of children is more straightforwardly controllable on the basis of the 'rights of others' derogation (actual harm to a child).

(e) possessing child pornography in a computer system or on a computer-data storage medium.

2. For the purpose of paragraph 1 above, 'child pornography' shall include pornographic material that visually depicts:

(a) a minor engaged in sexually explicit conduct;

(b) a person appearing to be a minor engaged in sexually explicit conduct;

(c) realistic images representing a minor engaged in sexually explicit conduct.

3. For the purpose of paragraph 2 above, the term 'minor' shall include all persons under 18 years of age. A Party may, however, require a lower age limit, which shall be not less than 16 years.

4. Each Party may reserve the right not to apply, in whole or in part, paragraph 1(d) and 1(e), and 2(b) and 2(c).

114 *Handyside* v *UK* (1979–80) 1 EHRR 737.

115 *Ibid.*, at paras 48 and 57.

116 *Wingrove* v *UK* (1997) 24 EHRR 1

117 *Ibid.*, at para. 58.

118 *Ibid.*, at para. 64.

On the more controversial matter of virtual pornography, although Article 9.2 of the *Cybercrimes Convention* clearly envisages liability for the simple possession of virtual or morphed images of children, the proportionality of any restriction would be critical. The Court would presumably expect to see a rational link between possession and harm to young persons. Of considerable importance here is the state of empirical evidence about the use made by paedophiles of virtual imagery. Even though an individual possessor might not be shown to have attempted to have sexual relations with children at the time of detection, the leeway afforded to the state to protect vulnerable persons might be thought to permit some infringement via the criminal law of possessors' Article 8 and Article 10 rights.[119] If, as the empirical evidence tends to suggest, virtual pornography is used by a significant proportion of adults to whet their appetite for sexual activity with children, to convince children to engage in sexual relations, and for trade with other adults so that the latter may do likewise, then the basis of the possession offence would seem sound.[120] A contrary finding that virtual pornography was, in some circumstances, protected under Article 8 and/or Article 10 would have the unfortunate effect of allowing possessors of actual child pornography to claim that the images were in fact computer-generated and thus evade liability. As O'Connor J recognized in *Ashcroft* v *Free Speech Coalition*, with advances in technology it may be extremely difficult for evidential purposes to distinguish between actual and computer-generated images.[121]

Virtual Child Pornography – A Conclusion

The case for allowing legislatures a certain leeway to regulate sexually explicit speech can now be stated. Viewed against the central concerns of constitutional guarantees of freedom of expression, the freedom to disseminate and acquire pornography must

119 It should be stressed that not all possessors of child pornography go on to commit sexual abuse crimes against children. Some have argued that it acts as a safety valve to prevent sexual abuse, see B Kutchinsky, 'The Effect of Easy Availability of Pornography on the Incidence of Sex Crimes: The Danish Experience' (1973) 29 *J of Social Sciences* 163.

120 See i§121, 110 Stat. 3009–26, Congressional Findings (4), (10) (B) during passage of the *Child Pornography Prevention Act* 1996. A US Senate Sub-Committee Report, *Child Pornography and Pedophilia*, concluded that child pornography has a 'central role in child molestations by paedophiles, serving to justify their conduct, assist them in seducing their victim and providing a means to blackmail the children they have molested in order to prevent exposure'; at 44. See also in this regard the report of the International Association of Prosecutors Working Group 1, *Combating the Use of the Internet to Exploit Children*, available electronically at http://www.iap.nl.com/exploit.htm. The group is composed of prosecutors from Australia, Brazil, Canada, The Netherlands, Sweden, Thailand and the US with over 70 years' combined experience in prosecuting cases. An excellent review of the research literature is to be found in a study for the Canadian Department of Justice by Dr LJ Rettinger, *The Relationship between Child Pornography and the Commission of Sexual Offences against Children: A Review of the Literature* (2000, Department of Justice, Canada).

121 535 US 234 (2002).

surely rank as of peripheral importance only. In respect of child pornography, any benefits to individual self-fulfilment of this lesser value expression are countered by the undisputed empirical evidence of its role in the sexual abuse of children. Statutory regulation of virtual sexually explicit imagery of children seeks to address new technological means available to those wishing to harm children and uphold this vulnerable group's constitutional entitlements to privacy, dignity and non-violence. Of course, deference to elected bodies' rule-making must not be carried to the extent that it relieves the state of the burden of demonstrating that the limits placed on expressive freedom advance a substantial government interest in a proportionate manner. That said, in a fast-developing area such as virtual child pornography, judicial intervention in legislative policy-making must still be carefully thought through. After all, not even the First Amendment requires Congress to wait for harm to occur before legislating against it. As the Court noted in *Turner* v *FCC*,

> Even in the realm of First Amendment questions where Congress must base its conclusions upon substantial evidence, deference must be accorded to its findings as to the harm to be avoided and to the remedial measures adopted for that end, lest we infringe on traditional legislative authority to make predictive judgments when enacting nationwide regulatory policy.[122]

The record of legislative interventions in the US and Canada indicates that an awareness of the constitutional questions raised by sexually explicit speech has played some role in ensuring that legislative policies are based on reliable empirical evidence. That respective Supreme Courts have not always accepted that specific legislative schemes were narrowly tailored to meet states' legitimate interests in protecting the welfare of young persons should not deflect attention away from critical questions about the intensity of scrutiny applied by judges.[123]

By contrast, laws restricting speech that advocates the legalization of paedophilia will rarely be justified, even where the majority find this viewpoint repulsive. This is political speech par excellence, intended to change people's attitudes towards current laws and thus worthy of the highest protection from state interference. However, much sexually explicit expression involving actual/apparent imagery of children does not even attempt to engage in social deliberation.

---

122 *Turner Broadcasting System Inc.* v *FCC* 520 US 180, 212 (1997).

123 In the UK, conversely, the absence of principled parliamentary debate prior to October 2000 whenever legislative restrictions on sexually explicit imagery of children have been proposed would seem to make our domestic laws more vulnerable to constitutional challenge.

Chapter 7

Advertising, Autonomy and Proportionality: Constitutional Arguments Surrounding the Regulation of Commercial Expression

Introduction

Communications designed to persuade consumers to buy goods or services are typically subject to a range of legislative and extra legal restrictions. In the UK more than 150 statutes and statutory instruments impact upon commercial speech.[1] The *Trades Descriptions Act* 1968, for example, makes it a criminal offence to make false or misleading oral or written statements about goods and services.[2] Similarly, the *Property Misdescriptions Act* 1991 criminalizes the making of false or misleading statements in the course of an estate agency or property development business.[3] In other measures, statutory instruments which mandated the metrication of weights and measures make it an offence for traders to refuse to advertise their wares in metric units.[4] Businesses that continued to communicate information about their products in imperial units only after, at the latest, 1 January 2000 have been successfully prosecuted.[5] In addition, rules governing the advertising of harmful though lawful products have been tightened. European Union directives have sought (sometimes in an *ultra vires* manner) to harmonize rules on the promotion of tobacco products and sponsorship by tobacco manufacturers across member states. In the UK, the *Tobacco Advertising and Promotion (Point of Sale) Regulations* 2004 imposed limits on the

1 C Rohsler and A Willis, 'Pan European Advertising Clearance' (2004) 15 *Ent L R* 249.

2 See further I Ramsay, *Consumer Protection – Text and Materials* (1989, Weidenfeld and Nicolson, London) Ch. 6, and also I Ramsay, *Advertising, Culture and the Law* (1996, Sweet & Maxwell, London) 86 *et seq*.

3 The scope of the Act is set out in detail in the Property Misdescriptions (Specified Matters) Order SI 1992/2834.

4 The *Weights and Measures Act* 1985 (Metrication)(Amendment) Order 1994 implementing Council Directive 89/617/EEC, itself amending Directive 80/181 EEC. See further G Marshall, 'I Speak Your Weight But Only in Kilograms: Is Mandatory Metrication Lawful?' (1996) *PL* 1.

5 *Thoburn* v *Sunderland City Council* [2003] QB 151.

freedom of tobacco companies to advertise their products. Predictably, this measure was promptly challenged in *R (on the application of British American Tobacco & others)* v *The Secretary of State for Health* as a disproportionate means of promoting the state's legitimate interests in public health.[6] The outcome of that challenge is discussed later in this chapter. Extra-legally, self-regulatory codes of practice in the non-broadcast media set out standards of acceptable marketing communications and are policed by the Advertising Standards Authority and the Committee on Advertising Practice.[7] Professional bodies representing the interests of solicitors, barristers, architects, surveyors, and so on, also have their own sets of rules which limit the advertising of services by their members.[8] These have been challenged in a series of actions before the European Court of Human Rights with varying degrees of success. In international law, public health concerns over the consumption of tobacco led the World Health Organization to develop a *Framework Convention on Tobacco Control*. The Convention came into force in February 2005.[9] Obligations undertaken by ratifying states include the adoption of measures on health warnings on tobacco products and, where permitted under national constitutions, the imposition of a comprehensive ban on tobacco advertising, promotion and sponsorship.[10]

From the perspective of comparative constitutional law, it is instructive to examine the outcomes of disputes where statutory controls are tested in the courts for compliance with constitutional guarantees of freedom of expression on account of the differences of principle thrown up across different regimes, each of which proclaims a constitutional commitment to freedom of expression.[11] Thus, a fundamental question posed by any constitutional challenge relates to the *level* of protection to which commercial expression is entitled. Specifically, it may be asked whether such expression is on a par with political expression such as the criticism of government or elected officials, or whether it ranks more lowly as an inherently less valuable type of speech that may accordingly be regulated (even where the expression in question is truthful as in the case of tobacco advertising) by legislatures along with other issues of social policy without prompting the full range of constitutional objections

6 [2004] EWHC 2493.

7 On the ASA's expanded powers to regulate broadcast advertising, see A Willis, 'The Future Regulation of Broadcast Advertising' (2004) 15 *Ent L R* 255.

8 Of course, in the UK a number of these restrictions have been relaxed in the last 30 years. The Monopolies Commission may be credited with pushing the case for liberalization in 1970. See *A report on the general effect on the public interest of certain restrictive practices so far as they prevail in relation to the supply of professional services* Cmnd 4463.

9 *WHO Framework Convention on Tobacco Control*. On the date it came into force, the treaty bound the 40 states who became contracting parties before 30 November 2004.

10 *WHO Framework Convention on Tobacco Control* – Article 13.2. Ratifying states whose constitutions do not permit a complete ban undertake to apply restrictions to advertisements, promotion and sponsorship, Article 13.3.

11 See in general RA Shiner, *Freedom of Commercial Expression* (2003, OUP, Oxford); M Redish, 'Tobacco Advertising and the First Amendment' (1996) 81 *Iowa L Rev* 589; E Barendt, 'Tobacco Advertising: The Last Puff' (2002) *PL* 22.

that limitations on political speech provoke. The argument that will be made in this chapter is that, despite occasional doubts about whether in a particular instance the speech in question is commercial or not,[12] the interests of speakers and audience in much commercial expression put this speech type well outside the core reasons why free speech is valued in liberal democracies, although not so far from the core as to deny constitutional protection altogether as some have argued.[13] The core reasons why free speech is valued have to do with a well-functioning system of democratic deliberation and the desire to have informed popular control over office holders. It follows from this that, whilst we ought to be highly sceptical of restrictions upon political expression that the government believes to be false or misleading, we should be less troubled by the idea of restrictions on false or misleading commercial expression. In other words, the constitutional burdens that lie in the way of legislatures when seeking to regulate political expression should be much more formidable than those facing legislatures that opt to control the activities of estate agents, double-glazing salespersons or tobacco promoters. Admittedly, a more difficult issue is raised by purely truthful commercial expression that conveys useful information about the product (such as price and availability) to consumers who can then make a more informed decision about whether to buy or not. What attitude should the courts adopt towards governmental restriction of the communication of accurate product information? Should limits on freedom of expression here be treated with as much scepticism as those pertaining to political information? Before analysing the distinctive treatment of commercial speech claims in constitutional litigation, this chapter addresses some of the definitional and conceptual issues that are raised by commercial expression.

Commercial Expression Defined

Commercial expression may be defined as expression that is intended to further the economic interests of the speaker, usually in the form of an advertisement that communicates information about a product or service or expressing an opinion about the same (either in the form of praising the speaker's product/service or denigrating those of a competitor). Not all communications from such speakers will be motivated directly by the drive to increase market share alone, however. On occasion, it is conceivable that an individual or company may wish to participate in

12 This has been a recurrent problem in ECHR jurisprudence where a commercial entity seeks to contribute to a debate on a matter of public interest in a manner that also promotes services or goods offered by the speaker, see *Markt Intern and Beerman* v *Germany* (1989) 12 EHRR 161; *Stambruk* v *Germany*; *Jacobowski* v *Germany* (1994) 19 EHRR 64; *Hertel* v *Switzerland* (1998) 28 EHRR 534; *Verein gegen Tierfabriken* v *Switzerland* (2002) 34 EHRR 159 – all of which are discussed in further detail below. For an alternative view to that advanced in this chapter see C Munro, 'The Value of Commercial Speech' (2003) 62 *CLJ* 134.

13 RA Shiner, *Freedom of Commercial Expression* (2003, OUP, Oxford).

an ongoing public debate about (say) certain related ethical or product safety issues. In recent times, for example, Nike has been criticized for labour conditions in its Chinese, Indonesian and Vietnamese factories. A variety of monitoring bodies have reported *inter alia* that Nike forced its employees to work 11–12 hour days, required compulsory overtime, breached minimum wage laws and exposed staff to dangerous levels of toxic fumes and dust. The company responded to the allegations by way of issuing strenuous denials. It was then sued by Kasky under Californian state law for engaging in unfair and deceptive practices. Nike moved to have the claim dismissed on the grounds that Kasky's suit was barred under the First Amendment. Unfortunately, the US Supreme Court refused to hear the matter, ruling that Nike's move was premature.[14] As a result, the Court was not required to classify the speech type at issue in the case. In September 2003, the parties announced an out-of-court settlement in which they agreed that 'investments designed to strengthen workplace monitoring and factory worker programs are more desirable than prolonged litigation'.[15]

In other settings a member of a profession (practising lawyer/veterinary/pharmacist, and so on) may wish to initiate or contribute to a public debate about the adequacy of professional services. Whilst seen as an informed input to public debate, criticism (whether implicit or explicit) of the level of provision offered by rival professionals may also be thought to be intended in part to boost the speaker's own business interests.[16]

The categorization of these instances of expression as belonging to the purely commercial or political/public interest sphere is then all-important. If treated as commercial expression, any statutory restrictions which impinge upon the speaker's freedom to make certain claims or convey information may, for reasons that are explored below, pass constitutional examination relatively easily. On the other hand, if the expression is deemed to be more straightforwardly political expression, legal constraints will usually be made subject to much closer judicial scrutiny.[17]

Underlying Philosophical Arguments – Autonomy, Corporations, Listeners and Maximizing Market Efficiency

On what basis in free speech terms is the right to engage in commercial expression considered valuable? A moment's reflection upon the major rationales for freedom of expression reveals that advertisements for goods and services do little to serve the interests of an informed democracy exercising intelligent control over the holders of public office or, more broadly, a Millian search for truth. A claim, for example, that a

14 http://supct.law.cornell.edu/supct/html/02-575.ZC.html.

15 See http://www.nike.com/nikebiz/news/pressrelease.jhtml?year=2003&month=09&letter=f for Nike's version of the settlement.

16 Even if not directly intended, the speaker may well realise that the contribution is reasonably likely to advance his/her business interests.

17 See thus *Nike Inc. et al.* v *Kasky* 539 US (2003).

certain product will make the user instantly more attractive to the opposite sex is so patently false as to be qualitatively different from more obviously contestable claims in political, societal or moral matters where Mill's argument is more often applied. Much advertising is, as Barendt observes,

> ... inherently misleading, promising results in terms that are at best vague and at worst clearly false. Even factual statements by doctors or lawyers concerning the range and quality of services offered will often require supplementary information if they are not to give false impressions ...[18]

A more promising (and commonly recognized) basis for protecting commercial expression is offered by the notion of listener autonomy, understood as enhancing through the provision of information the ability of consumers to realize their potential to lead fulfilling and happy lives. Before considering this argument in more detail however, it is necessary to comment upon the autonomy claims of the producers of goods and services to freedom of commercial expression as speakers. The point of granting autonomy, it is generally agreed, is to further the values of happiness, dignity and flourishing. It is easy enough to envisage natural persons (individuals or groups of persons) as the beneficiaries of autonomy in these terms. What is less obvious is how corporations and other forms of commercial organization could be said to have interests *in the same way* in the pursuit of happiness, dignity and flourishing. Outside the context of freedom of expression claims, courts in Canada and the US have thus acknowledged that corporations and business organizations do not possess the same autonomy interests that natural persons have in other autonomy-based constitutional freedoms. Take, for example, s.7 of the *Canadian Charter of Rights and Freedoms* which states:

> Everyone has the right to life, liberty and security of the person and the right not to be deprived thereof except in accordance with the principles of fundamental justice.

An attempt by a toy manufacturer to claim the protection of s.7 failed in *Irwin Toy Ltd* v *AG Quebec*.[19] The Supreme Court of Canada found that the section

> ... was intended to confer protection on a singularly human level. A plain, common sense reading of the phrase 'Everyone has the right to life, liberty and security of the person' serves to underline the human element involved; only human beings can enjoy these rights. 'Everyone' then, must be read in light of the rest of the section and defined to exclude corporations and other artificial entities incapable of enjoying life, liberty or security of the person, and include only human beings.[20]

---

18 E Barendt, *Freedom of Speech* (1985, Clarendon Press, Oxford) 56.

19 [1989] 1 SCR 927.

20 *Ibid.*, at 1004. For a US example see *United States* v *White* 322 US 694 (1944), in the context of the Fifth Amendment privilege against self-incrimination. See further RA Shiner, *Freedom of Commercial Expression* (2003, OUP, Oxford) 166–78.

One possible response or qualification to this denial of autonomy-based rights is to look down the organizational scale away from multinational and national corporations to instances of individual proprietorship and small partnerships. Here, it may be harder to rule out autonomy-type values in the decisions and acts of smaller-scale commercial entities.

Whatever the force in this qualification, it remains the case that the more potent form of the autonomy-based argument for freedom of commercial expression lies in the audience or listener interest in receiving information about goods and services. To begin with, listener autonomy does not make distinctions between political speech, commercial expression and artistic work. The state interferes with the moral independence of citizens when it prevents them hearing what speakers on *any topic* have to say. Indeed, as compared to levels of apathy that exist in relation to political processes in many Western liberal democracies, it may be plausibly claimed that the attention and interest of the average citizen is considerably more engaged by the free flow of information about products and services.[21] The philosophical grounding for commercial expression rests on the view that informed consumer choices constitute an important feature of individual self-fulfilment. Constitutional protection for the commercial expression of others assists the self-realization of the recipients of expression in the sphere of personal economic decision-making.[22] Governmental interference with commercial expression (outside of preventing false and misleading advertising) is objected to because it obstructs the self-realization of recipients in making lifestyle choices. Whilst there is truth in this assertion, it may be doubted whether self-realization in the arena of economic decision-making really deserves to be put on equal footing with self-realization in other arenas such as religious affiliation or the decision to have children. The kind of human flourishing promoted by the exercise of autonomy in these latter spheres is best thought of as qualitatively different from, and more fundamental to individuals than, the flourishing that follows from the choices of motor car, washing powder or deodorant also made in individuals' lives. That is not to say that informed economic decision-making cannot contribute to individual growth, just that it will often rank as less important than other lifestyle choices and, that for this reason alone, might deserve less constitutional protection.[23] It is also right to note that autonomy alone cannot guarantee individual flourishing.

21 A point made by the US Supreme Court in *Virginia State Board of Pharmacy* v *Virginia Citizens Consumer Council* 425 US 748 (1976) at 763 *per* Blackmun J. However, it is doubtful whether this heightened interest in itself can sustain the argument for putting commercial expression on an equivalent constitutional footing to political expression or even conferring protection on commercial expression within a free speech principle at all. As Barendt argues, the mere fact of a high level of demand for pornography or state secrets does not mean that the expression in question is covered by the free speech principle; *Freedom of Speech* (1985, Clarendon Press, Oxford) 55.

22 See thus the Canadian Supreme Court in *Ford* v *Quebec (Att Gen)* [1988] 2 SCR 712.

23 Compare with Shiner in *Freedom of Commercial Expression* (2003, OUP, Oxford), who goes further than this in arguing that commercial expression does not qualify for any constitutional protection, at Chs. 10–12.

Low levels of educational attainment, poverty and even mental and physical ill health will variously hinder the forming and/or implementation of an individual's life plans.

Any analysis of the support offered by appeals to listener autonomy for commercial expression must also occur within a broader context of the complex relationship between autonomy and freedom of expression. Where the basis of a claim to expressive freedom is rooted in the value of autonomy and individual self-development, the very width or open-endedness of autonomy is such that it is apt to embrace making the most out of oneself or making oneself as wise as possible. Once this is granted, it is then difficult to see how the listener's interest in receiving speech is especially valuable alongside other autonomy-enhancing freedoms so as to confer on speech the status of an independent principle.[24] In terms of personal growth, other interests apart from receiving commercial speech are clearly important too. It might be conceded in particular that entitlements to individual privacy, religious freedom and freedom of association are all relevant to individual development. On what basis, if any, might commercial speech be regulated when its exercise infringes say a privacy-type interest in not being made subject to unsolicited advertising or cold-calling by telephone?

States plainly rely upon a number of justifications to support intrusions into truthful commercial expression. Two main types of justification can be usefully identified. The first is derived from paternalist concerns – namely to prevent the individual from self-inflicted harm. The second type of justification is non-paternalist in nature – namely, the prevention of harm to a societal interest. Shiner has made the valuable point that, in the context of restrictions on commercial expression, courts frequently and wrongly categorize constraints as springing from paternalist motives on the part of the state. In truth, he argues, regulation will often be partially or even primarily prompted by non-paternalist reasoning.[25] Take, for example, restrictions on the advertising of gambling. Clearly there is a paternalist basis to such controls but there is a societal interest at stake here as well in the form of preventing/limiting certain harms to family life that are commonly associated with addictive gambling. Limits placed on the advertising of tobacco products may also have a significant non-paternalist rationale in the form of reducing harm to persons other than the individual user/potential user of tobacco products (the health of those sharing an enclosed space with the smoker) and the public interest in freeing up limited economic resources for other health priorities. Likewise, restrictions upon the advertisement of lawyers' professional services are justified by broader public interest concerns

24 J Lichtenberg (ed.), *Democracy and the Mass Media* (1990, CUP, Cambridge) at 108. Constitutional writers in the US have expressed much the same point, see G Gunther, *Constitutional Law* (1985, The Foundation Press Inc., New York) Ch. 11.

25 In what follows, I focus on non-paternalist arguments for limiting commercial expression for the reason that they feature more commonly in constitutional litigation. For a discussion of possible paternalist arguments *within* an autonomy paradigm, see Shiner, *ibid.*, at Ch. 11.

such as maintaining the dignity of the profession and the special status of lawyers as intermediaries between the public and the courts.[26] It follows that arguments against paternalism, even if convincing, will not always address the full panoply of reasons behind a restriction on commercial expression.[27]

In the case of restrictions imposed for reasons beyond the mere prevention of harm to the intended consumer, state interference with truthful commercial expression may be justified from outside the autonomy paradigm altogether by reference to legitimate and substantial state interests that trump listener autonomy claims. These might include social policy concerns such as a claimed adverse effect of the product/service upon family life, the economic costs to society of treating the users of a product and the tendency for criminal activity to cluster around the commercial activity in question. As shall be seen below, a number of liberal democratic constitutions do permit restrictions on truthful advertising provided that the means chosen do in fact advance those interests and are no more extensive than is necessary to further the same.

Before turning to consider the stances taken in a number of Western liberal democratic regimes, it is important to consider a further rationale for affording commercial expression protection as a matter of constitutional principle, namely that the free flow of information about products and services is important to the efficient operation of competitive markets and, as such, important to society as a whole. When consumers have access to information about price, quality and availability of goods, each individual buyer can search out and purchase the product whose combination of price and quality suits best their budget. This ability of buyers in turn stimulates sellers to compete with each other for custom by improving what they have to offer consumers. Restricting access to information about price or some other attribute undermines consumers' abilities to locate 'best' products and thereby lessens the incentive upon sellers to compete.[28] As a result, market efficiency is diminished. As will be seen below, judicial appeals to the public interest in well-functioning competitive markets do feature in constitutional litigation as a check on governmental regulation of product information. It is not clear, however, that the system benefits of an unregulated flow of commercial information are as straightforward as its supporters would have us believe.

In disputing the benefits of an unregulated flow of commercial information in market efficiency terms, critics have pointed to the 'bounded rationality' of consumers to make appropriate use of the sheer volume of unrestricted expression. Making reference to empirical psychological studies, Ramsay has noted that consumers

---

26 *Casado Coca* v *Spain* (1994) 18 EHRR 1 para. 54.

27 For discussion of various attempts to construct paternalist arguments that are purportedly ultimately autonomy respecting, see Shiner, *ibid.*, at Ch. 11. One arena in which paternalism would appear to offer a reasonable basis for control concerns bans on tobacco advertisements aimed at, or likely to be seen by, children and young persons.

28 H Beales *et al.*, 'The Efficient Regulation of Consumer Information' (1981) 24 *Journal of Law and Economics* 492.

typically accept the form in which factual claims are made by the speaker (such as monthly interest rate rather than a yearly rate which might cause a would-be purchaser to think more carefully before deciding to buy).[29] Also, consumers tend to attach excessive reliance on small data samples presented by sellers and prefer to rely upon anecdotal evidence over mathematically respectable statistical information. These findings endorse claims that factually accurate advertising can nonetheless prove misleading. Moreover, it appears that consumers' research is limited to a few of the alternative products/services on offer. Some buyers might recoil from the large volume of information available and screen out some relevant data. The studies suggest that, far from creating the conditions for optimal functioning, unregulated information flows may undermine the reasoning capacity of consumers. Even if there were no failures in consumers' reasoning, an unregulated system might still fail to maximize purchaser utility. In such a system, sellers would not be required (and have no incentive) to disclose product information which was either costly to ascertain or showed the product in a bad light (such as the level and type of toxic ingredients in a brand of cigarette). This would plainly prejudice consumers' capacities to make best choices, impacting most severely especially where the buyer is unlikely to make a repeat purchase or unaware after initial purchase of the product's full attributes. It follows that, consistent with maximising utility, the state may be entitled to force sellers to make certain disclosures about their products that would not otherwise readily come to light in an unregulated market.

National Legal Systems' Treatment of Constitutional Claims to Commercial Expression

The United States

In a previous chapter dealing with hateful expression, I suggested that, of late, the US Supreme Court had began an assault on the tiered nature of expression types that had hitherto been a generally accepted feature of First Amendment jurisprudence. Particular emphasis was placed on the Court's decision in *RAV* v *City of St Paul, Minnesota* where, in relation to the 'fighting words' doctrine, the majority led by Justice Scalia, embarked upon a fundamental revision of established doctrine.[30] After *RAV*, fighting words became entitled to First Amendment protection where previously they had been entirely outside the First Amendment. The ordinance at issue in the case had targeted racial epithets and other particular subsets of 'fighting words' (rather than imposing a blanket prohibition on all fighting words). This meant that speakers who wished to air their views on disfavoured subjects were caught by the ordinance whilst others who provoked anger, alarm or resentment on the bases of political affiliation, trade union membership or homosexuality were not brought

29 I Ramsay, *Consumer Protection – Text and Materials* (1989, Weidenfeld and Nicolson, London) 46–7.

30 505 US 377 (1992).

within its ambit. In short, the authorities were proposing to treat race-based fighting words differently from other types of fighting words. Such contents-based regulation was not permitted.

Does *RAV* reflect a broader dissatisfaction with the hierarchical categorization of speech types under the First Amendment? In particular, in relation to the doctrine of commercial expression has there been any re-evaluation of the appropriate level of protection for promotional advertising? Currently, the regulation of commercial speech is subject under the rule enunciated in cases such as in *Ohralik* v *Ohio State Bar Association*[31] and *Central Hudson Gas & Electricity* v *Public Service Commission*[32] to a less strict standard of scrutiny than political speech 'commensurate with its subordinate position in the scale of First Amendment values'.[33] As will be shown below, this lesser status has been subject in the intervening years to serious challenge. At the time of writing, however, *Central Hudson* is still authoritative.

Viewed through a historical lens, the current subordinate status of commercial expression nonetheless represents an enhancement in the protection for commercial expression on the 1942 ruling in *Valentine* v *Chrestensen* where the respondent unsuccessfully challenged a New York City ordinance outlawing the distribution of commercial advertising on city streets.[34] Acknowledging in passing that the communication of information and opinion on matters outside of public interest was constitutionally protected, a unanimous Court went on unequivocally to declare that 'the Constitution imposes no such restraint on government as respects purely commercial advertising.'[35]

This exclusion was ended some 34 years later in *Virginia State Board of Pharmacy* v *Virginia Citizens Consumer Council* when by a majority of 8–1 the Court struck down a state law that had declared the advertisement by licensed pharmacists of the prices of prescription drugs to constitute unprofessional conduct.[36] Since then, constitutional challenges to the regulation of commercial expression have obliged the Court to address the question of when state interference is First Amendment-compliant. In *Virginia State Board of Pharmacy* the initial decision to afford constitutional protection for commercial information rests upon a variety of rationales. The Court alluded at the outset to the listener autonomy claims of the recipients of commercial information to be free to make purchasing decisions. Individual consumers, the Court noted, particularly the poor, sick and aged, had a clear interest in learning about where best to spend 'their scarce dollars' on healthcare needs.[37] When drugs prices varied as strikingly as they did, access to accurate information

31 436 US 447 (1978).

32 447 US 557 (1980).

33 *Ohralik* v *Ohio State Bar Association* 436 US 447, 456 (1978). See further C Munro, 'The Value of Commercial Speech' (2003) 62 *CLJ* 134, 135–8.

34 316 US 52 (1942).

35 *Ibid.* at 54. See also *Breard* v *City of Alexandria* 341 US 622 (1951).

36 425 US 748 (1976).

37 425 US 748, 763 (1976).

'could mean the alleviation of physical pain or the enjoyment of basic necessities.'[38] In some cases, the Court recognized that commercial advertising would also contain information of more general public interest entitling such expression to heightened protection under established First Amendment norms. Blackmun J cited the Court's ruling in *Bigelow* v *Virginia* one year previously where a state law that criminalized the selling or circulating of newspapers containing advertisements that encouraged abortions was struck down. The advertisement in *Bigelow* had announced to readers that abortions were lawful in New York and provided the name of a referral agency in New York. This was considered to contain information on a matter of public interest about a lawful service.[39] Finally, *Virginia State Board of Pharmacy* recognized a public interest in the myriad number of private economic decisions being taken in an 'intelligent and well informed' manner.[40]

On this view, some restrictions on advertising may constitute not only an unjustified form of paternalism on the part of the state which prevents consumers perceiving their own best interests but also damage the separate public interest in aggregate informed consumer decision-making.[41] The latter suggestion met with scorn from the dissenting member of the Court, Justice Rehnquist in his forceful rebuke to the majority:

> I had understood this view to relate to public decision making as to political, social and other public issues, rather than the decision of particular individual as to whether to purchase one or another kind of shampoo. It is undoubtedly arguable that many people in the country regard the choice of shampoo as just as important as who may be elected to local, state or national political office, but that does not automatically bring information about competing shampoos within the protection of the First Amendment.[42]

---

38 *Ibid.* at 764. The argument about facilitating consumer choice has been applied to advertising the monopoly supply of a product. In *Central Hudson Gas & Electricity Corporation* v *Public Service Commission of New York* 447 US 557, 567–8 (1980) which is discussed in greater detail below, the fact that the advertiser held a monopoly in electricity supply in its service area did not mean that speech restriction impacted only negligibly. A consumer might need the information to decide whether to use the service at all (there being rival energy sources in fuel oil and natural gas) or how much of the service should be used.

39 421 US 809 (1975). *Bigelow* should be seen in its proper context – following fast on the heels of *Roe* v *Wade* 410 US 113 (1973) which had upheld a constitutional right to abortion under certain circumstances. On the willingness to find a public interest component within ostensibly commercial speech forms, see *Bates* v *State Bar of Arizona* 433 US 350 (1977) and *Bolger* v *Youngs Drug Products Corp.* 463 US 60 (1983).

40 425 US 748, 765 (1976).

41 *Ibid.* at 770. For background to the development of First Amendment doctrine (and criticism of the 'paternalism' that is claimed to lie behind state regulation of harmful products such as tobacco) see M Redish, 'Tobacco Advertising and the First Amendment' (1996) 81 *Iowa L Rev* 589.

42 *Ibid.* at 786–7. Rehnquist J doubted whether door-to-door 'pot-sellers' came within the protective ambit of the First Amendment.

Nonetheless, *Virginia State Board of Pharmacy* having settled that commercial speech was protected under the First Amendment, the Court in subsequent litigation has had opportunities to consider more fully the issue of just how much protection from governmental interference commercial speech is entitled to. In *Central Hudson Gas & Electricity* v *Public Service Commission*, a four-part analysis was applied to determine constitutionality in commercial speech cases, namely:

> For commercial speech to come within … [the First Amendment], it must at least concern lawful activity and not be misleading. Next we ask whether the asserted government interest is substantial. If both inquiries yield positive answers, we must determine whether the regulation directly advances the governmental interest asserted, and whether it is not more extensive than is necessary to achieve that interest.[43]

Reflecting international concerns over insufficient energy supplies in the mid 1970s, the Public Service Commission of New York had sought to prohibit factually accurate promotional advertising by the monopoly electricity supplier for the purposes of conserving limited energy resources.[44] Before the Supreme Court, it was accepted that the state's interest in conserving energy was substantial, given the national dependence on energy resources from outside the US. There was also a direct connection between advertising and electricity consumption. The court felt sure that Central Hudson would not be contesting the ban unless it considered that advertising was likely to increase electricity consumption. Logically, it followed that a ban on advertising would directly advance the substantial government interest in energy conservation. This left unresolved the critical issue of proportionality. Was the ban no more extensive than necessary to advance the goal of energy conservation? Concluding that the regulator had not shown that a less restrictive speech restriction would not have adequately served the state's legitimate interests, the total ban on all advertising was adjudged to violate the appellant's First Amendment rights. Specifically, the Court found that the all-encompassing nature of the prohibition prevented Central Hudson from advertising energy-saving devices that would actually advance the cause of energy conservation.

Despite the result in *Central Hudson*, the judgment may be characterized as allowing some leeway to the state when regulating the communication of truthful commercial information. This width was made manifest perhaps most controversially in *Posadas de Puerto Rico* v *Tourism Co* when the Supreme Court upheld by 5–4 a partial ban imposed by the Puerto Rico legislature on advertisements for casino gambling.[45] As construed by the lower courts, the restrictions prohibited advertising aimed at the residents of Puerto Rico whilst allowing publicity in tourist publications targeted at foreign visitors. The majority view reasoned that the state had a substantial interest in reducing gambling among its citizens. The legislature

43 447 US 557, 566 (1980) *per* Powell J.

44 An embargo by Arab Middle East oil exporters in the 1970s hit countries such as the US which were generally perceived to have been pro-Israeli in their foreign policy stances.

45 478 US 328 (1986).

had reasonably concluded that excessive gambling would damage the health, safety and welfare of the people. The measure it had chosen to lessen demand for gambling among its citizens directly advanced this interest in a proportionate manner. The fact that advertisements for other gambling activities (including horse-racing and cock-fighting) remained outside the scope of the prohibition did not invalidate the measure. The legislature had considered that the threats posed by casino gambling warranted tighter advertising controls than other forms of gambling. In any event, there was no constitutional right to gamble. The state could, if it had so chosen, have completely banned gambling by the residents of Puerto Rico. If the power to ban gambling completely existed, the lesser power to ban advertising of casino gambling must also be granted.

By contrast, the minority led by Brennan J queried the application of *Central Hudson*'s looser scrutiny standard. When government attempted to manipulate private behaviour by depriving citizens of truthful information about lawful products, the resulting interference with consumer autonomy must be made subject to strict scrutiny. On the facts here, the state had not established to the standard required under the strict scrutiny standard that gambling did bring about the harmful effects that its detractors alleged.[46]

Perhaps emboldened by the sharply split Court in *Posadas*, opponents of the regulation of truthful commercial speech were back before the Supreme Court in a further challenge to state regulations in *44 Liquormart et al.* v *Rhode Island et al.*[47] Once more, the Court split 5–4 on the appropriate scrutiny standard. The entire Court agreed that the Rhode Island Legislature's virtual blanket ban on the advertisement of all retail alcohol prices had violated the First Amendment.[48] Once more, a majority of the Court adhered to the *Central Hudson* 'looser' scrutiny approach and found on this occasion that the means used to further the legitimate and substantial state interest of dampening demand for alcohol was not narrowly tailored to that interest.[49] Other, less intrusive (and non-speech curtailing) means were open to the authorities, including raising taxes on alcohol, educating the public about the dangers associated with alcohol consumption and limiting per capita purchases.

Whilst agreeing that the restriction lacked narrow tailoring, the minority opinion took issue with the looser scrutiny standard in *Central Hudson*. Justice Stevens who was joined by Justices Kennedy and Ginsburg doubted whether the Court should apply that standard when confronted, as was the case here, with a complete ban on the communication of truthful, non-misleading information about a lawful product. According to Justice Stevens, the First Amendment required the Court to

46 *Ibid.* at 350–60 and joined by Marshall and Blackmun JJ.

47 517 US 484 (1996).

48 The ban was not comprehensive since the price of alcohol could be displayed at the point of sale.

49 The majority view upholding *Central Hudson* is constructed from the opinion of Justice O'Connor (joined by Rehnquist CJ, Souter and Breyer JJ) and the separate concurrence of Scalia J who, despite expressing unease with the 1980 ruling, was not prepared to overrule it.

be 'especially sceptical of regulations that seek to keep people in the dark for what the government perceives to be their own good'. Making clear his commitment to a listener autonomy defence of commercial communications, he argued as follows:

> Precisely because bans against truthful, non-misleading commercial speech rarely seek to protect consumers from either deception or overreaching, they usually rest solely on the offensive assumption that the public will respond 'irrationally' to the truth.[50]

Although *44 Liquormart* was hailed by some as the occasion when the constitutional basis of paternalist controls on truthful advertising was seriously undermined and hopes raised that strict scrutiny of such communications might soon be a reality,[51] neither in fact has come to pass. Although the Court in *Lorillard Tobacco* v *Reilly AG Massachusetts* subsequently invalidated a partial ban on the outdoor advertising of tobacco products within 1,000 feet of schools or playgrounds and, indoors, on adverts placed lower than five feet from the floor,[52] it did so within the parameters of *Central Hudson*. Notwithstanding the fact the state's interest in preventing under-age tobacco use was undoubtedly a substantial interest and the means chosen did directly advance that interest, the restrictions in question were still excessive, impacting as they did on tobacco companies' lawful communications with adult consumers.[53]

It may be thought that, despite the formal adherence to *Central Hudson*, bans of the sort attempted by Massachusetts face severe hurdles in practice in demonstrating compliance with the fourth limb of *Central Hudson*. The Court in *Lorillard* was at pains to dispel any such impression. Emphasizing that the requirement under the fourth part of that test of a 'fit' between the end objective of regulations and the means chosen to secure that end, *Lorillard* reiterated the point that this did not require the adoption of the 'least restrictive' means, simply a reasonable relationship between ends and means.

The survival of *Central Hudson* against recent onslaughts is to be welcomed. The denial of equivalent status with political expression not only reflects the ambivalent nature of the autonomy claims that underpin the leading arguments for strict scrutiny of purely commercial expression, but also signals the primacy of speech about matters relating to public affairs. A further encouraging strand that may be detected in *Posadas* and *44 Liquormart* is a degree of deference to the policy decisions of popularly elected assemblies. There are two interconnected suggestions at play here: first, that legislatures may be better placed in institutional terms to make social

---

50 517 US 484, (1996).

51 KM Sullivan, 'Cheap Spirits, Cigarettes and Free Speech: The Implications of *44 Liquormart*' [1996] *Sup Ct Rev* 123; Note, 'The Elephant in the Room: Evolution, Behavioralism and Counter-Advertising in the Coming War against Obesity' (2003) 116 *Harv L Rev* 1161.

52 533 US 525 (2001).

53 A recurrent theme in First Amendment jurisprudence is that adult-to-adult communications cannot be burdened merely out of wish to protect children from accessing such materials. See Chapter 6 and, *inter alia*, *Reno* v *ACLU* 521 US 844 (1997).

policy choices on the basis of the available empirical evidence; and second (and in consequence), that they enjoy a margin within which to adopt one among a range of possible policy stances without fear of judicial intervention. Questions about the extent of deference to legislative policy-making have also featured heavily in the Canadian Charter materials on commercial expression to which attention is now given.

Canada

In Chapter 2 of this book, the structure of constitutional adjudication under the s.1 'reasonable limits' clause of the *Canadian Charter of Rights and Freedoms* was discussed.[54] It will be recalled after *R* v *Oakes*[55] that, once an infringement of a Charter right has been established, it must be shown not only (i) that the objective of the infringement is of sufficient importance, but also that the chosen measure is (ii) rationally connected to the aforementioned objective and (iii) impairs the right as minimally as is necessary to meet the objective. Finally, (iv) the effect of the measure must not be out of all proportion to that which is gained by securing the objective.[56] I commented in Chapter 2 that the extent to which s.1 ensures the supremacy of legislative infringements of individual rights depends critically upon the intensity of judicial scrutiny applied by the Court, especially at stages (ii) to (iv) above.

In contrast to the initial tranche of First Amendment rulings, the Canadian Supreme Court made clear from the outset that advertising was protected by s.2(b) of the Charter's freedom of expression guarantee. This was explained on the basis that advertising and other forms of commercial expression fostered informed economic choices on the part of the recipients of speech.[57] Nonetheless, the same period also witnessed the Court conferring a wide discretionary zone on legislatures' regulation of pure commercial expression.[58] Thus, in *AG of Quebec* v *Irwin Toy Ltd*, the Court left intact Quebec's *Consumer Protection Act* which banned advertisements directed at persons under 13 years of age.[59] The legislation had a legitimate aim of protecting a group vulnerable to manipulation and did not advance this aim in a disproportionate manner. The makers of children's products remained free to direct their advertising to the true purchasers, namely adults. Whilst there was evidence that other, even

54 Section 1 states that Charter rights are subject to 'such reasonable limits prescribed by law as can be demonstrably justified in a free and democratic society'.

55 [1986] 1 SCR 103.

56 [1986] 1 SCR 103.

57 See thus *Ford* v *Quebec (Att Gen)* [1988] 2 SCR 712.

58 I do not consider here the striking down in *Ford* v *Quebec (Att Gen)* of Quebec's requirement that all public signs, posters and commercial advertising be expressed in the French language only. There are issues of national identity and political status that take the case out of the realm of standard commercial expression disputes. For analysis of the case and the legislative override in Canadian Constitutional law, see G Marshall, 'Taking Rights for an Override: Free Speech and Commercial Expression' (1989) *PL* 4.

59 [1989] 1 SCR 927.

less intrusive means were open to the state, provided there was a 'sound evidentiary basis' for the legislative policy, the majority in the Court

> … would not in the name of minimal impairment, take a restrictive approach to social science evidence and require legislatures to choose the least ambitious means to protect vulnerable groups.[60]

This relaxed scrutiny standard was appropriate in cases where the government was best seen as having to mediate between competing individuals and groups and evaluate conflicting scientific evidence and calls on scarce resources. The courts were not well equipped to make rival and supervening evaluations in these types of case. The case for judicial restraint was especially strong where the beneficiaries of the policy stance were considered especially vulnerable.[61] By contrast, where the government was the 'singular antagonist of the individual whose rights had been infringed', as was true in criminal law,[62] the courts could, with much greater certainty, engage in the relevant proportionality analysis. The myriad range of views and policy options before the legislature on how to deal with the nuisances caused by (or associated with) street soliciting by prostitutes justified a similarly deferential approach by the majority in *Reference re ss.193 & 195(1)(c) of the Criminal Code (Manitoba)* in respect of a restriction on communications in public for the purpose of prostitution.[63] Compared to the core reasons why expression was accorded constitutional protection, communications about sex for money could only be said to enjoy a peripheral status, making the state's task of demonstrating a 'reasonable limit' all the easier.

The leading counter-example from the early period of an unreasonable limit on freedom of commercial expression occurred in *Royal College of Dental Surgeons of Ontario et al.* v *Rocket et al.*[64] Significantly, the case concerned a prohibition on the advertisement of dental services set down in professional misconduct rules rather than an Act of Parliament. Although the purpose behind the prohibition was legitimate (namely, the maintenance of high standards of professionalism in dentistry and the prevention of irresponsible and misleading advertising), the prohibition went beyond the control of misleading advertising and the making of claims not susceptible to verification to catch the provision of accurate information of use to customers, including the hours of opening and the languages spoken at individual practices. For that reason, a unanimous Court declared that the prohibition did more than minimally impair dentists' and consumers' freedom of expression

60 *Ibid.*, at 934.

61 The majority relied upon the remarks of Dickson CJ in *Edwards Books & Art Ltd* v *The Queen* [1986] 2 SCR 713, 779: 'In interpreting and applying the Charter I believe that the courts must be cautious to ensure that it does not simply become an instrument of better situated individuals to roll back legislation which has as its object the improvement of the condition of less advantaged persons.'

62 *Ibid.*, at 933.

63 [1990] 1 SCR 1123.

64 [1990] 2 SCR 232.

entitlements and thus constituted a disproportionate interference with s.2(b) of the Charter. Although not explicit in the judgment, one reason the offending provision was cast aside relatively easily may owe something to the fact that it lacked the democratic credentials of either set of restrictions in *Reference re ss.193 & 195(1)(c) of the Criminal Code (Manitoba)* and *AG of Quebec* v *Irwin Toy Ltd.*[65] The policy choices selected in these latter instances reflected the outcome of considered and well-publicized debates among elected representatives after input from interested parties, pressure groups, individuals and the media. Social science evidence on the likely impact of rival policy solutions formed an essential part of the background to policy formation. These features were absent from the promulgation of dentists' professional misconduct rules in *Rocket*.

Judicial interference with the federal Parliament's social policy did occur in *RJR McDonald Inc.* v *Canada*[66] which concerned penal restrictions on tobacco advertising and sales imposed by the *Tobacco Products Control Act*. The law prevented all advertising and promotion of tobacco products unless accompanied by a list of a product's toxic constituents and a prescribed unattributed health warning. By the narrowest of majorities, the legislation was held to be unreasonable limit on s.2(b) of the Charter. In reaching their opposing conclusions, both the majority and minority judgments grappled with the relationship between the value of particular expressive acts and the degree of deference to legislative policy-making.

In the majority judgment, McLachlin J warned her colleagues of the dangers of what she perceived as excessive deference:

> … care must be taken not to extend the notion of deference too far. Deference must not be carried to the point of relieving the government of the burden which the Charter places on it of demonstrating that the limits it has imposed on guaranteed rights are reasonable and justifiable.[67]

Whilst Parliament was entrusted to enact social policy choices, the Court still had a crucial role to play in determining the constitutionality of those policy choices. McLachlin J also queried the distinction advanced by the Court in *Irwin Toy* to explain different degrees of deference towards legislative enactment.[68] Some statutes,

65 In support of the view that the courts ought, as a matter of principle, to show greater deference to an Act of Parliament than is appropriate in the case of a decision of the executive or subordinate legislation is due, see (in England) Laws LJ in *International Transport Roth Gmbh* v *Secretary of State* [2002] 3 WLR 344 at paras 82–3.

66 [1995] 3 SCR 199. For contrasting responses to *RJR McDonald* see M Jackman, 'Protecting Rights and Promoting Democracy: Judicial Review under Section 1 of the Charter' (1996) 34 *Osgoode Hall LJ* 661 and AC Hutchinson, 'Supreme Court Inc. – The Business of Democracy and Rights' in GW Anderson (ed.), *Rights and Democracy – Essays in UK–Canadian Constitutionalism* (1999, Blackstone Press Ltd, London).

67 *Ibid.*, at 332.

68 For academic criticism of the distinction, see D Beatty, 'The Canadian Charter of Rights: Lessons and Laments' in GW Anderson (ed.), *Rights and Democracy – Essays in UK–Canadian Constitutionalism* (1999, Blackstone Press Ltd, London) at 19–21.

she argued, might straddle the categories of regulating the competing rights/interests of different groups in society and engaging the state as a principal antagonist of the rights of the individual. This was particularly true in the case of criminal legislation such as the provisions presently before the Court.[69] Excessive deference was also problematic in constitutional terms since it attenuated the s.1 burden on the State to the point where, as the infringer of a Charter right, it was effectively relieved of the task of showing that limitations on Charter rights were reasonable and justified. Accordingly, McLachlin J ruled that the legislature's total prohibition on advertising Canadian tobacco products constituted a more than minimal impairment of the tobacco companies' expression entitlements.[70] The government had failed to show that the less intrusive measure of a partial ban (that would have allowed information and brand preference advertising) or attributed health warnings might equally have met the government's legitimate goal of preventing people from being persuaded to use tobacco products. Alive to the criticism that her stance may have overstated the protection for a form of speech which was considered less important than other speech forms, McLachlin J stressed the informational content of such speech which empowered consumers to make informed choices between brands.[71] The fact that such speech was profit-motivated was not relevant to a determination of the level of constitutional protection to which it became entitled.

For the minority,[72] the sole purpose of the appellant's expression was to promote the use of a product that was harmful and often fatal to its users. Together,

> … (t)he harm engendered by tobacco and the profit motive underlying its promotion place this form of expression as far from the 'core' of freedom of expression values as prostitution, hate-mongering and pornography … [73]

Addressing McLachlin J's point about the lack of definitive evidence linking advertising with tobacco consumption, LaForest J countered that it was simply unrealistic to expect Parliament to produce definitive social scientific evidence every time it wished to legislate in an area of pressing social concern. The peripheral value of tobacco advertising to core freedom of expression values and the demonstrable link between tobacco consumption and harm to health meant that the state need only show an attenuated level of s.1 justification for the advertising ban to pass constitutional muster. On the facts, the minority found that the purpose behind the measures was pressing and substantial and that the measures themselves were

69 Compare with LaForest J who chose to endorse the distinction in *Irwin Toy* and categorize the federal legislation as social policy aimed at striking a balance between conflicting interests, *ibid.*, at 279.

70 The prohibition was deemed to be rationally connected to the objective of dampening demand for tobacco products.

71 Although such a position assumes that the claims made for the product do not mislead purchasers in any way.

72 LaForest J, joined by Gonthier and L'Heureux-Dubé JJ.

73 [1995] 3 SCR 199, 281–4 for this section of reasoning.

rationally connected to their objective, constituted a minimal impairment of the appellant's Charter rights and were not otherwise disproportionate.

In a legislative sequel to the ruling, the *Tobacco Act* 1997 was passed. The Act follows closely the guidance set out by the majority in *RJR MacDonald* to meet the 'minimal impairment' criterion under the reasonable limits clause of the Charter. Thus, lifestyle advertising and advertising that appeals to minors were prohibited. On the other hand, informational and brand-preference advertising were permitted. The Act also permitted the Governor in Council to make regulations to further the objects of the Act.[74] These powers were used to require tobacco companies to place warnings and details about toxic emissions on cigarette packets. The warnings alone had to take up 50 per cent of the total surface area of a packet. In addition, information on how to stop smoking was also to be provided. Conscious that any tightening of conventional advertising rules would further accelerate the trend towards tobacco sponsorship in sports and cultural activities to convey 'lifestyle' messages, the 1997 Act (as amended) also prevented from October 2003 the display of a tobacco product related brand or manufacturer's name in association with a sports or cultural event or activity.[75]

The Act was thereafter challenged before the Quebec Superior Court in *JTI MacDonald and others* v *Att Gen of Canada*. In December 2002, the Act and its associated regulations were upheld.[76] Although this is unlikely to be the last word on the matter, the scope enjoyed by tobacco companies under the Canadian Charter to disseminate commercial information about their products has been substantially curtailed.

European Convention Article 10 Jurisprudence

As discussed in previous chapters, the Strasbourg Court and (in pre-November 1998 cases) the European Commission on Human Rights have consistently adopted a tiered view of freedom of expression in which political forms of expression have been accorded prime importance and given a considerable level of protection from national authorities' interference. In contrast, commercial and artistic expression have tended to receive much less protection from Strasbourg in respect of interference by national authorities.[77] Commercial expression may thus be regulated by national

74 The regulations were made under powers set out in ss.17 and 33 of the 1997 Act. They were approved by the Canadian Parliament in June 2000.

75 S.25 of the 1997 Act (inserted by amendment in SC 1998 c.38, s.1).

76 *Case No. 500-05-031299-975 et al.* (Judgment of 13 December 2002). Ruling available electronically at:
http://www.tobaccolaw.org/documents/english/cases/JTIMacDonaldCorpvAGfoCanada2002.htm.

77 Harris, O'Boyle and Warbrick suggest that commercial expression may even rank below artistic expression in Convention jurisprudence: DJ Harris, M O'Boyle and C Warbrick, *Law of the European Convention on Human Rights* (1995, Butterworths, London) at 402–3. For an argument that there may in fact be a substantial overlap between commercial and

authorities to prevent dishonest or misleading claims, unfair competition and, in respect of particular classes of product, even truthful advertising.[78]

In one of the earliest rulings on the point – *X and Church of Scientology* v *Sweden* – commercial expression (in the form of the church's advertisement for an 'E-meter' which purportedly measured the 'mental state of an individual') was recognized by the Commission to be within the ambit of Article 10 but entitled to a lesser level of protection than its political equivalent (understood in its broadest sense) since the latter was more closely connected to underlying Convention purposes.[79] Confirmation that commercial expression did enjoy protected expression status was subsequently provided by the Court in *Barthold* v *Germany*.[80] The concurring opinion of Judge Pettiti is worth highlighting because of his assertion of a direct connection between commercial speech and the right to receive and impart information and ideas. Advertising, he noted, provided the financial backing for private media organizations. As such, the courts should be wary of limits placed on commercial expression. The clear implication which his concurrence carried was that, without advertising revenues, there would be a reduction in communicative activity on the part of private sector broadcasters, a reduction which would impact negatively in spheres beyond advertising, striking at artistic and even political forms of expression. This implication needs close examination. What it fails to acknowledge is that the safeguarding of corporate media expression through advertising revenues cannot guarantee a *range* of artistic and political expression. It is more likely in practice to generate a narrow class of expressive activity that is considered to boost ratings. The goal of protecting diversity of opinion and ideas is arguably already much better served by Internet and web-based technologies where unorthodox views can co-exist alongside more mainstream speech.

Mirroring the structure of constitutional adjudication elsewhere and having established that commercial expression does lie within the ambit of Article 10, it is crucial to ascertain when national authorities might limit advertisements and other commercial speech consistently with the terms of Article 10. As the vast majority of domestic law restraints are likely to be prescribed by law[81] and for a legitimate purpose (the safeguarding of consumers' interests), the critical question in challenges

artistic expression, see C Munro 'The Value of Commercial Speech' (2003) 62 *CLJ* 134, 149–50.

78 *Stambuk* v *Germany* Application No. 37928/97, Judgment of 17 January 2003, at para. 39.

79 Application No. 7805/77 16 D.R. 68 (1979) at 73. Interestingly, the authority cited by the Commission for this view is *Handyside* v *United Kingdom* (1976) 1 EHRR 737. However, *Handyside* does not point unequivocally to the primacy of political expression. I discuss this point further below.

80 (1985) 7 EHRR 383.

81 It is important to remember that the 'prescribed by law' limb of Article 10(2) requires that any legal restriction be both accessible and stated with sufficient clarity as to enable citizens to regulate their conduct, see further *Sunday Times* v *United Kingdom* (1979) 2 EHRR 245.

to national authorities' controls will centre upon whether domestic provisions are 'necessary in a democratic society' and this requires analysis of the issues of (i) the proportionality of any restriction and (ii) the margin of appreciation enjoyed by municipal actors. Strasbourg case law indicates that applicants have fared better when they have been able to establish that the restricted communication went significantly beyond telling the public about a particular good or service but sought primarily to raise issues of general concern. Overall however, the leeway conceded to national authorities in cases such as *Markt intern Verlag and Beerman* v *Germany* (albeit on the casting vote of the President Ryssal) has been criticized in a number of places as excessive.[82] It has been argued, for example, that deference of the sort witnessed in *Markt intern* constitutes

> … a retreat from the fundamental principle of *Handyside* and *Sunday Times* cases that an interference with expression is necessary only if the state presents convincing evidence of a pressing social need for it.[83]

The argument in this part of the chapter seeks conversely to defend an attenuated standard of review in commercial expression cases as consistent with fundamental ECHR norms. It will be argued that, generally speaking, the Court has drawn appropriate distinctions between, on the one hand, expressive forms intended to be (and received as) a contribution to public debate which in a largely incidental manner publicize the speaker's business or professional interests and, on the other hand, communications which are primarily intended to generate business advantages to the speaker.[84]

To begin, however, it is necessary to examine the claim that restrictions on commercial expression are deserving of the same (or at least similar) intensity of scrutiny from the Strasbourg Court as limitations applied to speech that is critical of politicians or public institutions. This claim rests upon the view that consumer empowerment through access to information about products and services is tied closely to (and is a concrete manifestation of) individual development. *Handyside* did indeed emphasize a dual rationale for protecting freedom of expression, noting that it was 'one of the basic conditions for the progress of democratic societies

---

82 (1989) 12 EHRR 161 and see comments by JG Merrills and AH Robertson, *Human Rights In Europe – A Study of the European Convention on Human Rights* (3rd edn, 1994, Manchester University Press, Manchester) 153–4; M Hunt in his paper 'Commercial Freedom of Speech, Advertising and Human Rights' delivered at a conference entitled *Human Rights, Privacy and the Media*, held at University College London on 8 January 1998; DJ Harris, M O'Boyle and C Warbrick, *Law of the European Convention on Human Rights* (1995, Butterworths, London) at 404–5. D Pannick, 'Article 10 of the European Convention on Human Rights' in P Birks (ed.), *Pressing Problems in the Law* (1995, OUP, Oxford).

83 Harris, O'Boyle and Warbrick, *ibid.*

84 Of course it is possible to point to counter-examples. Consider *Open Door Counselling and Dublin Well Woman Centre* v *Ireland* (1992) 15 EHRR 244, where the Court did not distinguish between the types of speech involved in the publication of leaflets in Ireland that detailed the availability of abortion services in the UK.

and for the development of each individual'.[85] The democracy-enhancing and individual development functions of freedom of expression have since been reiterated on numerous occasions including in *Lingens* v *Austria*[86] and *Oberschlick* v *Austria*.[87] It would be mistaken, however, to infer from these remarks that the individual autonomy/development rationale is considered by the Court to be on an equal footing with its democracy-enhancing counterpart. To begin with, the quoted extract from *Handyside* above needs to be read in the context of the remarks preceding it:

> The Court's supervisory functions oblige it to pay the utmost attention to the principles characterising a 'democratic society'. Freedom of expression constitutes one of the essential foundations of such a society and one of the basic conditions for its progress and for the development of every man.[88]

Virtually the entire emphasis in this passage indicates that Article 10 is valuable for the role it plays in maintaining and progressing democratic society. It is only the last phrase which points up an additional benefit of freedom of expression, namely individual development. Given the background circumstances leading to the formation of the Council of Europe, the primacy accorded to democracy-related expression is hardly surprising. As Merrills and Robertson have observed, the Council was formed shortly after 1945 by statesmen involved in the struggle against totalitarianism. These framers all too keenly appreciated that the first steps on the road back towards a dictatorship began with the curtailment of key individual rights such as freedom of the press, assembly and open trials. Accordingly, it was crucial to 'lay down in advance the rights and freedoms that must be respected in a democratic society…'.[89] The primacy of the democracy-enhancing rationale for freedom of expression in Strasbourg's Article 10 jurisprudence has been noted by the current Registrar of the Court – Paul Mahoney. Writing in 1997, he referred to the two major purposes for which freedom of expression has been valued by the Court and Commission as (i) enabling participation in decision-making by all members of society; and (ii) ensuring individual and group fulfilment.[90] He then commented:

> … [t]he Court and the Commission have, however, made it clear in subsequent case law that for them the main argument for free speech is the one derived from the first

85 (1979–80) 1 EHRR 737. For some interesting insights into the dynamics of Article 10 jurisprudence in general, see M Oetheimer, *L'Harmonisation de la Liberté d'Expression en Europe* (2001, Editions A Pedone, Paris).

86 (1986) 8 EHRR 407, 418.

87 (1995) 19 EHRR 389, 421.

88 (1979–80) 1 EHRR 737 at para. 49.

89 JG Merrills and AH Robertson, *Human Rights In Europe – A Study of the European Convention on Human Rights* (3rd edn, 1994, Manchester University Press, Manchester) at 3.

90 P Mahoney, 'Universality versus Subsidiarity in the Strasbourg Case Law on Free Speech: Explaining Some Recent Judgments' (1997) EHRLR 364.

purpose, namely providing one of the main pillars for the effective functioning of political democracy … .[91]

Apart from the immediate historical legacy and the Court's own rhetoric, the primacy of the democracy-enhancing rationale for freedom of expression is further pointed up (albeit negatively) by the ambivalent relationship between freedom of expression and individual autonomy outlined earlier in this chapter. To recapitulate: a serious weakness in the claim for expression speech as essential for individual self-development is that the latter notion is very broad, encapsulating as it does the ideas of making the most out of oneself or making oneself as wise as possible. Viewed thus, autonomy becomes so open-ended as to fail to mark out speech in particular and confer on it the status of an independent principle.[92] Thus, in terms of self-fulfilment, other interests apart from speech are important too. It might be conceded that individual privacy, religious freedom and freedom of association are all relevant to individual development. An overriding concern for autonomy might conceivably lead us to contemplate drastic inroads into freedom of expression. Thus analysed, and in contrast to the enhancement of democracy rationale, autonomy fails to offer unequivocal support for freedom of expression.

If the foregoing argument is correct, claims to freedom of expression such as commercial expression which rest solely on autonomy grounds must necessarily lack the core status which political speech forms acquire. One consequence of this is that, consistent with Article 10, states can control the contents of commercial expression in ways that would not survive scrutiny in respect of more obviously political forms of expression. The questions to which attention must now be given are whether and, if so, to what extent does the Strasbourg Court's jurisprudence reflect this ordering?

In the analysis which follows, it is argued that the Court's treatment of the commercial expression claims has been properly nuanced. For the most part, it has been alive to the importance of contributions to debate on matters of public interest (and hence political expression) made by speakers in circumstances where any resulting economic advantage/disadvantage has properly been categorized as an incidental or secondary consequence of the contested communication.

Examples of Unlawful Domestic Interference with Expression Interests

An early example of the Court's awareness on this point is evident in *Barthold* v *Germany* which arose from an interview given to a Hamburg evening newspaper by the director of a veterinary practice providing 24-hour emergency vet service. In the interview he revealed how busy his evening surgeries were. The resulting article criticized the lack of evening services in Hamburg and published a list of vets

---

91 *Ibid.*, at 372.

92 J Lichtenberg (ed.), *Democracy and the Mass Media* (1990, CUP, Cambridge) at 108. Constitutional writers in the US have expressed much the same point; see G Gunther, *Constitutional Law* (1985, The Foundation Press Inc., New York) Ch. 11.

offering emergency services and their telephone numbers. Dr Barthold's photograph also appeared in the article although the caption incorrectly gave the name of another vet.[93] After complaints were made by fellow veterinaries, an injunction was granted by the regional court (and confirmed by the Court of Appeal) on unfair competition grounds preventing Dr Barthold from speaking to journalists about his clinic's experiences of veterinary provision at night.[94] By a margin of five votes to two, the European Court followed the unanimous verdict of the Commission in holding that the injunction violated Dr Barthold's Article 10 rights. The newspaper article was judged to be primarily about the level of evening veterinary services. Any publicity to Dr Barthold's clinic was purely a secondary consequence of the article. It followed that the injunction did not accord sufficient importance to a matter of public interest and would, on the contrary, have the damaging effect of discouraging members of the professions from joining public debate. This was a particularly serious risk on the present facts because German domestic law allowed the grant of injunction on the ground of unfair competition where the publicity resulting from any published article was a minor consequence *only* of the article.

In a similar factual context, the Court in *Stambuk* v *Germany* was required to assess the dominant/secondary effect of a newspaper article about laser techniques which referred to the applicant's ophthalmology practice and his success rate in using laser techniques.[95] The applicant's photograph was included in the published story. On being fined for a breach of professional conduct rules regarding the advertising of services,[96] the applicant challenged this sanction under Article 10. As in *Barthold*, the dispute centred upon the proportionality of the domestic penalty. Once more, the Court conceded that the article did give publicity to the applicant. However, the dominant impact of the article was to inform the general public on a matter of considerable interest – the risks and success rates of corrective laser eye surgery.

The Court has also had to confront situations where, although the applicant has nothing to sell, the economic interests of others are adversely affected by the information and/or opinions expressed by the applicant. One such example was *Hertel* v *Switzerland*, where the applicant wrote a paper that pointed in qualified terms to a connection between food cooked in microwave ovens and the development of cancer in humans.[97] The paper's findings were published in a journal and used by the editor to support much less guarded claims that microwave ovens were harmful.[98] Subsequently, a Swiss manufacturers' association obtained an order to restrain the applicant from repeating his claims. Whilst accepting that the expression

93 The error was corrected in the following day's edition of the newspaper.

94 The terms of the injunction did allow communication with professional journals.

95 [2002] ECHR 674 Application No. 37928/97.

96 The article was considered to go beyond the bounds of an objective presentation of information.

97 (1999) 28 EHRR 534.

98 The front cover of the magazine was entitled 'The danger of microwaves: scientific proof' and had an image of the Grim Reaper with an outstretched hand pointing to a microwave oven.

was likely to have an adverse impact on the rights of microwave manufacturers, the Court declared the order to constitute a disproportionate interference with Mr Hertel's Article 10 rights, substantially inhibiting as it did the applicant's freedom to contribute to a public debate about the safety of microwave ovens. The fact that his views were not generally accepted in the scientific community did not render the order Article 10-compliant.[99]

Examples of Permitted Interference with Commercially Related Expression

The Court's pronouncements in *Barthold*, *Stambuk* and *Hertel* doubtless satisfied those onlookers concerned at national authorities' attempts to silence discussion of matters of interest to consumers, the public and policy-makers alike. Disappointingly for such observers, the Court has not always been prepared to find domestic restrictions in breach of Article 10. As was acknowledged earlier, the margin of appreciation that was afforded to the national authorities in *Markt intern & Beerman* v *Germany*[100] has come in for particular criticism as an instance where the Court mistakenly abandoned the application of a rigorous scrutiny standard in favour of a deferential approach. For reasons that will now be set down, it is argued that this criticism is misconceived and that the majority of the Court properly understood the less vital nature of claims to freedom of commercial expression.

The applicant was the publisher of a weekly bulletin whose purpose was to defend the business interests of small and medium-sized retail outlets against larger competitors such as supermarkets and mail order companies. One issue of the bulletin in November 1975 included details of an 'angry' complaint made by a chemist who expressed dissatisfaction with the quality of cosmetics she had ordered from an English mail order company and the failure of the company to honour a promise to reimburse the purchaser. The bulletin encouraged its readers to report their experiences with the mail order company in order to determine whether this was an isolated incident or part of a more general pattern. This issue of the bulletin was the fourth time in two months that the publisher had criticized the English company. On one of the previous occasions, it had urged readers to boycott the company. In response, the latter obtained an injunction under Germany's unfair competition laws which prevented repetition of matters referred to in the November issue unless any future article also made clear that (i) there was no reason to doubt the company's statement that it had no knowledge of receiving the goods; (ii) upon receiving the complaint, the company had reiterated its promise to reimburse the purchaser; and

99 See further *VGT* v *Switzerland* (2002) 34 EHRR 159, where a clear public interest element in the expressive activity (a 'television commercial' against meat production and promoting animal welfare) meant that the Swiss authorities' margin of appreciation to prohibit the 'commercial' was less extensive than would apply to more straightforwardly commercial advertising for a particular product. Under this narrowed margin of appreciation, the Court concluded that Switzerland had not demonstrated relevant and sufficient reasons for the ban.

100 (1989) 12 EHRR 161.

(iii) finally, that the company was not suspected of accepting payment for goods without immediately supplying the same. Before the Strasbourg Court, the applicants alleged that the injunction constituted an improper interference with their right to freedom of expression.

By the slimmest of majorities (10–9) made possible by the casting vote of President Ryssal, the injunction was held by the Court not to have infringed the applicants' Article 10 rights. This finding was based largely on the relatively broad margin of appreciation necessarily left to national authorities on commercial questions in general and competition law in particular. The complexity of that body of laws and constantly changing market conditions meant that the Strasbourg Court was not well placed to engage in a re-examination of the facts of each disputed case. Instead, it was confined to asking whether the measures were 'justifiable in principle and proportionate'.[101] On this basis, the applicants had failed to establish a breach of Article 10.

In a joint dissent, seven judges articulated their disagreement in the following terms:

> It is just as important to guarantee the freedom of expression in relation to the practices of a commercial undertaking *as it is in relation to the conduct of a head of government.*[102] [Emphasis added]

The unsoundness of this stance is evident upon brief reflection. As a matter of logic, the dissent has to be committed to one of two positions to attain parity of protection between commercial expression and its political equivalent: either the raising of the level of protection for commercial expression or, alternatively, the lowering of the level of protection for political expression. If the former position were adopted, commercial organizations ought to be free to make any false or misleading statement about their product or those of their competitors. If the latter position were adopted, we should allow the suppression of all false and misleading speech about political matters in much the same way as false and misleading advertisements are regulated.

On the facts in *Markt intern* it is hard to discern a strong public interest in the subject matter of the bulletin that would elevate it into the realms of political expression. The publication was intended to further the commercial interests of small businesses in their dealings with economically more powerful trading organizations. It was not suggested that the bulletin was either read by the public at large or dedicated to raising matters of obvious public interest. The Court's analysis might well have been different if the publishers had aired to a wider audience concerns, say, about a toxic component allegedly present in the make-up kits.

101 (1989) 12 EHRR 161 at para. 33.

102 Judges Golucklu, Pettiti, Russo, Spielmann, De Meyer, Carrillo Salcedo and Valticos. Judges Martens and McDonald issued a separate joint dissent also disputing the proportionality of the injunction.

The wide berth afforded to national authorities in *Markt intern* is apparent in the subsequent rulings of *Casado Coca* v *Spain*[103] and *Jacobowski* v *Germany*.[104] In the former, the Court declined to interfere with the Barcelona Bar Council's punishment of the applicant for having published a notice about his practice in a newsletter. In so doing, the Court pointed to the varying rates at which rules on professional advertising by lawyers were being relaxed across member states and considered that national authorities were best placed to strike the appropriate balance between upholding the administration of justice, maintaining the dignity of the profession, the interests of users of legal services in receiving accurate information and the interests of lawyers in advertising their services. Similarly, Germany's rules on unfair competition were again subject to a relaxed scrutiny standard in *Jacobowski* v *Germany* where the applicant – a journalist – was prevented under the terms of an injunction from distributing a circular sent out to broadcasters and other journalists which criticized a former employer and a letter offering to meet his fellow professionals to discuss 'not only the past but also future developments in the German "news market". I will ask for an appointment in due course'. The circular followed published criticism of the applicant by his former employer. The German courts all took the view that the communication was intended primarily to disparage a competitor and to establish personal business contacts, an interpretation supported by the fact that, prior to sending the circular, the applicant had manifested his intention to create his own rival news agency. In a 6–3 majority ruling, the European Court of Human Rights found that the injunction was within the national authority's margin of appreciation in matters to do with unfair competition. The majority agreed that the main purpose of the mailing was to solicit new business for the applicant rather than simply to defend his reputation. The proportionality of the injunction was evident from the fact that, under its terms, Jacobowski was not prevented from criticizing his former employer in any circumstances whatsoever. Criticism was permitted provided it was not done for 'the purposes of competition'.

Tobacco Advertising in EU and UK Law

The focus of much recent regulatory effort in respect of commercial expression in the EU and domestically has centred on attempts to dampen demand for harmful tobacco products. The various sets of restrictions have tended in the main to survive legal scrutiny suggesting in turn that the autonomy arguments advanced to support the freedom to make non-misleading statements about harmful products are treated by the EU and national courts as subordinate to the state's substantial interest in health promotion via reasonably tailored controls on advertising and sponsorship. Indeed, as will be seen below, the European Court of Justice has even turned the autonomy argument *against* tobacco manufacturers by upholding disclosure provisions that

103 (1994) 18 EHRR 1.

104 (1995) 19 EHRR 64.

oblige tobacco manufacturers to reveal levels of toxic components of cigarettes so that consumers might make more informed choices.

EU Law

Tobacco advertising on television across EU member states has been unlawful since national implementation of the *Television without Frontiers Directive*.[105] The sponsorship of television programmes is also prohibited under this 1989 measure. In May 2003, a new directive on the advertising and sponsorship of tobacco products requires member states to ensure that national laws prohibit the sponsorship by tobacco companies of international events such as Formula One motor racing.[106] A previous directive that would have imposed a complete ban on all forms of tobacco advertising and sponsorship was however nullified in *Germany* v *European Parliament and European Union*. The European Court of Justice ruled in 2000 that there was no legal basis for *Directive 98/43EC* in Community law.[107] Significantly for present purposes however, Advocate-General Fennelly did express the view in that case that a comprehensive media ban on tobacco advertising would not have violated Article 10 of the ECHR.[108] There were reasonable grounds for believing that a complete ban would achieve a significant reduction in the consumption of a dangerous product. Moreover, such a ban would also be proportionate since manufacturers would remain free to engage in point-of-sale advertising (if permitted by national laws) and campaign for the view that smoking was not harmful to its users.[109]

Other EU initiatives have tackled labelling issues in tobacco promotion with more success. *Directive 2001/37 EC concerning the manufacture, presentation and sale of tobacco products* required member states to bring into domestic law measures obliging manufacturers to display on packets tar, nicotine and carbon monoxide levels and also to print on packets more severe health warnings covering a larger proportion of the packet than had hitherto been required. Elsewhere, the directive banned the use of descriptors 'mild' and 'light'. The ECJ was called upon to examine the validity of the directive in *R (on the application of British American Tobacco (Investments) Ltd)* v *Secretary of State for Health*.[110] The directive was held to be within the competence of Community institutions under Article 95 (internal market).

105 *Council Directive 89/552* of 3 October 1989.

106 *European directive on advertising and sponsorship of tobacco products* 2003/33 26 May 2003. The same measure also outlaws cross-border promotion of tobacco products via radio and Internet advertising.

107 [2000] ECR I – 8419 *Case C 376/98*. For comment see (2003) 113 *EU Focus* 2.

108 This part of the opinion is relevant for the reason that the rights protected in the European Convention on Human Rights enjoy 'fundamental' status in EU law.

109 Para. 166. Also relevant to this conclusion was the argument that partial bans had been shown to be ineffective. Note however that the ECJ did not have to rule on the Article 10 point.

110 C491/01 reported at *The Times* 13 December 2002.

Existing laws and regulations on tobacco products' manufacture, sale and advertising varied significantly across member states. The directive sought lawfully to remove these variations which had created obstacles to a properly functioning internal market. As to the proportionality of the measures, the ECJ noted that Community institutions enjoyed a wide discretion within political, economic and social policy questions that could only be impugned by the Court if the directive was 'manifestly inappropriate'. The increased size and severity of health warnings as well as the forced disclosure of specific toxicities were not disproportionate to the permissible goal of attaining high levels of health protection across the EU. The ban on the descriptors 'mild' and 'light' was also justified for products marketed solely within the EU. Consumers were entitled to objective information about toxicity rather than misleading labels and no alternative, less intrusive means of securing that interest could have done so as efficiently.

Tobacco Bans in UK Law

The Labour Government was elected to office in 1997 with an express commitment to ban tobacco advertising.[111] It had been preparing to implement *Directive 98/43 EC* when the ECJ upheld a challenge to the directive's legality. As a result, the Government pressed on with its own Bill in an effort to make good its manifesto commitment. This initiative was lost when the 2001 General Election was called. In the next Parliament, an identical measure was introduced as a Private Member's Bill in the House of Lords and subsequently became law as the *Tobacco Advertising and Promotion Act* 2002.[112]

The Act imposes a comprehensive if not quite total ban on the various forms of tobacco advertising. Section 2 of the Act, for example, makes it an offence for a person in the course of a business to publish, print, devise or distribute a tobacco advertisement.[113] This prohibition is subject to certain exemptions, including a freedom to engage in limited point-of-sale advertising where regulations permitting such advertising are made under the Act.[114] In the absence of a regulation explicitly authorizing a specific type of publicity, point-of-sale advertising will generally be caught by the ban in s.2. In *The Queen* v *British American Tobacco UK Ltd and others*[115] a challenge was taken to the legality of regulations made under the Act that restricted point-of-sale advertising to an A5 size, two-dimensional sign 'on a "gantry", display cabinet tray or other product in which a tobacco product is held pending

111 For background, see the White Paper *Smoking Kills* Cm 4177 (1998).

112 For an anticipatory discussion in 2002 of how the then Bill might have been received in the courts, see E Barendt, 'Tobacco Advertising: The Last Puff' (2002) *PL* 22.

113 S.2, 2002 Act brought into force on 21 December 2004 for actual point-of-sale advertising and 31 July 2005 in respect of website point-of-sale advertising, SI 2004/3138. Other forms of tobacco advertising became subject to s.2 on 14 February 2003, SI 2002/2865.

114 S.4(3), 2002 Act.

115 [2004] EWHC 2493; (2004) 101 LSG 33.

sale…'.[116] The sign was also required to incorporate a health warning covering 30 per cent of the surface area. The claimants argued that the point of sale regulations amounted to a disproportionate interference with tobacco companies' freedom of expression for three main reasons. First, it was contended that the reduced size of advertisement permitted under the new rules was simply too drastic an interference with commercial expression. Secondly, given the legitimate objective of preventing children being exposed to tobacco advertising, the restrictions impacted too broadly across a range of retail outlets, including hotels, bars and nightclubs, where children were unlikely to be present. The suggestion being made here was that, drawing on First Amendment notions of a measure improperly burdening lawful adult-to-adult communications as recognised in *Lorillard*, the reach of the present regulations intruded too far into protected expression.[117] Finally, the Secretary of State had failed to direct his mind to the possibility of devising less intrusive regulations to advance his purposes.

In upholding the regulations as *Human Rights Act*-compliant, McCombe J noted that the legislative scheme set out in the 2002 Act by Parliament clearly countenanced measures that were 'substantially stricter' than the point-of-sale regulations at issue in the dispute before him. The claimants had not in any event sought a s.4(2) *Human Rights Act* declaration of incompatibility, a concession which confirmed that restrictions made under the Act could have curtailed even more commercial speech. McCombe J also observed that commercial freedom had tended to be treated as being of less significance than political or even artistic expression. The Government's regulations were intended to address a serious public health issue. According to Government figures, some 120,000 people died annually from smoking-related illnesses. The cost of National Health Service treatment amounted to some £1.7 billion each year. In these circumstances, the Court had to be 'particularly wary of imposing its own value judgments upon a legislative scheme'.[118] In what constituted the fatal blow to the claimants' submissions, the judge accepted that, whilst the point-of-sale regulations were intended to protect children and young persons in particular, their aim went further than this. Expert evidence existed to show that patterns of consumption among adults were also influenced by point-of-sale advertising and that the Government wished also to dampen demand among adults. On this basis, the fact that the regulations impacted on bars, hotels and nightclubs did not render them 'too blunt' an instrument. Moreover, the limit laid down by the regulations of one A5-size advert was not disproportionate. Displays of cigarettes would continue and price lists were permitted in addition to the A5 advert, all of which would indicate to customers which products were on sale, pack sizes and prices. Lawful adult-to-adult communication was not thereby unduly hindered. In these circumstances, the Secretary of State's regulations could not be said to have exceeded the bounds of

116 SI 2004/3138.

117 *Lorillard Tobacco* v *Reilly AG Massachusetts* 533 US 525 (2001) and discussed above.

118 [2004] EWHC 2493, at para. 36.

discretion in balancing the interests of public health promotion and commercial speech.

Conclusion

Thirty years ago, Justice Blackmun stated that the interest of an individual consumer in the unencumbered flow of information concerning products and services might be 'as keen, if not keener by far, than his interest in the day's most urgent political debate'.[119] There is no reason to suppose today that this interest has declined. If anything, we live in a more consumerist society in which a bewildering array of goods are placed before our eyes and offer the prospect of leading more fulfilled lives upon purchase. At the same time, incontrovertible evidence about harms caused by tobacco products have generated tighter legislative controls on the advertising of these goods. This chapter has sought to focus on the constitutional issues that arise when limits are placed on commercial expression. Some of these limits have been fairly uncontroversial. Few persons would dispute the need for misleading and dishonest advertising to be regulated. The harder cases are those where a speaker wishes to convey accurate information about a lawful, though undeniably harmful product and also those instances in which the expression goes beyond publicity for a product/service and raises questions of broader public concern. Ought the state be able to limit/ban altogether these sorts of communications? Can the state require producers to carry warnings about the harms associated with consumption?

The central argument in this chapter is that none of the rationales offered in support of the view (that commercial expression is entitled to as much protection as political expression) withstand close examination. The weaknesses inherent in autonomy and public-interest-based arguments for parity of constitutional protection were demonstrated. It was also noted that a number of restrictions are premised upon non-paternalist grounds, a fact not always appreciated by the judges. I did not seek to argue that commercial expression is entirely outside the realms of speech protection, merely that its distance from the core reasons why we value freedom of expression meant that it was susceptible to regulation in circumstances when political expression was not. The remainder of the chapter looked to assess the extent to which, if at all, this understanding accords with settled interpretations of the US, Canadian, ECHR, EU and domestic UK legal systems. Here, much constitutional argument centres upon the proportionality of restrictions upon commercial expression. Whilst few states have difficulties in demonstrating a legitimate purpose behind restraints, the critical inquiry is usually one about the relationship between means and ends and the availability of less draconian methods of pursuing state objectives. I suggested that questions of deference to legislative policy-making touched on in Chapter 2 were to the forefront at this stage of analysis. In seeking to defend an attenuated standard of review in cases of pure commercial expression, I argued that community

119 *Virginia State Board of Pharmacy* v *Virginia Citizens Consumer Council* 425 US 748, 763 (1976).

judgments (as reflected in legislative policy stances), after detailed debate among the interested parties and with the benefit of empirical evidence, ought to be accorded a degree of immunity from rights-based judicial intervention. Each legal system examined in this chapter does indeed permit scope for legislative policy-making. Even the US Supreme Court continues laudably to resist the claims of those who would have us believe that commercial speech matters as much in a democracy as political expression. Lately, as the evidence on harmful effects of tobacco has mounted, so too has the willingness of judges to defer to legislative assessments about advertising and sponsorship.

Chapter 8

Conclusion: Protecting Expression as a Constitutional Value

At the outset of this monograph, I noted that the boundary between constitutionally protected expression and proscribable expression in modern liberal democracies is highly contested. Since starting work upon this manuscript, intervening events have tended to confirm this claim. At the time of writing, the UK Government's determination to enact an incitement to religious hatred law has been given a fresh impetus in the aftermath of suicide and attempted suicide bombings by British Muslims and others in London. The Government believes that the case for supplementing existing incitement to racial hatred laws has become stronger in the aftermath of the terrorist attacks as a means of protecting Muslim communities from those who seek to induce hatred of them.[1] The measure has reawakened concerns that strongly worded criticism or even satirical treatment of others' religious beliefs and practices will be subject to the full force of the criminal law in what some maintain is a clumsy attempt to suppress threats to community cohesiveness. Whether, as the Government argues, a line can be successfully drawn between that which remains permitted (namely, attacks on religious ideas and practices) and that which is forbidden (inducing hatred against the followers of a particular faith) will continue to be debated. Alongside a new provision on religious hatred, further restrictions on freedom of expression are proposed as part of the Government's counter-terrorism strategy. These include the creation of a new offence of 'indirect incitement to terrorism'. The proposal will criminalize those who 'glorify and condone terrorist acts, knowing full well that the effect on their listeners will be to encourage them to turn to terrorism'.[2] An intention to incite others to commit acts of terrorism will also have to be proved for liability to arise under the measure. The primary targets of the new offence include Islamic fundamentalist preachers and persons responsible for websites where the speech in question stops short of directly endorsing the actions of suicide bombers and other violent insurgents and thus remains beyond the reach of existing criminal laws. Although the proposed offence enjoys cross-party support in principle, the Government has run into difficulties over the precise ambit of the

---

1 See now the *Racial and Religious Hatred Act* 2006, inserting s.29A-N into the *Public Order Act* 1986.

2 Home Secretary Rt Hon. Charles Clarke MP (2004–5) HC Debs. Vol. 436, col. 1254 and see now the *Terrorism Act* 2006, s.1.

new offence.[3] In other expression-related measures, accessing websites that contain bomb-making instructions would be construed as an act preparatory to terrorism.

The trade-offs that are deployed by legislators and judges to resolve these and other free speech problems in open societies entail a weighing of individual, collective and societal interests engaged by each particular expressive act. Freedom of expression, we are frequently and rightly reminded, is one of the core freedoms required for democratic, informed self-government to function. At the same time, this freedom may on occasion have to yield to more pressing interests in national security, public order, public morals, health, crime prevention and the administration of justice as well as individual rights and interests (such as the right to reputation). Needless to say, a number of excellent comparative treatments of the constitutional regulation of freedom of expression have already been published. For example, in the case of work by UK scholars, Loveland's edited collection[4] on aspects of UK and US free speech jurisprudence built on earlier comparative work by Barendt.[5] Both works have brought insightful analyses to bear on the subject matter.

The distinctive contribution that the present book seeks to make is to offer a comparative account of selected topical free speech problems, the constitutional issues they provoke and their resolution in courts and legislatures *within* an analytical framework that draws upon the political philosophies of liberalism, communitarianism and civic republicanism. I suggest that a fuller understanding of the legal treatment of claims to freedom of expression may best be arrived at by reference to the wider political culture and constitutional traditions within which these claims are made. Part of this monograph is therefore necessarily descriptive. It does not, however, set out in comprehensive detail all relevant rules in each jurisdiction. Rather, the selective treatment of specific laws is intended to shed light on the broader themes of political culture and philosophy. However, beyond this descriptive account the reader is presented with a normative approach to the problem of free speech regulation in liberal democracies. Thus I argue that libertarian objections to contents-based restrictions on expression of the sort frequently encountered in First Amendment literature are flawed on account of the fact that they understate other, equally important constitutional values such as equality and dignity. Libertarian scholarship tends to approach limits on expression in terms of the damage done to unpopular or unorthodox speech rather than attempting to understand the harms (beyond physical acts) done to sections of the community through official tolerance of hateful and denigratory words and images. The distrust in libertarian free speech discourse of contents-based regulation of expression means that representations of ethnic minorities and women by economically powerful speakers

3 For detailed criticism of the measure, see the Joint Committee on Human Rights' *Third Report of Session 2005-06* (2005, HL Paper 55-I; HC 561-I) at paras. 18-49 and further I Cram, 'Regulating the media: some neglected freedom of expression issues in the United Kingdom's counter-terrorism strategy (2006) 18 *Terrorism & Political Violence* (forthcoming).

4 *Importing the First Amendment – Freedom of Expression in American, English and European Law* (1998, Hart Publishing, Oxford).

5 *Freedom of Speech* (3rd edn, 2005, OUP, Oxford).

may pander to, and reinforce prejudiced attitudes in ways that deny the equal worth of individuals and groups without constraint. Libertarian thinking also underplays the damaging consequences of allowing wealthy speakers unlimited access to the public in political debate, namely that of dominating the terms of public discourse with the attendant risks of skewing. The disparity in resources between competing viewpoints serves also to cast doubt upon the much-aired 'more speech' solution favoured by opponents of regulation. In the absence of legal controls, those with access to greater wealth invariably enjoy greater access to, and influence upon, the general population. The communication possibilities opened up by the Internet cannot yet be said to have produced in overall terms a level playing field among differently resourced speakers.

A substantial portion of this book is given over to discussion of the implications for freedom of expression of liberalist, communitarian and civic republican alternatives to libertarianism. In particular, I identify aspects of speech regulation in a number of jurisdictions that are consistent with the central commitment in civic republicanism to an inclusive community of political equals actively participating in a system of deliberative decision-making. The ideal of a more inclusive deliberative democracy is common to both liberal and communitarian thinking. Each is concerned by the ongoing decline in civic virtue that is considered to threaten the long-term future of representative government. The problem for liberals is that the state is required to be neutral as between competing accounts of the good life. Individuals may not be coerced into behaving virtuously. Communitarians on the other hand envisage that the state will act to promote the 'public good' sometimes at the expense of individual autonomy. The civic republican variant of communitarianism identified in Chapter 1 places considerable emphasis upon the importance of public deliberation and plainly envisages a role for the courts in maintaining the conditions required for deliberative democracies to function. This chimes with ideas of constitutionalism discussed in Chapter 2. At the core of constitutionalism lies the claim that certain fundamental values are so central to democratic self-government that they should be off-limits, that is not alterable by passing political majorities. Most closely associated with John Hart Ely's *Democracy and Distrust*, the imposition of restraints on political majorities can be justified by an appeal to maintaining the conditions in which informed control over elected office holders is exercised. Thus, in the case of freedom of expression, the possibility that executive authorities and legislative majorities will be tempted to censor speech for self-interested motives can never be discounted. Even where the ground of interference rests more obviously upon an appeal to 'offensiveness', as it did most controversially in *R* v *BBC ex parte ProLife Alliance* to a party election broadcast during an election campaign, the propriety of resulting restraints is no less questionable.

In making the case for judicial review of executive discretion/legislative rule-making, Chapter 2 responded to the assault on 'legal constitutionalism' mounted by Adam Tomkins and others. I suggested that Tomkins's position was founded somewhat shakily upon the twin pillars of an over-hasty dismissal of the record of judicial contributions in human rights cases and an unrealistically upbeat account of parliamentary politics that ignored the tendencies of temporary and whipped majorities to force through populist, liberty-infringing measures without necessarily engaging in principled debate. In setting out the case for a nuanced form of judicial oversight, Chapter 2 highlighted the central importance which liberal democracies attach to political expression. If the electorate is to retain ultimate sovereignty in representative democracies over elected office holders, it follows that contributions to political debate must be accorded the greatest degree of protection from legislative/executive abridgment. Thus expressed, judicial review is anathema to those like Waldron who prefer to entrust constitutional safekeeping to elected majorities unfettered by judicial oversight. Waldron, it will be recalled, prefers majoritarian processes on institutional grounds, arguing that rule-making processes in legislative assemblies are more respectful of the various factions' contending positions in disputes where there are no right answers. His characterization of legislative process as an arena in which there is a careful (if not judicious) weighing up of alternative policy options in an atmosphere of mutual respect was queried. Political scientists have long noted how access to the policy-making processes by interested parties at the important pre-legislative stage is often notoriously unequal, reflecting differences in resources, expertise and insider contacts among lobbying and pressure groups. I further argued that the role played by structures of party discipline in ensuring the progress of governments' legislative programmes is also overlooked in the institutional defence of majoritarian processes. In stressing the importance of evaluating the competing *institutional* claims of courts and legislatures to have the ultimate say on constitutional questions, I sought to move away from a purely results-based approach to the matter which it was argued lacked a proper basis in constitutional principle.

If a case for some form of judicial review in principle can be made out, it becomes vital to consider how this power might be used in rights disputes. The open-ended nature of rights declarations in constitutional documents means that little or no guidance in individual cases is forthcoming from the text itself. In the second half of Chapter 2, I argued that the practice of judicial review in a particular jurisdiction needed to show a 'fit' with the constitutional traditions and values of that jurisdiction as manifested by the underlying political culture and the outcomes of previous constitutional litigation. To consider within the confines of one jurisdiction featuring prominently in this work whether such a 'fit' was evident, a detailed account of the match between Canadian political culture, the *Canadian Charter of Rights and Freedoms* and Supreme Court jurisprudence was then set down. The commitment to representative democracy and an emphasis upon collective values and community interests were said to be reflected in both the structure and content of constitutional guarantees. Particular attention was paid to the s.33 override clause and the extent to which the existence of this clause (rather than its use) has prompted a dialogue between the courts and legislatures. The Charter's s.1 'reasonable limits' clause provides another means by which majoritarian policy-making that infringes Charter rights might ultimately prevail. The point was made that the determination of whether legislative curtailment amounts to a 'reasonable limit' is conducted by the Supreme Court on tests laid down by the Court. Thus, only in a very qualified way, might s.1 be said to enshrine a preference for legislative regulation of rights.

The brief analysis of political expression cases which followed indicated that the Canadian Supreme Court's reading of the s.2(b) freedom of expression guarantee had demonstrated a commitment to upholding a participative and representative democracy. In other aspects of its rights adjudication, the Court's pronouncements on the outer limits of hateful expression, sexually explicit speech and commercial advertising were more equivocal. Arguably, these more peripheral forms of expressive activity were accorded at times an unduly high level of judicial protection against legislative abridgement. The debates around these rulings were considered in more detail in subsequent chapters.

The underlying political culture of the UK bears some similarities to that identified in Canada. Notions of accountable parliamentary government and representative democracy allied to a more positive conception of the state in pursuing community goals may be said to describe our own political system and its values. Unlike the Canadian constitutional settlement however, the *Human Rights Act* 1998 stopped short of authorizing judicial review of primary legislation. Despite this fact, it is clear that the enhanced role of the judges in 'interpreting' legislation (even, it should be said, according to those judges inclined to be more deferential to legislative rule-making) offers the prospect of more intense scrutiny over the content of legislative rule-making and the exercise of executive discretionary powers where important constitutional rights are engaged. Where, in the alternative, a declaration of incompatibility is issued, this too speaks of a heightened role for the judiciary in bringing rights violations to the attention of the legislature.

Judicial oversight of restraints on a variety of forms of political expression (broadly construed) formed the central unifying theme of Chapters 3 and 4. In this section of materials, having outlined the important functions played by political parties in democracies, I looked at restrictions upon political parties, including at one extreme the dissolution of political organizations judged to pose a real threat to democratic society, through lesser restrictions upon communicative activities such as party election broadcasts, advocacy advertising by pressure groups and others as well as controls on party donations and election expenditure. In Chapter 3, I took particular issue with the deference shown by the House of Lords to broadcasters' judgments of offensiveness in *R* v *BBC ex parte ProLife Alliance* in respect of a proposed party election broadcast consisting of images of the contorted remains of aborted foetuses. That their Lordships could see nothing in the circumstances of the broadcast to indicate why ordinary taste and decency considerations should not apply to this broadcast suggested an obvious failure to afford the electorate access to the widest possible range of candidates' statements and opinions at this crucial time. The better argument, I suggested, was to be found in the Court of Appeal which had required the broadcasters to show exceptional grounds for interfering with the electoral expression of the ProLife Alliance.

Limitations placed on the rights of citizens to participate in elections as voters and candidates were discussed in the remaining sections of Chapter 3. Specifically, the stringent level of oversight applied by the Canadian Supreme Court and, more lately, at supra-national level by the European Court of Human Rights to prisoner disenfranchisement laws was noted. In the case of Canada, this development was traced to underlying concerns on the part of the court to promote the values of inclusiveness, equality and dignity. In the UK, the extension of candidacy restrictions to local government officers in 1990 following the Widdicombe Committee of Inquiry into Local Authority Business proved highly controversial. Despite an initial ruling by the European Commission on Human Rights that these constituted a disproportionate interference with the applicants' Article 10 ECHR freedoms, the Court (by six votes to three) upheld the regulations as falling within the UK Government's margin of appreciation. Whilst the objective of the 1990 regulations is entirely legitimate – namely, safeguarding the political neutrality of local government – the restrictions impinge in truth across a large number of public servants unconnected to the provision of advice to councillors, preventing their participation as candidates for election and denying the public access to officers' political opinions.

The tension between liberalist and communitarian approaches to the regulation of freedom of expression were brought out sharply in Chapter 4 where a selective analysis of some recent changes to electoral finance laws in the UK, US and Canada was offered. Noting first the broad measure of agreement across these jurisdictions about the importance of maintaining/restoring public confidence in elected officials and political parties and the role played by reporting and disclosure requirements in these tasks, the discussion in this chapter also raised more controversial questions of 'equality' and 'fairness' in election finance laws. The threat to informed voter decision-making posed by unlimited expenditure is a major concern in this area. The extra-communicative reach of wealthier political parties may be considered to skew voters' access to information about the full range of policies and programmes on offer. In addition to the distorting effect of uncontrolled expenditure during general election campaigns, supporters of controls point to the especial difficulties in referendums where a large imbalance in financial support may exist between the two sides. A commitment to the principle of the political equality of all citizens would seem to require the placing of curbs on the communicative powers of some and perhaps enabling the voices of less wealthy individuals/groups to be heard. The redistribution by the state of private wealth, lawfully acquired, is of course objected to in libertarian thinking and this view finds its clearest articulation by the US Supreme Court in *Buckley* v *Valeo*. There the autonomy of individuals who choose to spend their wealth to promulgate their political views was upheld. In contrast, the UK has opted under the *Political Parties, Elections and Referendum Act* 2000 for limits on national expenditure. I argued that this represented an attempt to lessen the distorting effect of the parties' unequal financial resources. Nonetheless, ceilings on expenditure alone cannot guarantee equal spending or access to voters. Less well endowed parties may well fail to reach the spending ceiling and require considerable sums of public money to match the expenditure of rivals or, alternatively, the ceiling might be set so low as to allow poorly resourced parties to compete but severely hampering the ability of any party to communicate effectively with voters. Although various forms of state assistance exist in the form of *Short* monies, free PEBs, mailshots and use of election rooms, the sheer range of European, national, regional and local electoral campaigns that UK parties are expected to contest in this post-devolution era means that these difficult issues cannot be expected to go away.

The claim examined in Chapter 4 that the speech of some may have to be silenced in order that the voices of others be heard links neatly with the materials on hateful expression in Chapter 5. This section of the book looked at the different constitutional traditions and political philosophies that underpin distinctive attitudes to the regulation of abusive expression targeted at specific groups in society. Alongside long-standing concerns over anti-black and anti-Semitic expression, the issue has been given fresh impetus in the wake of anti-Muslim sentiment after 11 September 2001. Civic republican thinking emphasizes decision-making by an inclusive community of political equals and can more readily accept constraints on invective that inhibit participation than its libertarian counterpart. For the latter, contents-based regulation of expression by the state (no matter how worthy the cause) is, in the absence of physical harm, impermissible. The thrust of Chapter 5 was to suggest that constitutional values beyond freedom of expression are implicated in the regulation of hateful expression. These include the concepts of equality between citizens and individual dignity. Thus, supporters of regulation argue with some force that to frame an analysis of speech curbs *solely* in terms of the damage inflicted upon the unfettered exchange of ideas (as occurs in much First Amendment discourse) is misconceived. The loss in qualitative terms to public debate that flows from not having access to hateful expression is perhaps small when set alongside gains that result from legal interventions that define rules of civility in public discourse and strive to signal the equal worth of all community members. The silencing impact on target communities of tolerating hateful expression has been acknowledged in social science literature. Knowing how much expression to silence is, however, problematic. There are no scientific indicators or mathematical formulae that will measure the gains to an inclusive and genuinely deliberative democracy yielded by any particular set of speech restraints. Important questions about the precise formulation of rules and the scope of any defences need to be considered carefully. Given the marginal contribution (at best) to societal discourse made by hateful speech forms, an appropriate starting point for any analysis of the level of constitutional protection to which it is entitled should recall the peripheral value of hateful expression to democratic deliberation.

The argument that the degree of constitutional protection conferred by the courts upon expressive activity must be context-dependent runs through the final two chapters on the regulation of sexually explicit and commercial expression forms. Here, we encountered two types of expression that usually lack a close connection to the demands of a well-functioning democracy and that are grounded instead on claims to individual autonomy and self-fulfilment. I chose in Chapter 6 to take a particularly close look at arguments for conferring constitutional protection upon the producers and consumers of sexually explicit imagery of children and young persons. In the era of digitally produced materials, the production of computerized images need not entail the sexual abuse of a living person. To criminalize the mere possession of such materials might be thought to interfere with the right to receive others' expressive work and/or to engage privacy claims. That communities might be allowed to impose criminal liability on the basis of an offensiveness standard without the prospect of proper constitutional control is, with this view, troublesome. Certainly, the technical and unprincipled way in which English law has regulated this area is open to criticism and liable to be revisited under the *Human Rights Act*. At the same time, to treat claims to freedom of sexually explicit expression as equally deserving of constitutional protection from legislative restraint as contributions to debate on matters of public interest is misguided. If, as a body of research now appears to show, virtual child pornography is used by adults variously to whet their appetites for sexual activity with children, to persuade children of the 'normality' of adult–child sex relations and to trade images with other adults, then a more relaxed attitude on the part of the judges towards legislative controls is probably justified. Apart from the undoubted interests of children and young persons themselves in being free from molestation, the state's own interest in safeguarding the welfare of children argues in favour of some leeway being available to legislatures.

The claims of producers of goods and services and their consumers to freedom of commercial expression were considered in Chapter 7. The major focus of inquiry in this chapter was the regulation of truthful advertising – a subject of current interest in the light of restrictions on tobacco promotion. Observing that corporations cannot in any meaningful sense make autonomy-based claims to publicize their products, arguments for unfettered commercial expression rely principally on the audience interest in receiving information about goods and services. Through such information, consumers are empowered to make informed choices that contribute to individual self-fulfilment. Government regulation of factually accurate statements hinders personal growth, representing either a form of paternalism or a prioritization of societal interests above those of the consumer. Chapter 7 questioned the assumption that unlimited commercial information will always enhance informed consumer choice and thus promote autonomy. Empirical studies have shown that consumers display 'bounded rationality' when it comes to making purchasing decisions, accepting uncritically information in the way it is presented to them by sellers and relying upon statistical claims derived from small data samples. Even if consumers' reasoning was more rational and critical, it is doubtful whether sellers would voluntarily disclose information that showed their product in an unfavourable light or simply cost too much to ascertain. Finally, assuming for the sake of argument that regulation does indeed equate to diminished autonomy, it is appropriate to ask whether countervailing societal interests might trump autonomy concerns under any circumstances. The adverse effects of gambling on family life, the economic costs to the taxpayer of treating the users of a potentially harmful product (such as alcohol) or the tendency for criminal activity to attach itself to product/service might all suggest plausible rationales for regulation. The analysis of the commercial speech cases litigated in the US, Canada, the UK and the European Court of Human Rights inevitably centred upon the proportionality of contested restrictions. The application of a more relaxed approach on the part of the courts to scrutiny of expression claims across a number of jurisdictions was welcomed. As with the sexually explicit case law examined in the previous chapter, the argument in respect of harmful products such as tobacco was that, given the difficulties in demonstrating definitive social science evidence linking the control of advertising and reduced consumption, legislative rule-making after detailed debate among interested parties was entitled to an attenuated standard of judicial oversight.

Where Now? – Some Implications for the Theory and Practice of Freedom of Speech

Some of the conclusions reached in this book are jurisdiction-specific. I have claimed that the US Supreme Court was wrong to abandon its hierarchical approach to speech types and that the resulting anxious scrutiny of race-hate ordinances and child pornography laws confers a mistakenly high level of judicial protection on speech that has low value in deliberative democracies. The Canadian Supreme Court may have fallen into similar error in upholding challenges to restrictions on tobacco advertising and child pornography. Our own House of Lords has conversely failed to bestow sufficient protection on party political expression in the face of broadcast regulators' determinations of 'offensiveness'.

The arguments in this book have broader implications that go well beyond criticisms of individual instances of line-drawing. First, the centrality of political speech forms in modern liberal democracy would seem to require the emboldening of constitutional courts in their scrutiny of legislative/executive restrictions of expression where the latter is made and received as a contribution to political debate. Second, the mere absence of restraint on political expression will not by itself ensure a more deliberative system of democratic self-governance. Imbalances in private power and access to resources in capitalist/mixed economies pose an ever-present threat to the effective dissemination of diverse forms of political expression. This threat explains why, during election/referendum campaigns, a number of states accept some forms of limits, either on contributions by persons or political parties' expenditure. Some of these states may also relieve parties of the costs entailed in producing mailshots, party election broadcasts or the hire of meeting rooms. It may be questioned, however, whether the commitment on the part of states to promote greater diversity of political speech should cease when the electoral campaign is over. After all, distortions in political debate that are attributable to differentials in wealth among private individuals/organizations do not cease to operate on the morning after election day. These imbalances are most evident in the print media. Broadcasters in the UK remain under duties of impartiality in their news and current affairs coverage and so may not openly endorse one side in political debate.[6] A

---

6 I do not claim, however, that a fair representation of divergent views is always achieved by the broadcast sector. There is much empirical work in the field of communications studies that points to media organizations' influence in shaping the terms of public discourse. Thus, for a polemical analysis of mainstream media coverage of the Iraq war, see D Miller (ed.),

genuine willingness to facilitate the communication of a variety of viewpoints raises profound issues about the principal and possible mechanisms of assistance to less well endowed political parties, pressure groups and others. State assistance in this context might, for example, mean taxpayer-funded speech and it should be expected that efforts to 'equalize' (or, more accurately, make less unequal) the conditions in which political debate occurs will be met with considerable resistance from those whose taxes fund the attempt to equalize. To these persons, it should be pointed out that the principle has already been conceded and that their taxes have for some time been used for this purpose at election time. Public service broadcasting is one obvious route through which a range of viewpoints could be allowed greater access to the public. More imaginatively, a lighter-touch regulatory style might oblige a newspaper or website advocating a particular policy line to inform its readers of the name of a publication or website advocating an alternative approach (or, in the case of websites, a hyperlink to the same).

Factors other than disparate levels of spending power contribute to the under-representation of certain groups in structures of deliberative decision-making. That hateful expression (in the case of ethnic minorities, gays and lesbians, disabled persons) and the representation of women as primarily sexual beings contribute to a withdrawal from participation in political life can probably never be causally demonstrated. The fact that we cannot know precisely *how* hostile expression or misogynist imagery inhibits or silences its victims (or to what extent this occurs among members of the targeted group) should not, however, lead us to abandon the entirely rational belief that in a variety of subtle and less subtle ways such speech is a hindrance to the goal of an inclusive community of political equals. The need for mutually respectful or civilized dialogue within political decision-making might thus justify the imposition of curbs (legal, non-legal) on hostile invective so that, as a condition of participation in all discursive forums, each speaker would have to show respect to other speakers and to support his/her position by means of reasoned argument and empirical evidence. On this account, the design of respectful procedures for political debate is a worthy objective of constitutional scholarship.

In an earlier era, freedom of expression was commonly invoked by political dissenters to oppose capitalism, war and the Establishment. Today it is more frequently claimed by multinational corporations, the producers, disseminators and users of pornography and the propagators of racial and religious hatred. Ritual invocation on the part of these groups of the right to freedom of expression has sometimes served to obscure the non-absolute or qualified nature of this freedom and to obstruct debate about countervailing individual and societal interests. Perhaps it is time to acknowledge that membership of a constitutional democracy requires us to confront more squarely the variety of harms that specific forms of freedom of expression may produce. It is to be doubted whether the 'more speech' solution beloved of some in the civil liberties movement will always be effective in countering these

Tell Me Lies – Propaganda and Media Distortion in the Attack on Iraq (2004, Pluto Press, London).

expressive forms. Speech that is inimical to democratic and constitutional values such as equality and human dignity needs to be recognized as such and regulated accordingly. The challenge for liberal democracies is to articulate in principled terms the basis of these limits. So stated, we may thus be able to explain why the religious fundamentalist website that glorifies (but stops short of directly encouraging) the actions of suicide bombers in killing innocent non-believers cannot shield behind a constitutional guarantee of freedom of expression.

Bibliography

Ackerman, B, *We the People* (1991, Harvard University Press, Harvard MA)

Akdeniz, Y, 'Child Pornography' in Y Akdeniz, C Walker and D Wall (eds), *The Internet, Law and Society* (2000, Longman, Harlow)

Alemann, U von, 'Die Parteien und das Geld oder: Sind alle Politiker korr' (2000) *Gewerkschaftliche Monatscheft: Zeitschrift fur Theorie und Praxis* 51

Allan, J, 'The Author Doth Protest Too Much' (2003) 20 *New Zealand Universities Law Review* 519

Amar, A, 'The Case of the Missing Amendments' (1992) 106 *Harvard Law Review* 124

Anderson, GW, 'Understanding Constitutional Speech: Two Theories of Expression' in GW Anderson (ed.), *Rights and Democracy: Essays in UK–Canadian Constitutionalism* (1999, Blackstone Press Ltd, London)

Anonymous, 'The Elephant in the Room: Evolution, Behavioralism and Counter-Advertising in the Coming War against Obesity' (2003) 116 *Harvard Law Review* 1161

Barendt, E, *Freedom of Speech* (1985, Clarendon Press, Oxford)

Barendt, E, 'Tobacco Advertising: The Last Puff' (2002) *Public Law* 22

Barnum, D, *The Supreme Court and American Democracy* (1993, St Martin's Press, New York)

Beales, H *et al.*, 'The Efficient Regulation of Consumer Information' (1981) 24 *Journal of Law and Economics* 492

Beatty, D (ed.), *Human Rights and Judicial Review – A Comparative Perspective* (1994, Kluwer Academic Publishers, Dordrecht)

Beatty, D, 'The Canadian Charter of Rights: Lessons and Laments' in GW Anderson (ed.), *Rights and Democracy – Essays in UK–Canadian Constitutionalism* (1999, Blackstone Press Ltd, London)

Bickel, AM, *The Least Dangerous Branch – The Supreme Court at the Bar of Politics* (1962, Bobbs-Merrill Co., Indianapolis IN)

Bickel, AM, *The Morality of Consent* (1975, Yale University Press, New Haven CT)

Bindman, G, 'Incitement to Racial Hatred' (1982) *New Law Journal* 299

Bindman, G, 'Outlawing Holocaust Denial' (1997) 147 *New Law Journal* 466

Blackburn, R (ed.), *Constitutional Studies – Contemporary Issues and Controversies* (1992, Mansell Publishing, London)

Bollinger, L, *The Tolerant Society – Freedom of Speech and Extremist Speech in America* (1986, Clarendon Press, Oxford)

Bork, R, *The Tempting of America: The Political Seduction of America* (1990, Touchstone Books Ltd, New York)

Boyle, K, 'Religious Intolerance and the Incitement of Hatred' in S Coliver (ed.), with K Boyle and F D'Souza, *Striking a Balance – Hate Speech, Freedom of Expression and Non-discrimination* (1992, Article 19, London Human Rights Centre, University of Essex, Colchester)

Bradley, A, 'The Sovereignty of Parliament – Form or Substance?' in J Jowell and D Oliver (eds), *The Changing Constitution* (5th edn, 2004, Oxford University Press, Oxford)

Bradley, A and Ewing, K, *Constitutional and Administrative Law* (13th edn, 2003, Longman, Harlow)

Brennan, W, 'The Supreme Court and the Meiklejohn Interpretation of the First Amendment' (1965) 79 *Harvard Law Review* 1

Brennan, W, 'The Constitution of the United States: Contemporary Ratification' (1986) *South Texas Law Review* 433

Broadhead, J, 'Votes for Prisoners' (2004) 154 *New Law Journal* 437

Burke, E, *The Works of the Right Honourable Edmund Burke* (1854–56, Henry G Bohn, London)

Burney, E and Rose, G, *Home Office Research Study 244: Racist Offences – How is the Law Working?* (2002, Home Office Research, Development and Statistics Directorate, London)

Burns, R, *An Overview of the Protection of Freedom of Expression under Canadian Constitutional Law and Section 2(b) of the Canadian Charter of Rights and Freedoms* (1996, Research Paper No. 3, Centre for Media, Communications and Information Technology Law, Melbourne University)

Butler, A, 'Interface between the Human Rights Act 1998 and Other Enactments: Pointers from New Zealand' (2000) *European Human Rights Law Review* 249

Butler, A, 'Implied Repeal, Parliamentary Sovereignty and Human Rights in New Zealand' (2001) *Public Law* 586

Byron, RJ and Lenton, RL, 'The Distribution of Anti-Semitism in Canada in 1984' (1991) 16 *Canadian Journal of Sociology* 411

Chalmers, D, *Hooded Americanism: The First Century of the Ku Klux Klan 1865–1965* (1965, Doubleday & Company Inc., New York)

Chesterman, M, *Freedom of Speech in Australian Law – A Delicate Plant* (2000, Ashgate, Aldershot)

Choper, J, *Judicial Review and the National Political Process* (1980, University of Chicago Press, Chicago IL)

Coliver, S (ed.), with Boyle, K and D'Souza, F, *Striking a Balance – Hate Speech, Freedom of Expression and Non-discrimination* (1992, Article 19, London Human Rights Centre, University of Essex, Colchester)

Coliver, S, 'Hate Speech Laws: Do They Work? in S Coliver (ed.) *et al.*, *Striking a Balance – Hate Speech, Freedom of Expression and Non-discrimination* (1992, Article 19, London Human Rights Centre, University of Essex, Colchester)

Cooper, J and Williams, AM, 'Hate Speech, Holocaust Denial and International Human Rights Law' (1999) 6 *European Human Rights Law Review* 593

Cram, I, *A Virtue Less Cloistered* (2002, Hart Publishing, Oxford)

Cram, I, 'Criminalizing Child Pornography – A Canadian Study in Freedom of

Expression and Charter-led Judicial Review of Legislative Policy Making' (2002) 66 *Journal of Criminal Law* 359

Cram, I, 'Beyond Madison? The Supreme Court and the regulation of sexually explicit expression' (2002) *Public Law* 743

Cram, I, 'Hate Speech, the First Amendment and Cross-Burning in the United States' (2003) 8 *Communications Law* 389

Cram, I, 'Judicial Intervention in Democratic Policy-making – The Case of Free Speech' in A Celada *et al.* (eds), *El Impacto de la Carta Canadiense de Derechos y Libertades (1982–2002) Perspectivas Europeas* (2003, Kadmos, Salamanca)

Cram, I, 'Unconstitutional Conditions? – Public Libraries, Federal Subsidies and the Internet' (2004) 8 *Communications Law* 417

Cram, I, 'Film Licensing in New Zealand and the Limits of Constitutional Protection for Artistic Expression' (2004) 15 *Entertainment Law Review* 243

Cram, I, 'Hate Speech and Disabled People: Some Comparative Constitutional Thoughts' in A Lawson and C Gooding (eds), *Disability Rights in Europe: From Theory to Practice* (2005, Hart Publishing, Oxford).

Cutts, D, 'Did Local Activism Really Matter? Liberal Democrat Campaigning and the 2001 British General Election' (2004) *Political Studies Association* conference April 2004

Davis, D, Chaskalason, M and De Waal, J, 'Democracy and Constitutionalism: The Role of Constitutional Interpretation' in D van Wyk, J Dugard, B de Villiers and D Davis, *Rights and Constitutionalism – The New South African Order* (1995, Clarendon Press, Oxford)

Delgado, R, 'Words that Wound: A Tort Action for Racial Insults, Epithets and Name-Calling' (1982) 17 *Harvard Civil Rights – Civil Liberties Review* 133

Delgado, R and Stefancic, J, *Understanding Words That Wound* (2004, Westview Press, Oxford)

Dershowitz, AM, *Why Terrorism Works* (2002, Yale University Press, New Haven CT)

Dickey, A, 'Prosecutions under the Race Relations Act 1965 s.6' (1968) *Criminal Law Review* 489

Donnerstein, E and Linz, D, 'Mass Media Sexual Violence and Male Viewers: Current Theory and Research' (1986) 29 *American Behavioral Scientist* 601

Dorsen, N, 'Is There a Right to Stop Offensive Speech? The Case of the Nazis at Skokie' in L Gostin (ed.), *Civil Liberties in Conflict* (1988, Routledge, London)

Drew, E, *The Corruption of American Politics: What went Wrong and Why* (2000, Overlook Press, New York)

Dryzek, J, *Deliberative Democracy and Beyond: Liberals, Critics and Contestations* (2000, Oxford University Press, Oxford)

Dworkin, R, *A Matter of Principle* (1996, Clarendon Press, Oxford)

Dworkin, R, *Freedom's Law – The Moral Reading of the American Constitution* (1996, Oxford University Press, Oxford)

Eastman, K, 'Racial Vilification: The Australian Experience' in S Coliver (ed.) *et al.*, *Striking a Balance – Hate Speech, Freedom of Expression and Non-*

discrimination (1992, Article 19, London Human Rights Centre, University of Essex, Colchester)

Edwards, R, 'Reading Down Legislation under the Human Rights Act' (2000) 20 *Legal Studies* 353

Elster, J (ed.), *Deliberative Democracy* (1998, Cambridge University Press, Cambridge)

Errera, R, 'Group Libel, Hate Speech, and other Fighting Words: Civility and the Uses of Law' in B Markesinis (ed.), *Law Making, Law Finding and Law Shaping: The Diverse Influences, Vol. 2, The Clifford Chance Lectures* (1997, Oxford University Press, Oxford)

Etzioni, A, 'On Protecting Children from Speech' (2004) 79 *University of Chicago-Kent Law Review* 3

Evans, J, 'Questioning the Dogmas of Realism' (2001) *New Zealand Universities Law Review* 145

Ewing, K, *The Funding of Political Parties in Britain* (1987, Cambridge University Press, Cambridge)

Ewing, K, 'The Legal Regulation of Campaign Financing in American Federal Elections' (1988) 47 *Cambridge Law Journal* 370

Ewing, K, 'Legal Control of Party Political Finance' in I Loveland (ed.), *A Special Relationship – American Influences on Public Law in the UK* (1995, Clarendon Press, Oxford)

Ewing, K, 'Human Rights, Social Democracy and Constitutional Reform' in C Gearty and A Tomkins (eds), *Understanding Human Rights* (1996, Mansell Publishing Ltd, London)

Ewing, K, 'Transparency, Accountability and Equality – The Political Parties, Elections and Referendums Act 2000' (2001) *Public Law* 542

Feldman, D, *Human Rights and Civil Liberties in England and Wales* (2nd edn, 2002, Oxford University Press, Oxford)

Feldman, D, 'The Internationalization of Public Law and its Impact on the United Kingdom' in J Jowell and D Oliver (eds), *The Changing Constitution* (5th edn, 2004, Oxford University Press, Oxford)

Fiss, O, *The Irony of Free Speech* (1996, Harvard University Press, Harvard MA)

Flauss, JF, 'L'action de L'Union Européenne dans le Domaine de la Lutte contre le Racisme et la Xénophobie' (2001) 12 *Revue Trimestrielle des Droits de L'Homme* 487

Ford, PL (ed.), *Writings of Thomas Jefferson* (1892, GP Putnam's Sons, New York)

Forde, P and Patterson, A, *Paedophile Internet Activity* (Trends and Issues in Crime and Criminal Justice Paper No. 97) (1998, Australian Institute of Criminology, Canberra)

Foster, N, *German Law and Legal System* (1993, Blackstone Press Ltd, London)

Freeman, M, 'Are There Collective Human Rights?' in D Beetham (ed.), *Politics and Human Rights* (1995, Blackwell, Oxford)

Fudge, J, 'The Canadian Charter of Rights: Recognition, Redistribution and the Imperialism of the Courts' in T Campbell, KD Ewing and A Tomkins (eds),

Sceptical Essays on Human Rights (2001, Oxford University Press, Oxford)

Galston, W, *Liberal Purposes* (1991, Cambridge University Press, Cambridge)

Gearty, C, 'Reconciling Parliamentary Democracy and Human Rights' (2002) 118 *Law Quarterly Review* 248

Geddis, A 'What Future for Political Advertising on the United Kingdom's Television Screens?' (2002) *Public Law* 615

Geddis, A, 'If Thy Right Eye Offend Thee, Pluck it Out': *R v BBC ex parte ProLife Alliance*' (2003) 66 *Modern Law Review* 885

Gelber, K, 'Free Speech, Hate Speech and an Australian Bill of Rights' (2002) 2 *The Drawing Board: An Australian Review of Public Affairs* 107

Gey, S, 'The Unfortunate Revival of Civic Republicanism' (1993) 141 *University of Pennsylvania Law Review* 801

Gey, S, 'What if *Wisconsin* v *Mitchell* had Involved Martin Luther King Jr? The Constitutional Flaws of Hate Crime Enhancement Statutes' (1997) 65 *George Washington Law Review* 1014

Gillespie, A, 'Sentences for Offences Involving Child Pornography' (2003) *Criminal Law Review* 81

Gillespie, A, 'Child Pornography: Balancing Substantive and Evidential Law to Safeguard Children Effectively from Abuse' (2005) 9 *International Journal of Evidence and Proof* 29

Gottlieb, M J, 'Developments in the Law "One Person, No Vote: the Laws of Felon Disenfranchisement"' (2002) 115 *Harvard Law Review* 1939

Grant, A, 'The 1996 Elections and Campaign Finance in the United States' (1997) 10 *Talking Politics* 56

Greenawalt, K, *Fighting Words; Individuals, Communities and Liberties of Speech* (1995, Princeton University Press, Princeton NJ)

Gunther, G, *Constitutional Law* (1985, The Foundation Press Inc., New York)

Guttman, A, 'The Challenge of Multiculturalism in Political Ethics' (1993) 22 *Philosophy and Public Affairs* 171

Guttman, A and Thompson, D, 'Deliberative Democracy Beyond Process' in JS Fishkin and P Laslett (eds), *Debating Deliberative Democracy* (2003, Blackwell, Oxford)

Hanley Kosse, S, 'Virtual Child Pornography – A United States Update' (2004) 9 *Communications Law* 39

Hanschmann, F, 'Federal Constitutional Court to Review NPD Party Ban Motion' (2001) 2 *German Law Journal* 17

Hare, I, 'Legislating Against Hate – The Legal Response to Bias Crimes' (1997) 17 *Oxford Journal of Legal Studies* 415

Hare, I, 'Is the Privileged Position of Political Expression Justified?' in J Beatson and Y Cripps (eds), *Freedom of Expression and Freedom of Information – Essays in Honour of Sir David Williams* (2002, Oxford University Press, Oxford)

Hare, I, 'Inflammatory Speech: Cross-Burning and the First Amendment' (2003) *Public Law* 408

Hare, I, 'Method and Objectivity in Free Speech Jurisprudence: Lessons from

America' (2005) 54 *International and Comparative Law Quarterly* 49

Harris, DJ and Joseph, S, *The International Covenant on Civil and Political Rights and United Kingdom Law* (1995, Clarendon Press, Oxford)

Harris, DJ, O'Boyle, M and Warbrick, C, *Law of the European Convention on Human Rights* (1995, Butterworths, London)

Hart Ely, J, *Democracy and Distrust* (1980, Harvard University Press, Harvard MA)

Hennessy, N and Smith, P, 'Have We Got It Right? NSW Racial Vilification Laws Five Years On' (1994) *Australian Journal of Human Rights* 6

Heywood, P, 'Political Corruption; Problems and Perspectives' (1997) XLV *Political Studies* 417

Hofmann, R, 'Incitement to National and Racial Hatred: The Legal Position in Germany' in S Coliver (ed.) *et al.*, *Striking a Balance – Hate Speech, Freedom of Expression and Non-discrimination* (1992, Article 19, London Human Rights Centre, University of Essex, Colchester)

Hogg, P and Bushell, A, 'The *Charter* Dialogue between Courts and Legislatures' (1997) 35 *Osgoode Hall Law Journal* 75

Hogg, P and Bushell, A, 'Reply to Six Degrees of Dialogue' (1999) 37 *Osgoode Hall Law Journal* 529

Holmes, S, *Passions and Constraints: On the Theory of Liberal Democracy* (1995, University of Chicago Press, Chicago IL)

Horwitz, P, 'Citizenship and Speech. A Review of Owen M Fiss' (1998) 43 *McGill Law Journal* 445

Hunt, M, *Using Human Rights Law in English Courts* (1998, Hart Publishing, Oxford)

Hunt, M, 'Commercial Freedom of Speech, Advertising and Human Rights', paper presented at *Human Rights, Privacy and the Media* conference held at University College London on 8 January 1998

Hutchinson, A 'Supreme Court Inc. – The Business of Democracy and Rights' in GW Anderson (ed.), *Rights and Democracy – Essays in UK–Canadian Constitutionalism* (1999, Blackstone Press Ltd, London)

Hutchinson, A and Petter, A, 'Private Rights/Public Wrongs: The Liberal Lie of the Charter' (1988) 38 *University of Toronto Law Journal* 278

Idriss, M, 'Religion and the Anti-Terrorism, Crime and Security Act' (2002) *Criminal Law Review* 890

Jackman, M, 'Protecting Rights and Promoting Democracy: Judicial Review under Section 1 of the Charter' (1996) 34 *Osgoode Hall Law Journal* 661

Jepson, P, 'Tackling Religious Terminology that Stirs Up Racial Hatred' (1999) 149 *New Law Journal* 554

Johnston, R, *Money and Votes: Constituency Campaign Spending and Election Results* (1987, Croom Helm, London)

Joseph, PA, *Constitutional and Administrative Law in New Zealand* (1993, Law Book Company, Sydney)

Justesen, P, 'Liberté d'Expression et Props Racistes au Danemark' (2001) 12 *Revue*

Trimestrielle des Droits de L'Homme 343
JUSTICE *Briefing on the European Commission Proposal for a Council Framework Decision on Racism and Xenophobia* (2002, London)
Kant, I, *Perpetual Peace – First Supplement* (1903, Allen & Unwin, London)
Karst, K, 'Equality as a Central Principle of the First Amendment' (1975) 43 *University of Chicago Law Review* 20
Kavanagh, A, 'Statutory Interpretation and Human Rights after Anderson: A More Contextual Approach' (2004) *Public Law* 537
Kelly, J, 'Charter Activism and Canadian Federalism: Rebalancing Liberal Constitutionalism in Canada 1982–1997 (1998, PhD dissertation, McGill University)
Kelly, R, *Short Money* (2004, Parliament and Constitution Centre, London)
Klug, F, 'Judicial Deference under the Human Rights Act 1998' (2003) *European Human Rights Law Review* 125
Kutchinsky, B, 'The Effect of Easy Availability of Pornography on the Incidence of Sex Crimes: The Danish Experience' (1973) 29 *Journal of Social Sciences* 163
Kymlicka, W, *Contemporary Political Philosophy – An Introduction* (2nd edn, 2002, Oxford University Press, Oxford)
Lardy, H, 'Prisoner Disenfranchisement: Constitutional Rights and Wrongs' (2000) *Public Law* 524
Lasson, K, 'Racial Defamation as Free Speech: Abusing the First Amendment' (1985) 17 *Columbia Human Rights Law Review* 11
Lawrence, C, 'If He Hollers Let Him Go: Regulating Racist Speech on Campus' (1990) *Duke Law Journal* 431
Laws, J, 'Is the High Court the Guardian of Fundamental Constitutional Rights?' (1993) *Public Law* 59
Laws, J, 'Law and Democracy' (1995) *Public Law* 72
Leeson, H, 'Section 33, the Notwithstanding Clause: A Paper Tiger?' (2000) 6 *Choices* 17
Lester, A, 'The Art of the Possible – Interpreting Statutes under the Human Rights Act 1998' (1998) *European Human Rights Law Review* 665
Levy, L, *Original Intent and the Framers' Constitution* (1988, Macmillan, New York)
L'Heureux-Dubé, C, 'Judicial Independence and Judicial Activism' in FL Morton (ed.), *Law, Politics and the Judicial Process in Canada* (3rd edn, 2002, University of Calgary Press, Calgary)
Lichtenberg, J, (ed.), *Democracy and the Mass Media* (1990, Cambridge University Press, Cambridge)
Linton, M, 'The Funding of Political Parties' in R Blackburn and R Plant (eds), *Constitutional Reform: The Labour Government's Constitutional Reform Agenda* (1999, Longman, Harlow)
Lipstadt, D, *Denying the Holocaust: The Growing Assault on Truth* (1994, Plume, New York)
Livingstone, S, Owen, T and McDonald, A, *Prison Law* (3rd edn, 2003, Oxford

University Press, Oxford)
Loveland, I, 'The Criminalization of Racist Violence?' in I Loveland (ed.), *A Special Relationship? American Influences on Public Law in the UK* (1995, Clarendon Press, Oxford)
Loveland, I (ed.), *Importing the First Amendment* (1998, Hart Publishing, Oxford)
Ludlam, S and Smith, MJ (eds), *Governing as New Labour – Policy and Politics under Blair* (2003, Palgrave Macmillan, Basingstoke)
Macedo, S, *Liberal Virtues* (1990, Clarendon Press, Oxford)
Mackinnon, C, *Toward a Feminist Theory of the State* (1989, Harvard University Press, Harvard MA)
Mackinnon, C, *Only Words* (1993, Harvard University Press, Harvard MA)
Madison, J, Hamilton, A and Jay, J, *The Federalist Papers* (1987, Penguin Books, London)
Magnet, J, 'Hate Propaganda in Canada' in W Waluchow (ed.), *Free Expression – Essays in Law and Philosophy* (1994, Clarendon Press, Oxford)
Mahoney, KE, 'Destruction of Women's Rights through Mass Media' in K Mahoney and P Mahoney (eds), *Human Rights in the Twenty First Century: A Global Challenge* (1995, Martinus Nijhoff, Dordrecht)
Mahoney, KE, 'Hate Speech: Affirmation or Contradiction of Freedom of Expression' (1996) *University of Illinois Law Review* 789
Mahoney, P, 'Universality versus Subsidiarity in the Strasbourg Case Law on Free Speech: Explaining Some Recent Judgments' (1997) *European Human Rights Law Review* 364
Manchester, C, 'More about Computer Pornography' (1996) *Criminal Law Review* 645
Mandel, M, *The Charter of Rights and the Legalization of Politics in Canada* (1989, Wall & Thompson, Toronto)
Manfredi, C, *Judicial Power and the Charter – Canada and the Paradox of Liberal Constitutionalism* (2nd edn, Oxford University Press, Toronto, 2000)
Manfredi, C and Kelly, J, 'Six Degrees of Dialogue: A Response to Hogg and Bushell' (1999) 37 *Osgoode Hall Law Journal* 513
Manwaring, J, 'Legal Regulation of Hate Propaganda in Canada' in S Coliver (ed.) *et al.*, *Striking a Balance – Hate Speech, Freedom of Expression and Non-discrimination* (1992, Article 19, London Human Rights Centre, University of Essex, Colchester)
Marshall, G, 'Taking Rights for an Override: Free Speech and Commercial Expression' (1989) *Public Law* 4
Marshall, G, 'I Speak Your Weight But Only in Kilograms: Is Mandatory Metrication Lawful?' (1996) *Public Law* 1
Marshall, G, 'Two Kinds of Incompatibility; More about s.3 of the HRA 1998' (1999) *Public Law* 377
Marshall, G, 'The Lynchpin of Parliamentary Intention: Lost, Stolen or Strained' (2003) *Public Law* 236
Matsuda, MJ, 'Public Response to Racist Speech: Considering the Victim's Story'

(1989) 87 *Michigan Law Review* 2320

McAuslan, P and McEldowney, J, 'Legitimacy and the Constitution: The Dissonance between Theory and Practice' in P McAuslan and J McEldowney (eds), *Law, Legitimacy and the Constitution* (1985, Sweet & Maxwell, London)

McCluskey, JH, *Law, Justice and Democracy* (1987, Sweet & Maxwell and BBC Books, London)

McGoldrick, D and O'Donnell, T, 'Hate-speech Laws: Consistency with National and International Human Rights Law' (1998) 18 *Legal Studies* 453

McIntyre, A, *After Virtue: A Study in Moral Theory* (1981, Duckworth, London)

McKay, D, Houghton, D and Wroe, A, '*Controversies in American Politics and Society* (2001, Blackwell, Oxford)

McLachlin, B, 'The Canadian Charter and the Democratic Process' in C Gearty and A Tomkins (eds), *Understanding Human Rights* (1996, Mansell Publishing Ltd, London)

McLachlin, B, 'Courts, Legislatures and Executives in the Post-Charter Era' (1999) *Policy Options* 42

McNamara, L, *Regulating Racism: Racial Vilification Laws in Australia* (2002, Sydney Institute of Criminology, Sydney)

Meese, E, (1986) *Public Administration Law Review* 701

Meny, Y and Knapp, A, *Government and Politics in Western Europe* (3rd edn, 1998, Oxford University Press, Oxford)

Merrills, JG and Robertson, AH, *Human Rights in Europe – A Study of the European Convention on Human Rights* (2001, Manchester University Press, Manchester)

Michelman, F, 'Law's Republic' (1988) 97 *Yale Law Journal* 1493

Miller, D (ed.), *Tell Me Lies – Propaganda and Media Distortion in the Attack on Iraq* (2004, Pluto Press, London)

Monahan, P, *Politics and the Constitution – The Charter, Federalism and the Supreme Court of Canada* (1987, Carswell, Toronto)

Monahan, P, 'The Charter Then and Now' in P Bryden, S Davis and J Russell (eds), *Protecting Rights and Freedoms* (1994, University of Toronto Press, Toronto)

Monahan, P, 'The Supreme Court of Canada in the 21st Century' (2001) 80 *Canadian Bar Review* 374

Moon, R, 'Justified Limits on Freedom of Expression: The Collapse of the General Approach to Limits on Charter Rights' (2002) 40 *Osgoode Hall Law Journal* 337

Morris, GS, 'Local Government Workers and Rights of Political Participation: Time for Change' (1998) *Public Law* 25

Morton, FL, *Law, Politics and the Judicial Process in Canada* (3rd edn, 2002, University of Calgary Press, Calgary)

Munro, C, 'The Value of Commercial Speech' (2003) 62 *Cambridge Law Journal* 134

Murphy, T, 'Incitement to Hatred: Lessons from Northern Ireland' in S Coliver (ed.) *et al.*, *Striking a Balance – Hate Speech, Freedom of Expression and Non-discrimination* (1992, Article 19, London Human Rights Centre, University of

Essex, Colchester)

Neier, A, *Defending My Enemy: American Nazis in Skokie, Illinois and the Risks of Freedom* (1979, EP Dutton, New York)

Neill of Bladen, Lord, *Committee on Standards in Public Life* Cm 4057 (1998)

Neuborne, B, 'Ghosts in the Attic: Idealized Pluralism, Community and Hate Speech' (1992) 27 *Harvard Civil Rights – Civil Liberties Law Review* 371

Nicol, D, 'Gender Reassignment and the Transformation of the Human Rights Act' (2004) 120 *Law Quarterly Review* 194

Nieuwenhuis, A, 'Freedom of Speech: *USA vs Germany and Europe*' (2000) 18 *Netherlands Quarterly of Human Rights* 195

Oetheimer, M, *L'Harmonisation de la Liberté d'Expression en Europe* (2001, Editions A Pedone, Paris)

Oldfield, A, *Citizenship and Community: Civic Republicanism and the Modern World* (1990, Routledge, London)

Pannick, D, 'Article 10 of the European Convention on Human Rights' in P Birks (ed.), *Pressing Problems in the Law* (1995, Oxford University Press, Oxford)

Partington, M, 'Race Relations Act 1965; A Too Restricted View' (1967) *Criminal Law Review* 497

Perry, M, *The Constitution, the Courts and Human Rights: An Inquiry into the Legitimacy of Constitutional Policymaking by the Judiciary* (1982, Yale University Press, New Haven CT)

Pinto-Duschinsky, M, *British Political Finance 1830–1980* (1981, American Enterprise Institute, Washington DC)

Post, R, 'The Constitutional Concept of Public Discourse: Outrageous Opinion, Democratic Deliberation and *Hustler Magazine* v *Falwell*' (1990) 103 *Harvard Law Review* 601

Ramsay, I *Consumer Protection – Text and Materials* (1989, Weidenfeld and Nicolson, London)

Ramsay, I, *Advertising, Culture and the Law* (1996, Sweet & Maxwell, London)

Redish, M, 'Tobacco Advertising and the First Amendment' (1996) 81 *Iowa Law Review* 589

Redish, M and Lippman, G, 'Freedom of Expression and the Civic Republican Revival in Constitutional Theory – The Ominous Implications' (1991) 79 *California Law Review* 267

Renold, E and Creighton, S with Atkinson, C and Carr, J, *Images of Abuse: A Review of the Evidence on Child Pornography* (2003, NSPCC Publications, London)

Rettinger, LJ, *The Relationship between Child Pornography and the Commission of Sexual Offences against Children: A Review of the Literature* (2000, Department of Justice, Canada)

Ringhand, L, 'Concepts of Equality in British Election Financing Reform Proposals' (2002) 22 *Oxford Journal of Legal Studies* 253

Roach, K, *The Supreme Court On Trial: Judicial Activism or Democratic Dialogue* (2001, Irwin Law, Toronto)

Robson, JM (ed.), *Essays on Politics and Society, Vol XIX* (1977, University of

Toronto Press, Toronto)

Rohsler, C and Willis, A, 'Pan European Advertising Clearance' (2004) 15 *Entertainment Law Review* 249

Rolph, D, 'The Message, Not the Medium: Defamation, Publication and the Internet in *Dow Jones & Co v Gutnick*' (2002) 24 *Sydney Law Review* 262

Rosenfeld, M, 'Extremist Speech and the Paradox of Intolerance' (1987) 100 *Harvard Law Review* 1457

Rosenfeld, M, 'Hate Speech in Constitutional Jurisprudence: A Comparative Analysis' (2003) 24 *Cardozo Law Review* 1523

Rostow, E, 'The Democratic Character of Judicial Review' (1952) 66 *Harvard Law Review* 193

Rostow, E, 'The Supreme Court and the People's Will' (1958) 33 *Notre Dame Law Review* 573

Royal Commission on Electoral Reform and Party Financing, *Reforming Electoral Democracy: Final Report, Vol 1* (1991, Minister of Supply and Services, Ottawa)

Rush, M (ed.), *Parliament and Pressure Politics* (1990, Clarendon Press, Oxford)

Russell, P, 'Standing Up for Notwithstanding' (1991) 29 *Alberta Law Review* 293

Sadurski, W, 'Judicial Review and Protection of Constitutional Rights' (2002) 22 *Oxford Journal of Legal Studies* 275

Sandalow, T, 'A Skeptical Look at Contemporary Republicanism' (1989) 41 *Florida Law Review* 523

Sandel, M, *Liberalism and the Limits of Justice* (1982, Cambridge University Press, Cambridge)

Sandel, M, 'Morality and the Liberal Ideal' (1984) 190 *New Republic* 15

Sawyer, K, 'Rejection of Weimarian Politics or Betrayal of Democracy?: Spain's Proscription of Batasuna under the European Convention on Human Rights' (2003) 52 *Am Uni Law Rev* 1531

Scanlon, TM, 'A Theory of Freedom of Expression' (1972) 1 *Philosophy and Public Affairs* 204

Schauer, F, *Free Speech – A Philosophical Inquiry* (1982, Cambridge University Press, Cambridge)

Schauer, F, 'The Aim and the Target in Free Speech Methodology' (1989) 83 *Northwestern University Law Review* 562

Schrecker, E, *The Age of McCarthyism* (2001, Palgrave, New York)

Scott, A, '"A Monstrous and Unjustifiable Infringement"? Political Expression and the Broadcasting Ban on Advocacy Advertising' (2003) 66 *Modern Law Review* 224

Sedley, S, 'Human Rights: a 21st Century Agenda' in R Blackburn and J Busuttil (eds), *Human Rights for the 21st Century* (1997, Pinter, London)

Selzer, R and Lopes, GM, 'The Ku Klux Klan: Reasons for Support or Opposition among White Respondents' (1986) 17 *Journal of Black Studies* 91

Sherry, M, 'Don't Ask, Tell or Respond: Silent Acceptance of Disability Hate

Crimes' at http:///www.farnorthernrc.org/mylifemychoice/Hate%20Crimes-Mark%Sherry.pdf.

Shiner, RA, *Freedom of Commercial Expression* (2003, Oxford University Press, Oxford)

Skelly Wright, J, 'Politics and the Constitution: Is Money Speech?' (1976) 85 *Yale Law Journal* 1001

Smith, G, *Internet Law and Regulation* (3rd edn, 2002, Sweet & Maxwell, London)

South African Human Rights Commission, *Hate Crimes and Hate Speech in South Africa* (2003, South African Human Rights Commission, Johannesburg)

Starmer, K, 'Two Years of the Human Rights Act' (2003) *European Human Rights Law Review* 14

Steele, CM and Aronson, J, 'Stereotype Threat and the Intellectual Test Performance of African Americans' (1995) 69 *Journal of Personality and Social Psychology* 797

Stone, G, 'Content-Neutral Restrictions' (1987) *54 University of Chicago Law Review* 46

Strossen, N, 'Balancing Rights to Freedom of Expression and Equality: A Civil Liberties Approach to Hate Speech on Campus' in S Coliver (ed.) *et al.*, *Striking a Balance – Hate Speech, Freedom of Expression and Non-discrimination* (1992, Article 19, London Human Rights Centre, University of Essex, Colchester)

Strossen, N, *Defending Pornography* (1996, Abacus, London)

Strum, P, *When the Nazis Came to Skokie: Freedom for Speech We Hate* (1999, University Press of Kansas, Lawrence KS)

Sullivan, KM, 'Cheap Spirits, Cigarettes and Free Speech: The Implications of *44 Liquormart*' (1996) *Supreme Court Review* 123

Sumner, LW, 'Hate Propaganda and Charter Rights' in W Waluchow (ed.), *Free Expression – Essays in Law and Philosophy* (1994, Clarendon Press, Oxford)

Sumner, LW, 'Hate Crimes, Literature and Speech' in RG Frey and CH Wellman (eds), *A Companion to Applied Ethics* (2003, Blackwell, Malden MA)

Sunstein, C, 'Pornography and the First Amendment' (1986) *Duke Law Journal* 589

Sunstein, C, 'Beyond the Republican Tradition' (1988) 97 *Yale Law Journal* 1539

Sunstein, C, *The Partial Constitution* (1993, Harvard University Press, Harvard MA)

Sunstein, C, *Democracy and the Problem of Free Speech* (1993, The Free Press, New York)

Sunstein, C, 'Political Equality and Unintended Consequences' (1994) 94 *Columbia Law Review* 1390

Symes, M and Jorro, P, *Asylum Law and Practice* (2003, Butterworths, London)

Taylor, C, *Philosophy and the Human Sciences: Philosophical Papers, Vol. ii* (1985, Cambridge University Press, Cambridge)

Thayer, JB, 'The Origin and Scope of the American Doctrine of Constitutional Law' in *Legal Essays* (1908, The Boston Book Company, Boston)

Tomkins, A, *Our Republican Constitution* (2005, Hart Publishing, Oxford)

Tribe, L, 'Note: The Disenfranchisement of Ex-Felons: Citizenship, Criminality and the Purity of the Ballot Box' (1989) 102 *Harvard Law Review* 1300

Tushnet, M, 'Policy Distortion and Democratic Debilitation: Comparative Illumination of the Counter-Majoritarian Difficulty'(1995) 94 *Michigan Law Review* 245

Tushnet, M, *Taking the Constitution Away from the Courts* (1997, Princeton University Press, Princeton NJ)

Twomey, A, 'Laws against Incitement to Racial Hatred in the United Kingdom' (1994) 1 *Australian Journal of Human Rights* 5

Vickers, L, *Freedom of Speech and Employment* (2002, Oxford University Press, Oxford)

Wald, M, 'Children's Rights: A Framework for Analysis' (1979) 12 *University of California Davis Law Review* 255

Waldron, J, *Law and Disagreement* (1999, Oxford University Press, New York)

Walzer, M, *Spheres of Justice: A Defence of Pluralism and Equality* (1983, Blackwell, Oxford)

Weinrib, L, 'Learning to Live with the Override' (1990) 35 *McGill Law Journal* 541

Weinrib, L, 'The Supreme Court of Canada in the Age of Rights: Constitutional Democracy, the Rule of Law and Fundamental Rights under Canada's Constitution' (2001) 80 *Canadian Bar Review* 699

Weiss, C and Melling, L, 'The Legal Education of Twenty Women' (1988) 40 *Stanford Law Review* 1299

Whitfield, S, *The Culture of the Cold War* (2nd edn, 1996, Johns Hopkins University Press, Baltimore MD)

Wildhaber, L, 'The Right to Offend, Shock or Disturb? – Aspects of Freedom of Expression under the European Convention on Human Rights' (2001) 36 *Irish Jurist* 17

Willis, A, 'The Future Regulation of Broadcast Advertising' (2004) 15 *Entertainment Law Review* 255

Woolman, S, 'Riding the Push-Me Pull-You; Constructing a Test that Reconciles the Conflicting Interests which Animate the Limitation Clause' (1994) 10 *South African Journal of Human Rights* 60

Zillmann, D and Bryant, J, 'Pornography, Sexual Callousness, and the Trivialization of Rape' (1982) 32 *Journal of Communication* 10

Index